THE
BLACK
BULL

*FROM NORMANDY TO THE BALTIC
WITH THE 11TH ARMOURED DIVISION*

by
Patrick Delaforce

Pen & Sword
MILITARY

First published in Great Britain in 1993 by
Alan Sutton Publishing Ltd.

Republished in 2010 and in this format in 2020 and 2021 by
Pen & Sword Military
An imprint of
Pen & Sword Books Ltd
Yorkshire – Philadelphia

ISBN 978 1 52678 428 5

A CIP catalogue record for this book is
available from the British Library

Printed and bound in the UK on FSC accredited paper by 4edge Ltd, Essex, SS5 4AD

Pen & Sword Books Ltd incorporates the Imprints of Atlas, Archaeology,
Aviation, Discovery, Family History, Fiction, History, Maritime, Military, Military
Classics, Politics, Select, Transport, True Crime, Air World, Frontline Publishing, Leo
Cooper, Remember When, Seaforth Publishing, The Praetorian Press, Wharncliffe
Local History, Wharncliffe Transport, Wharncliffe True Crime and White Owl.

For a complete list of Pen & Sword titles please contact
PEN & SWORD BOOKS LIMITED
47 Church Street, Barnsley, South Yorkshire, S70 2AS, England
E-mail: enquiries@pen-and-sword.co.uk
Website: www.pen-and-sword.co.uk

Or
PEN AND SWORD BOOKS
1950 Lawrence Rd, Havertown, PA 19083, USA
E-mail: Uspen-and-sword@casematepublishers.com
Website: www.penandswordbooks.com

Contents

Acknowledgements

The Division fought as a closely-knit, well-trained team, so it is not surprising that representatives of all arms should have contributed to the making of this book. I am particularly grateful to Major-General G.P.B. Roberts DSO, MC, for allowing me to include extracts from his memoirs in this book. He was the outstanding leader of the outstanding division in the Normandy to the Baltic campaign. At the end of the book I have referred with many thanks to the score or two of Sharp End soldiers who have made this book so interesting. They have helped recreate the true images of war – the moments of noise, pain and death, the silence and the boredom, the contrast of happy leave and the occasional front-line humour. There have been contributions from the armour, infantry, reconnaissance, gunners, sappers, REME, RASC, RAChD, RAMC and CMP. Many photographs have been loaned for inclusion in *The Black Bull*, particularly from Ted Deeming, David Swiney and Bob Walmsley. Maps are reproduced by the Army Training Aids and Publications to the drawings of Major 'Ned' Thornburn MC 4KSLI.

If there are errors of names, dates and places they are mine alone.

Patrick Delaforce
Brighton, May 1993

CHAPTER ONE

The Sharp End

'Nobody enjoys fighting', Lieutenant-General Brian Horrocks, XXX Corps Commander, wrote in his autobiography, 'Yet the forward area in any theatre of war, the sharp end of the battle, as we used to call it, is inhabited by young men with a gleam in their eye who actually *do* the fighting. They are comparatively few in number and they are nearly always the same people.'

For nearly a year – from June 1944 to May 1945 – British, Canadian, American and Polish armies fought a dreadful, bloody campaign to free first France, then Belgium and Holland, of their Nazi occupants. And finally the Allies blasted their way across well-defended river barriers up to Schleswig-Holstein and the Danish borders. The British 11th Armoured Division, with its famous emblem of the black bull rampant, red hooves on a yellow ground, led the field.

This book contains accounts written by the twenty-year-old 'virgin' soldiers who took part in the dramatic battles. 'Virgin' because, with the exception of the distinguished GOC Major-General 'Pip' Roberts DSO, MC, who had won his spurs in the Desert, most regimental commanders and the gallant 3rd Royal Tanks, the rest of the Division had never been in action before.

In his book, *The Tanks*, Captain Liddell Hart wrote: 'within a few months, 11th Armoured achieved a reputation in Europe matching that which the long-famous 7th Armoured Division had gained in Africa. Its outstanding performance in 1944–5 owed much to the leadership of 'Pip' Roberts – who at thirty-seven was the youngest of all the divisional commanders in the campaign.' And the GOC British 2nd Army, Lieutenant-General Sir Miles Dempsey, wrote on 5 August 1945: 'The 11th Armoured Division proved itself throughout the campaign in North-Western Europe an outstandingly fine division. *I have never met a better.* Even after sustaining considerable losses [10,000 casualties including 2,000 killed] – and the 11th Armoured Division had heavier casualties than any other armoured division in Second Army – there was always a sound and well-trained nucleus to fall back on. The division was brimful of that priceless asset – confidence.'

In one day's brutal fighting east of Caen during Operation Goodwood, 115 tanks, nearly 50 per cent of the total, were brewed up or written off by assorted Tigers, Panthers, Mark IVs and 88-mm guns. Above all the Normandy campaign was a full-blooded war of attrition.

Twentieth-century front-line war is a curious mixture of terror, noise and fear mingled with interludes of rest, routine, even boredom, laced occasionally with humour. The forward troops would often consist of two very young men, crouching together in a fox-hole. Alone, for they might not be able to see the rest of the section. Probably cold, miserable and hungry, in a sinister emptiness. Safe as long as they stay in their slit trench, but very vulnerable once they are ordered to move forward into a violent future. Spandau, schmeisser, nebelwerfers, grenades and mines everywhere, but they almost certainly cannot see where the danger is located.

Private Battles

During most of the campaign a hundred or more nasty little private battles would be going on at the same time *each day*. The crew of a Sherman tank might be taking on a German Mark IV with modest confidence, a Panther with some optimism, or a Tiger with considerable trepidation. An infantry section carefully crossing a harvest field, possibly laced with teller or schu-mines, in order to clear a thick hedgerow in front of them, would be hoping not to be 'stonked' by 'moaning minnie' mortars. A troop of 25-pounders could be contributing furiously to an 'Uncle' Target on a well-defended Norman village occupied by German PZ grenadiers and a few SP guns. Engineers clearing a centre-line of mined verges hoped that they would make no mistakes. And the brave reconnaissance regiments with light-skinned armoured cars would be gingerly pushing their noses round corners and reporting back to Division and Corps. There were a dozen ways of getting killed. Snipers killed or wounded tank commanders, infantry and gun position officers with impunity, but when they were caught they were shot on the spot. Often eighteen-year-old SS lads longing to die for Das Reich, the snipers were everywhere. Our infantry officers, their chosen prey, learned to conceal all distinguishing marks, to carry rifles like their men (instead of the usual pistols), not to carry tell-tale maps or field glasses, and to wear pips on their sleeves instead of conspicuously on their shoulders. It was a case of stay anonymous or die. Bazookas (*panzerfaust*) brewed up Sherman and Cromwell tanks who ventured too close; and from time to time the Luftwaffe (and quite often the RAF and USAAF) bombed the living daylights out of everything that moved at the sharp end.

The Young Leaders

Lieutenant-General Brian Horrocks took command of XXX Corps, which included 11th Armoured Division, in early August 1944 in time for the final rolling battles of Operation Bluecoat. He wrote: 'Seven weeks hard slogging in the thick bocage country had taken their toll and the gloss had gone from the magnificently trained army which had landed in Normandy. I have always said that in a section of ten men, as a rough guide, two lead, seven follow and one would do almost anything not to be there at all. The two leaders take most of the risks and are usually the first to become casualties. When this happens on a large scale as it had occurred in the Normandy beachhead battle, so much better suited to defence than to attack, the cutting edge of a division becomes blunted.'

One infantry company commander described a typical action:

Down in his slit trench the defending infantryman saw little. Only the noise, the bangs and the crashes, the shrieks and whistles, gave some indication of what was happening. Rapid bursts of machine-gun fire were ominous: they were certainly German. The more measured beat of a Bren was reassuring. Men were hit; sometimes they shouted out, sometimes they gave no sound; they just slumped forward or collapsed into the bottom of the trench. The stronger supported the weaker to hold both the enemy and fear at bay. Courage, cowardice, leadership, all revealed themselves, sometimes where they had least been expected.

In their first three battles 2nd Northants Yeomanry, with their Daimler scout cars and Cromwell tanks, no match for Tigers or Panthers, lost fourteen officers killed, fourteen wounded and six missing – a scale as bad as First World War trench fighting. No wonder that by the end of the Normandy campaign, the young 'virgin' soldiers had lost their virginity and the Desert Army adage held good: 'An old soldier is a cautious soldier; that is why he is an old soldier.'

Courage

Private Ken Thorpe, 2nd Battalion The Royal Warwickshire Regiment, 185 Brigade under command of 159 Brigade (11th Armoured Division), wrote of the battle of Perrier Ridge on 7 August 1944:

Everyone assumes that he will be all right in an assault. After all, you must rely on God to protect you because if you think that at any moment you are going to be killed you would never leave the security of your slit trench. How does one maintain this feeling of invulnerability? Is it man's instinctive nature that makes him believe that death does not exist for him even while he sleeps next to it? What force compels a man to get out of his trench, to leave its security and offer himself to his executioners? Is it the discipline of duty or is it simply the dread of being a coward? I have often tried to understand this but I have never arrived at a conclusion. We all had fear, some more, some less, but we all went.

Private Thorpe was captured but survived to tell his tale.

Geoffrey Bishop, troop leader 23rd Hussars, wrote during Operation Bluecoat:

All is quiet for a while – brilliant sunshine – but the awful tension persists. *Prisoner in Paradise* suggests itself as the title for a story. This beautiful Normandy scene, the soft wooded hills, the good rich earth, a rich balmy summer's day: and yet fear is there – fear of the known – a tearing screaming shell blasting through your little iron fortress, taking with it your legs and your friends – fear of the unknown – a sniper in an adjacent hedgerow quietly preparing to kill you unawares. August the fourth – it is my sister's birthday, I think of a tennis party in England.

'The weakest part of any tank is its crew,' wrote Trooper Ernie Hamilton, 15/19th Hussars, 'especially after the unit receives casualties, the psychology of fear to a crew, when the words 'Tiger Tank' were heard over the radio, it was near panic in one's mind.'

On the Other Side of the Hill

The Germans defended their corner superbly. Devastated by the 'jabos' (jagd bombers) of the RAF (Typhoons) and USAAF (Thunderbolts) who had almost total air superiority, outgunned by the huge Allied artillery groups, and certainly outnumbered three to one, even five to one by Allied tanks, the Germans fought like fanatics. German historians recorded the Wehrmacht's reactions to the immense pressure put on them by the Allied air forces:

Unless a man has been through these fighter bomber attacks by the jabos he cannot know what the invasion meant. You lie there helpless in a roadside ditch, in a furrow in a field, or under a hedge, pressed into the ground, your face in the dirt – and then it comes toward you, roaring. . . . You feel like crawling into the ground. Then the bird has gone. But it comes back. Twice. Three times. Not until they think they've wiped out everything do they leave. Until then you are helpless. Like a man facing a firing squad.
    Even if you survive it is no more than temporary reprieve. Ten such attacks in succession are a real foretaste of hell.

Most German troop movements were thus made under cover of darkness.
    When a SS Panzer regiment was torn to pieces during the great battles, the survivors regrouped as KampfenGruppen. Admin. troops, cooks, engineers, signallers, Luftwaffe flak units, were quickly amalgamated, and with a couple of tanks, guns and mortars were once again a superb defensive unit. Indeed, when they lost ground they were always ordered to counter-attack. Colonel Wyldbore-Smith, GSO1 of 11th Armoured Division said:

'The Germans were great opportunists. They were prepared to act – always.' Of course attacking forces need superiority in all arms to succeed against a highly skilled defensive force, but war studies made immediately after the war showed that:

On a man to man basis, the German ground soldier consistently inflicted casualties at about a 50 per cent higher rate than they incurred from the opposing British, Canadian and American troops *under all circumstances.* This was true when they were attacking and when they were defending, when they had a local numerical superiority and when, as was usually the case, they were outnumbered, when they had air superiority and when they did not, when they won and when they lost. (Colonel Trevor Dupuy, *A Genius for War*)

Four German Mark IV tanks of the Panzer Lehr Division spent their first two weeks in action. Their commander wrote:

It was like a game of Red Indians – only deadly serious – this business of hide and seek to evade the sharp eyes of the fighter bombers. A tank commander got out to reconnoitre along a sunken lane. He crawled through the hedges. He inspected every inch of ground. He had moved up and down the lane about a dozen times. The tanks were concealed in sunken lanes, in orchards and in hayricks. The infantrymen around them were camouflaged by bushes, sheaves of oats, and broken-off branches and twigs. The first few hours were spent in camouflage. Time and time again a man would go off to see whether it looked genuine. The first two days were tolerable; water for washing and hot food were not yet missed. Mentally they surveyed their whole field of fire.

The ambush was set – but it might be rudely disturbed. A German historian wrote:

Once a tank was spotted (from the air) it was done for. Mercilessly it would be divebombed or attacked until a bomb or volley of rockets or cannon fire had finished it off. The planes dropped their 'eggs' among the soldiers and circled above them like birds of prey. They were hunting for the German tanks which lurked like fat grubs in the bushes or beneath the trees. They hunted and they found.

A Hostile Viewpoint

Views about the enemy's ability and experience were usually quite consistent. The SS were generally younger, tougher, more ruthless and would fight to the last. The Panzer divisions were usually the élite forces –

well-trained, disciplined and, in every sense, worthy foes. The run-of-the-mill Wehrmacht would contain a mixture of qualities, depending on their 'foreign' intake of Russians, Poles and a dozen other nationalities. But it is of course very interesting to discover what the enemy thought of us!

A British Army of the Rhine Intelligence review discovered an assessment based on the battle of France in 1940 called '*Wir fahren gegen England*', in preparation for the possible invasion:

> The English soldier was in excellent physical condition. He bore his own wounds with stoical calm. The losses of his own troops he discussed with complete equanimity. He did not complain of hardships. In battle he was tough and dogged. His conviction that England would conquer in the end was unshakeable. The English soldier has always shown himself to be a fighter of high standard. Certainly the territorial divisions are inferior to the regular troops in training, but this is compensated for by their morale. In defence the Englishman took any punishment that came his way. During the fighting, Fourth (German) Army Corps took fewer prisoners than in the fighting with French or Belgians. On the other hand the losses on both sides were bloody and high.

And another report said:

> The conduct of the battle by the Americans and English was, taken all round, once again very methodical. Local successes were seldom exploited. . . . British attacking formations were split up into large numbers of assault squads commanded by officers. NCOs were rarely in the 'big picture' so that if the officer became a casualty, they were unable to act in accordance with the main plan. The result was that in a quickly changing situation, the junior commanders showed insufficient flexibility. For instance when an objective was reached the enemy would neglect to exploit and dig in for defence. The conclusion is as far as possible go for the enemy officers. Then seize the initiative yourself.

During the campaign 11th Armoured Division had 174 officers killed in action and three times that number wounded. Nevertheless the division produced many examples of splendid dash and initiative, of which some are mentioned later in this book.

Happy Families

A modern twentieth-century armoured division is a complex beast. Consider this. The infantry take *and hold* ground, specifically villages, even cities. The armour are not capable of holding ground once taken. But the infantry are vulnerable to enemy armour and artillery. Armour can and do advance great distances – only they can make the brutal thrusts through the enemy defences. But the armour are vulnerable to better-equipped (and led) armour and nearby infantry equipped with bazookas or the equivalent. Neither infantry nor armour can cross river barriers if bridges are blown; Royal Engineers (Sappers) are vital for that operation. Neither armour nor infantry can reasonably cross minefields unless the Sappers clear them. The centrelines on which armour and infantry advance have to be marked and policed by the Military Police to avoid horrendous traffic jams. All arms will starve if no RASC-provided rations reach them. All arms will surrender if no ammo comes up at night. If the Luftwaffe is combative, the divisional AA is needed. If communications falter the division is at risk, and the Royal Corps of Signals was always at hand to keep the vital links open. The REME mended and repaired the broken AFVs (armoured fighting vehicles) after every action, so that tank strength was kept up for the morrow. Remember too the brave stretcher-bearers, who often collected the wounded while under fire and took them back by one means or another to the RAMC doctors. They patched them up – perhaps to fight another day, or perhaps to convalesce in Brussels or back across the channel.

A German intelligence report (PRO WO 208/3193) stated: 'It is better to attack the English, who are very sensitive to close combat and flank attack *at their weakest moment* – that is, when they have to fight without their artillery.' Lieutenant-General Horrocks wrote:

> I would say that the Royal Artillery did more to win the last war than any other arm. Time after time their young forward observation officers would step into the breach and take command of some forward infantry unit whose commanders had all become casualties, while the technical skill with which huge concentrations of fire were switched rapidly from one part of the front, was never equalled in any other army. The Germans never succeeded in achieving anything like it.

Of Operation Epsom General Paul Hauser i/c 2 SS Panzer Corps wrote: 'The murderous fire from the naval guns in the Channel and *the terrible British artillery* destroyed the bulk of our attacking force in its assembly area.' 13 RHA and 151 Field Regiment RA (Ayrshire Yeomanry) fired over half a million rounds of 25–pounder shells in the campaign, equivalent to forty rounds per gun per day.

Modern warfare demands command flexibility. Occasionally the two main fighting arms of 11th Armoured Division (29th Armoured Brigade and 159 Infantry Brigade) were separated and attached temporarily to other command structures (for instance in the Ardennes campaign). In each case the individual brigade activities have been included in this book. As indeed have the many occasions when Divisional artillery, still proudly wearing the sign of the Black Bull, were involved in battle when the two main fighting brigades were in reserve or resting or exchanging equipment.

The Butcher's Bill

The PBI – poor bloody infantry – in 159 Brigade suffered the worst. The 3rd Monmouthshires lost 292 killed, 4th Kings Shropshire Light Infantry 271, the 1st Herefords 223 and 8th Rifle Brigade 161. The armoured regiments too had a hard time. The 23rd Hussars lost 147 killed, 3rd RTR 90, 2nd Fife and Forfarshire Yeomanry 153, 15/19th Kings Royal Hussars 66 (post-Normandy) and the wretched 2nd Northants Yeomanry lost 87 killed in two months' fighting and had to be amalgamated with the 1st battalion. The Inns of Court recce regiment lost 63 killed, three supporting artillery regiments 152, the Sappers 47, Signals 19, RASC 29 and RAMC 13.

This book is written by one of the young 'virgin' soldiers. Pitched into the cauldron shortly after D-Day, aged twenty with one pip up, he was to spend over 300 days and most nights in action (the 13 RHA and 151 Field Regiment/Ayrshire Yeomanry were on call for almost 100 per cent of the year campaign.) Written with contributions, great help and encouragement from troopers, riflemen, privates, other troop leaders, troop commanders and last but certainly not least, our brilliant GOC, Major 'Pip' Roberts.

It is dedicated to the memory of the 2,000 members of the division who fell on the long centre-lines from Normandy to the Baltic.

CHAPTER TWO

In the Beginning

Much of the credit for the formation and early training of the 11th Armoured Division must go to Major-General P.C.S. Hobart. He was a hard taskmaster in Yorkshire in 1941–2 as the under-gunned 2-pounder Valentine tanks trundled over the dales, and even more so when 6-pounder Crusader tanks appeared in the summer of 1942 and training took place along the South Downs. When 'Hobo' left in September 1943 to take command of the new 79th Armoured Division with its dramatic mixture of 'Funnies', his successor was Major-General Brocas Burrows. Although it almost sailed to North Africa the division moved to East Anglia, where it was re-equipped with American Sherman tanks with 75-mm guns – reliable, fast and simple to maintain. The armoured reconnaissance regiment changed from armoured cars to light Centaur tanks and eventually to Cromwells. In December 1943 General Burrows left for Moscow to lead the British Military Mission and was succeeded by Major-General 'Pip' Roberts, who had earned DSOs and MCs in the desert commanding two armoured brigades in Monty's victorious 8th Army. He noted: 'In unblooded 11th Armoured Division I found everyone raring to go and with a few experienced officers in important positions, this was the ideal solution.' His 'Desert' veterans included Brigadier Roscoe Harvey, originally OC 23rd Hussars, now commander of 29th Armoured Brigade, Brigadier B.J. Fowler as Commander Royal Artillery, Lieutenant-Colonel F.B. Wyldbore-Smith GSO1 and Lieutenant-Colonel Bob Daniell, OC 13 RHA. And of course the 3rd Battalion, Royal Tank Regiment, perhaps the most experienced tank regiment in the Army after the North African campaigns.

Over nearly four years there followed rigorous training and yet more training, and exercises practising close infantry/tank combined operations. This was to prove itself time and time again in the year ahead.

An armoured division consists of roughly 15,000 men, including 724 officers, with an astonishing total of 3,414 vehicles. Of this total there were 246 tanks – Shermans including one in four Fireflies with the invaluable 17-pounder gun installed. They were divided between the three armoured regiments – 3 RTR, 23rd Hussars and 2nd Fife and Forfarshire Yeomanry. There were forty-four light tanks (Cromwells) and 100 scout cars, mainly with the armoured reconnaissance regiment, 2nd Northants Yeomanry and the Inns of Court. A total of 261 Bren gun carriers, many with 8th Battalion Rifle Brigade, and half tracks were scattered around the division. Finally

HQ Provost Section CMP, Germany, spring 1945

there were 2,100 trucks and lorries, which carried infantry, engineers, RASC, REME, RAOC, Royal Corps of Signals, RAMC and RMPs. The 'material' included 48 25-pounder guns, half with 13th (HAC) RHA as Sextons on a Ram chassis, and half towed with quad and limber with 151st Field Regiment RA (Ayrshire Yeomanry). The 75th Anti-Tank Regiment was equipped with two batteries of M10 tracked tank destroyers with 76-mm guns, and one battery towed 17-pounder gun. 58 LAA was equipped with a battery of self-propelled Bofors and two batteries of towed AA guns.

The four infantry regiments, including 8 RB, the lorried infantry regiment, were equipped with a total of 6,204 machine carbines, 1,376 light machine guns, 160 mortars and 302 PIATS (portable anti-tank guns). The 2nd Independent Machine gun company of the Royal Northumberland Fusiliers had twenty-two medium machine guns. Finally a total of 9,013 rifles and pistols was issued to an armoured division. This all sounds neat and tidy, but there were many exceptions. All tank crews carried pistols and many White armoured half tracks and Sextons carried ring-mounted 50-mm machine guns.

When the Division – heavily 'waterproofed' – sailed for France on 13 and 14 June (although advance recce parties had landed on Juno beach at D + 3), they were as British a unit as any in the Army. 8 RB were mostly Cockneys, and the fighting Scots were represented by two Yeomanry regiments, the 2nd Fife and Forfarshire and the 151 Field Regiment Ayrshire Yeomanry, who were often paired with each other in action. The Welsh had a strong contingent consisting of the 3rd Battalion Monmouthshire Regiment,

The 23rd Hussars A Squadron fitters, Sussex, June 1944

1st Battalion Herefordshire Regiment and the 4th Battalion King's Shropshire Light Infantry. The shires were represented by the 2nd Northamptonshire Yeomanry and the Royal Northumberland Fusiliers. The soldiers who fought with 23rd Hussars, 3 RTR, 13 RHA and the two armoured car regiments (initially 2nd Household Cavalry, then the Inns of Court), came from all over England. There was no fixed pattern other than the fact that the regiments had been together as units since 1941 or even earlier. And just as important they had, for the most part, trained together in Yorkshire, Surrey/Sussex and finally in East Anglia. It was perhaps the most highly trained division in the British Army.

CHAPTER THREE

Weaponry

For a variety of reasons tank design in the UK and, to a lesser extent in the USA, had one distinguishing feature. The tanks were always two years out of date. When the German armour had the equivalent of 4- or 6-pounder guns, the British tanks had 2-pounders. When the British upgraded to 6-pounders, the German tanks had the incredible 88 mm. When the three British armoured divisions and eight armoured brigades landed in Normandy their Churchills, Cromwells and Shermans were hopelessly outgunned.

Half the German tanks in Normandy were the Panzer Mark IV 'special'. It weighed 25 tons, moved at up to 25 mph, and its 75-mm Kwk 40 gun could penetrate 84 mm of armour at 1,000 yards. Its own front armour was 80 mm. The Panzer Mark V or Panther accounted for nearly 40 per cent of German tanks in Normandy; that is, one of every two tank regiments in most German armoured divisions was equipped with Panthers. It weighed 45 tons, could move at 35 mph, and its 75-mm Kwk 42 guns with a 14-pound shell could penetrate 118 mm of armour at 1,000 yards. Its own front armour was 100 mm. The Panzer Mark VI, or Tiger, was very nearly impossible to knock out. It weighed 54 tons with a maximum speed of 23 mph and carried 100 mm of frontal armour. Its 20-pounder shell from a 88-mm Kwk 36 gun could penetrate 102 mm at 1,000 yards.

Many German tank units had one Panther per troop of Mark IVs, a situation similar to the British units, which had one Sherman Firefly per troop. The Allied Sherman tank weighed 32 tons and could travel at 25 mph, but its front armour was only 76 mm thick. It could be knocked out by any German tank at 1,000 yards, even at 2,000 yards, and so was known as the 'Tommy-cooker'. Its 75-mm gun could at best penetrate 74 mm at 100 yards, 68 mm at 500 yards, and 60 mm at 1,000 yards. However, its Ford engine was reliable and easy to maintain.

Trooper John Thorpe was the 'Jack of all trades' in 4 Troop C Squadron, 2nd Fife and Forfarshire Yeomanry, equipped with Shermans:

> I could be called upon to take any other crew member's place and I was the disposable member of the crew. I was sent on foot reconnaissance to find the safest place to locate the tank without placing it in jeopardy when advancing slowly towards a vantage point in a hedge or out of a wood, or at a crossroads in a village, or to attach a tow rope to help extract a

disabled tank in the thick of battle. I developed not only a sixth sense but a super sense, a soldier's deepest sense, the sense to survive.

The reality of this equation was very disturbing. Unless a 76-mm Sherman could get *very close* to the opposition or by chance catch it sideways on (Tiger had 80 mm of *side* armour, Panther 45 mm and Mark IV 30 mm) the contest was inevitably one-sided. Only the 17-pounder Sherman Fireflies were capable of a level fight. A limited number of Challengers – 200 in all – were allocated to Guards Armoured Division and 15/19th Hussars in 11th Armoured. A 17-pounder anti-tank gun was mounted on a Cromwell chassis and allocated on the basis of one per troop, with a crew of five. However, the German dual-purpose 88-mm gun (ground and AA) was reckoned to be the best available during the Second World War. Its muzzle power could destroy any Allied tank at 2,000 m and its airburst fuse could put a shell on top of a crossroads eight times out of ten. Bill Close, squadron commander with 3 RTR throughout the campaign, was wounded three times and awarded two MCs. As author of *Panzer Bait*, and having had no fewer than eleven tanks knocked out from under him, his views on tanks have much authority!

Our ordinary 75-mm gun could not knock out either a Tiger or a Panther *except at about 500 yards range, and in the rear, and with a bit of luck in the flank!* The 17-pounder Firefly was our best tank but even it could not penetrate the Tiger head-on at over 1,000 yards. Whereas all our tanks would be knocked out at 2,500 yards by the German 88-mm gun.

Steel Brownlie, troop leader with 2nd Fife and Forfarshire Yeomanry, also fought throughout the campaign, was wounded and awarded the MC. He wrote *The Proud Trooper*, a story of the Ayrshire Yeomanry. His comments are:

The great snag was that the Sherman, mechanically reliable and available in great numbers, was inferior in many ways to the German tanks. The armour was thin, the ammunition was stowed in open bins so that it exploded if there was any penetration. *A hit almost inevitably meant a brew-up.* Some boffin hit on the idea of welding bits of extra armour to protect the bins but their effect was to provide an aiming mark. I certainly saw many brewed-up Shermans with a neat hole in the 'extra armour'. Even if you fixed spare track plates to the front of the Shermans, the basic weakness remained. You were in a 'Ronson' and if you were hit it was best to bale out p.d.q.

He also stressed the fear generated by the awareness of inferior armour: 'My crews got almost obsessive about NOT having a thick, sloping glacis plate in front like the Panther. I recall deliberately backing into a firing position so as to have the protection of the engine. There was the added advantage that if you had to get out in a hurry you had all the forward gears.'

'Sandy' Saunders, troop commander with 2nd Northants Yeomanry, wrote:

The regiment had been training since 1939 as an armoured regiment in both an anti-tank and reconnaissance role. It was a pity that their equipment was inadequate. The Cromwell was designated a cruiser tank, fast across country but under-armoured and under-armed. The 75-mm gun was only capable of knocking out German Mark IV and Panther tanks at *point blank* range while their 75 mm and 88 mm (converted AA guns) could knock out a Cromwell at extreme range. We only started to get 17-pounder guns in the Challenger version of Cromwells in August – too late for 2nd Northants Yeomanry to try out in action.

Simon Frazer, 15/19th Hussars, commented:

My appreciation of tank v. tank situations was coloured by three oversized factors *favouring* the enemy, *viz* silence, muzzle velocity and thick *sloped* armour. We had to match this with the speed, manoeuvrability and camouflaged outline of our Cromwells. 'David and Goliath' I told my dispirited crew to cheer them up. Our 75 mm became known as 'the sling' thereafter.

Reg Spittles, 2 Troop Corporal A Squadron, 2nd Northants Yeomanry, described some of his tactics:

I found that if in doubt to stand back and put a couple of 'smoke' shells into the area. If it was a possible anti-tank gun or infantry ambush that would often resolve the situation and cause an enemy withdrawal.

Tank maintenance itself gave few headaches because the Cromwell – Rolls Royce engine, transmission, tracks and traverse – was such a reliable vehicle. The 28-ton tank was reliable on the road, but its 75-mm gun shots bounced off Tiger full frontals. On dry hard fields Cromwell IVs and VIIs would do over 30 mph in fifth gear. But the story gets worse.

Every infantry battalion feared the noisy Nebelwerfer mortar, an ugly multi-barrelled brute on wheels, and easily towed. Its 'moaning minnie' stonks are said to have accounted for 75 per cent of infantry casualties in Normandy. They came in three sizes with a maximum range of 8,600 yards, and most of the five Nebelwerfer regiments (each of sixty projector-mortars) were concentrated on the British/Canadian front.

Only the British 25-pounder field guns with a range of up to 13,400 yards, and 4.5-in./5.5-in. medium guns meshed together in troop, battery and regimental and the larger 'Uncle' and 'Victor' targets were capable of inflicting dramatic large-scale protective barrages or defensive fire plans. Their pinpoint DF and DFSOS targets were praised by the infantry.

The Spandau was a faster firing weapon than the Bren, the Schmeisser better than the cheap little Sten gun. The Panzerfaust one-shot anti-tank missile was more effective than the British Piat. Major Ned Thornburn, Company Commander 4 KSLI, had these views: 'The Bren was adequate, the Sten did nothing to heighten our chaps' morale, the Piat was not reliable, often ineffectual – the Panzerfaust was better. Our 3-in. mortars were, however, as effective as their Nebelwerfers.'

The Germans laid hundreds of thousands of mines, mainly Teller mines, in roads or on verges. These could be gingerly excavated after location or lassooed with a long rope and towed away. Booby traps in houses were rarely defused by the REs, but simply blown up on the spot. But one of the greatest perils to infantrymen was schu-mines or S–mines planted randomly in fields and verges. The former were explosives contained in a wooden box more or less undetectable by the usual mine detectors. They exploded with the pressure of a foot on the buried lid. The latter were just as lethal – small anti-personnel mines activated by a trip wire, which exploded at waist height. The schu-mines would take your legs off and the S–mines would tear your whole body apart.

Field Marshal Montgomery, who had some capacity for deluding himself, wrote to Alan Brooke:

I have had to stamp very heavily on reports that began to be circulated about the inadequate quality of our tanks, equipment, etc. as compared with the Germans. . . . In cases where adverse comment is made on British equipment such reports are likely to cause a lowering of morale and a lack of confidence among the troops. It will generally be found that when the equipment at our disposal is used properly and the tactics are good, *we have no difficulty in defeating the Germans.*

Absolute rubbish of course, unless a ratio of five to one in tank losses was considered acceptable. Simon Frazer's 15/19th Hussar troop peppered a Mark V tank west of Argentan and hit it twenty-two times. They found the Mark V the next morning. It had been abandoned by its very gallant crew because it had run out of petrol. Admittedly its turret superficially resembled a cheese grater, *but not one hit had penetrated.*

Lieutenent-General Horrocks, XXX Corps Commander, knew the score. He wrote: 'Our Shermans and Cromwells had to approach within 500 m of the heavier Panther or Tiger tanks to knock them out, whereas the 88 mm or the Tiger could dispose of Allied tanks at 2 km. The Panther's gun was superior to Cromwell or Sherman, and Mark IV was certainly their equal.'

With the benefit of hindsight, there should have been many more 17-pounder Sherman Fireflies available before D-Day. The meagre supplies were 'reserved' for British armour despite belated American recognition of their superiority in the field. Bill Close, 3 RTR, commented: 'The Comet tank (finally issued early in 1945) was the last contributed by Britain's tank manufacture during the war. With a maximum 100 mm of armour, 77-mm gun and speed of 30 mph, it could tackle all but the King Tiger.'

But at least the Allies had almost total superiority in the air. Although at one time or another most units were bombed by the Luftwaffe and the RAF, and almost inevitably were shot up by USAAF prowling Thunderbolts, the universal view was 'Thank God for the Tiffies.' 155 Typhoon pilots were lost over the Normandy battlefields engaging in a very close support against Boche strongpoints, tanks, or dug-in 88-mm anti-tank guns, but many individual 'little' battles were won and precious lives saved by the RAF intervention. LIMEJUICE was the magic radio call that produced – often from a cab-rank of circling predatory Typhoons – almost miraculous support. The FOOs who were given the opportunity of calling for LIMEJUICE via the regimental radio network, had a feeling of power, of waving a magic wand. There is no doubt that the RAF was very highly regarded by the front line troops despite the occasional 'incidents'.

CHAPTER FOUR

Forming Up

Major Jimmy Carson, 2 i/c CREME, landed with advance parties beside the Canadians at Ouistreham on D + 3. He came ashore in heavy smokescreen and a shower of butterfly bombs as heavy enemy guns from Le Havre were bracketing troops on the beaches. The severely wounded Lord Lovat was shipped home on the same LST. Rifleman Roland Jefferson, 8th RB, recounts his pre-landing story.

We had been issued with French phrase books and money and went in convoy from Aldershot towards London. Every time we stopped the young East Enders would ask, 'Got any English money you don't want?' It seemed that they knew precisely where we were going. Anyway we travelled to the docks at Tilbury and spent a day in a wired off concentration camp. Our vehicles were embarked. Previously our days had been spent in equipment maintenance and the waterproofing of vehicles so that they could be driven through water. Pieces were added on the air intakes and exhaust pipes so that, in theory, they could be driven while almost submerged. Greasy substances had to be plastered all over the engines to prevent water from causing the engine to fail. Finally we walked up the gangplanks of the *India City*, a Liberty ship. We were issued with Mae West lifebelts which we had to inflate by blowing them up, and a paper 'vomit bag'. Thankfully these were merely a precaution and were not necessary.

Noel Bell, who commanded G Company in 8 RB, recalls:

We each drew 200 francs in the new Liberation notes and a little handbook entitled 'France'. On the front cover was a picture of the Arc de Triomphe. We were issued with various novelties for our first 'fend-for-yourself' hours ashore. We were soon the proud possessors of two 'twenty-four hour packs', those little packages which by dint of their contents of dehydrated porridge, dehydrated meat, some four bars of chocolate and some chewing gum were to keep us 'fighting fit' for our first forty-eight hours in France. Also a hexamite cooker heated by circular tablets two inches wide and half an inch deep – which when ignited by a match gave a very hot flame. And little tins of water-purifying tablets and a very fine pair of water-wings!

Arrival in Normandy: an
LCT off Arrowmanches

G Company travelled in the liberty ship *Samsit* together with some
divisional gunners and sappers:

> We were terribly crowded, the lighting was far from good and we were not
> allowed to smoke below. Off Southend we dropped anchor. A church
> service was held on the foredeck and in No. 4 hold two riflemen were
> turning their idle hours to much profit by operating, with considerable
> skill and much showmanship, a crown and anchor board!

Landing Craft Tanks (LCT) carried seven tanks, and Landing Ship
Tanks (LST) were bigger craft with two decks that carried wheeled vehicles.
Crews of course travelled with their vehicles. Lifebelts called 'Shirley
Temples', or the more buoyant 'Mae Wests', were issued to all ranks.

13 RHA went to war from Tilbury docks, with G Battery in a British
LCT, H and I in an American LCT. They landed on D + 9 on the westward
edge of Juno beach at Graye sur Mer, by the mouth of the River Selles,
noted for its tasty oysters and sandy beach. Their sister regiment, 151 Field
Regiment RA (Ayrshire Yeomanry) travelled across the channel split
between the *Empire Canyon* and the *Empire Farmer*. The advance party
sailed from Southampton. On arrival at Ouistreham beach on 13 June, guns
and 3-tonners were loaded on to huge self-propelled rafts known as Rhinos,
and most vehicles had an easy wade of about 3 feet. *Empire Farmer* spent the
night under fire from a mobile battery on the Le Havre coast.

Noel Bell noted:

We turned left and down along the beach, running parallel to the sea. The barbed wire hung in torn shreds and the sand dunes were pocked with shell holes and slit trenches. On a corner down a track was a little wooden cross made out of a 'compo' box inscribed 'A Canadian soldier lies here.' That was all. No name, no regiment. . . . We passed through a German minefield, still wired off and marked with the skull and crossbones sign. Halfway up the ridge was a crashed American fighter plane and just past three British graves in a line, with a khaki cap hung over each of the uprights of the cross. The rolling Normandy countryside opened out before us. Everywhere there were cornfields all gently waving in the summer breeze. Infantry were marching up the sides of the road in single file, sweat pouring off their faces as they laboured under their heavy loads of packs, rifles and shovels. They turned their red faces to the side as we passed in a vain effort to keep the swirling dust, sucked up by our half tracks, out of their eyes.

Roland Jefferson was much encouraged:

Apart from the great armada of ships, perhaps the most heartening sight that day was a very large group of German soldiers who had been taken prisoner and who had been gathered on the beach ready for shipment off to England . . . there were signs of the battles which had already taken place all around us, damaged houses, burned out tanks and other vehicles strewn about the roads and fields. Corpses of soldiers, British, Canadian and German, lying around unburied, and the bodies of cows. . . .

By contrast the 4 KSLI rifle companies who embarked from Tilbury Docks found the dockers on strike for 'danger money' because a flying bomb had fallen somewhere in the docks. KSLI then loaded their own vehicles. Captain Jack Clayton, B Company, an ex-London bobby, gave the sullen-looking group of dockers a piece of his mind. 'I think they thought I was going to draw my revolver on them,' he said.

Trooper John Thorpe was co-driver/hull gunner with C squadron, 2nd Fife and Forfarshire Yeomanry: 'When we set sail for Normandy the V-1 'Doodle Bugs' had just started and on the morning of embarkation one landed at the rear of our assembly camp. It was a reminder to all of us that we had to put every effort into the capture of the launching point to try and protect the civilian population.'

Lieutenant Steel Brownlie, troop leader 4 troop A squadron of the same regiment described his invasion:

We dozed in the (Sherman) tanks, had a wash in a nearby yard and took a quick meal before driving to the docks and reversing on to Tank Landing

Craft 399, along with the CO of 3 RTR. We lay there all day, bathed in the dirty water, ate and slept. We sailed in a huge convoy at dusk (D + 6). It was a rotten night, no cover from the rain and spray and a collision with another TLC about three in the morning. At five we loaded guns, primed grenades, ate biscuits and self heating soup. At eight France appeared as a misty black line, with a few houses and copses. At 9 a.m. on 16 June we 'waded' ashore in only three feet of water, after all that waterproofing designed for six feet. The beach was a hive of activity including a stall made of packing cases manned by two men *selling* Army rations. We pressed various buttons which by means of small explosive charges blew away some of the waterproofing and set off into the interior. I had no precise orders, just followed the tank tracks. They led us to the village of Cully, and there was the regiment.

The 4th KSLI sailed in American LSIs (landing ships infantry) from Newhaven and from Tilbury docks on 13 June. Major Ned Thornburn OC D Company noted: 'We embarked late in the afternoon in bright sunshine. The men were packed like sardines below deck,' but Ned and George Edwards OC C Company were poor sailors: 'We spent much of the night on deck lying like two heaps of garbage in the scuppers being violently seasick.' But despite some problems 4th KSLI arrived, one way or another, in three shipments, at Courseulles-sur-Mer and Ouistreham on 14 June. They marched inland for one mile and then travelled by truck another five miles to their concentration area in the village of Cainet. Most of the Division landed on 13–14 June between Bernières and Courseulles, just north of Bény sur Mer, and concentrated south of Creully – with wet feet but no casualties.

171 Company RASC arrived on 18 June off 'Juno' and Sergeant John Hooper recalls how on their way to Creully a *woman* sniper almost shot CSM Welch. Their harbour was a scene of 'lush meadows aglow with wild flowers, and the deep hedges combined with a strange quietness to produce a deceptively peaceful scene'. The main RASC depot for ammunition and petrol supplies was at Pierrepont. The depot at Rots was attacked by Typhoons. Three dispatch riders were lost: one was injured in a traffic accident, one drove into the enemy lines, and the third deserted back to the UK.

The 23rd Hussars sailed on the 20th. Their last serious action had been at Waterloo! Geoffrey Bishop wrote at the time: `

We move out to an anchorage. The water is literally alive with craft of all shapes and sizes, including one of our most famous battleships, HMS *Rodney*, which stands off proudly aloof from the rest, like a great dane among a crowd of terriers. Destroyers, minesweepers, MTBs, troopships, hospital ships, more and more ships fill the horizon, close on a thousand seen with binoculars.

He and Ted Harte, on board the LCT, shared a bottle of gin, some bread, cheese, onions and cake in the tiny wardroom with their naval hosts: 'We have a grand evening and there is a goodly show of bawdy stories.' Eventually on the 23rd they disembarked near shattered Courseulles and moved inland for 14 miles via Graye sur Mer.

CHAPTER FIVE

'War is Mostly about Waiting'

Looking back it was puzzling to realize that the finest armoured division in the Normandy bridgehead was kept champing in the wings between the villages of Cully and Lantheuil for nearly a fortnight. Monty had landed his 'professional' divisions – 7th Armoured, British 50th and 51st Highland – shortly after D-Day. On the day that 11th Armoured Division landed in Normandy, the famous Desert Rats suffered a humiliating defeat at Villers-Bocage. Tiger tanks of 501st Heavy Tank Battalion and 2 Panzer had brewed up twenty-five Sherman tanks and twenty-eight AFVs, mainly of 4th County of London Yeomanry. To be greeted by this dreadful news was distinctly not good for morale.

Ned Thornburn of 4th KSLI described Cainet as 'a quiet undistinguished little village, rather dusty with a number of apple orchards – a good place for a picnic'. Steel Brownlie wrote:

There was now a period of waiting, with sports and even bathing parties. We studied air photographs and visited nearby battlefields where there were brewed-up tanks still with bodies in their seats. I got to know a peasant family in the village, drank cider and ate artichokes. It rained. We became expert in cooking and making a watertight bivvy. As usual, postponed orders, so we hung about, wrote letters home, or dozed a bit. War is mostly about waiting.

Every junior officer performed the strange role of censor, 'vetting' the amazingly prolific mail engendered by all the soldiers. SWALK (signed with a loving kiss) was just one of a dozen 'secret' codes between husband and wife, trooper and girlfriend. Other more earthy endearments were BURMA ('be undressed ready my angel'), and NORWICH ('nickers off ready when I come home'). Reg Spittles, 2nd Northants Yeomanry, had his own private code to his wife – MIZPAH meant 'The Lord watch between me and thee while we are apart'. Reg survived the campaign and he and his wife lived happily ever after. Officer nicknames were freely used in the letters. It took troop leader Patrick Delaforce some time to realize who it was who was so frequently referred to as 'the lad'!

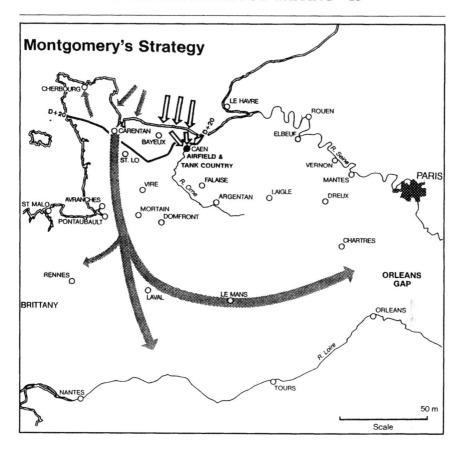

Montgomery's Strategy

Geoffrey Bishop, 23rd Hussars, organized a large dug-out slit trench near Coulombs, in which his camp bed fitted with a waterproof sheet on top, and christened it 'Chateau Ordinaire'. He and Desmond Chute inspected burnt-out British tanks to 'find out whether their destruction can teach us any lessons. A mile away, just burnt and charred ruins with evidence of the tragic end to most of their crews – desolate hulks in the middle of the dripping corn'.

Some officers with well-lined pockets went on the spree. Lieutenant Keith Jones and several other officers of 2nd Northants Yeomanry, with Charles Pidduck, the GOC's ADC, had a meal at a local auberge.

Lieutenant Keith Jones visited neighbouring units to tell them what the new British Cromwell tanks looked like, there being of course no photographs or drawings available. He took his scout car driver to the divisional dentist and admired the twenty comely RAMC ladies in uniform he saw there. At night the Luftwaffe dropped bombs. Occasionally the RAF or USAAF dropped bombs too. AA guns chattered and shell fragments caused most of the division to sleep well below ground at night.

The build-up of VIII Corps, of which 11th Armoured Division was the leading formation, was delayed by the mighty gales of 19–22 June, which damaged Mulberry harbours and prevented reinforcement and back-up troops, food and ammunition supplies from being landed.

There were many comments made about the French peasants moving sadly and forlornly about their ruined landscape, littered with dead cows and horses, corn crops ruined by minefields and tank tracks. British soldiers often milked cows abandoned by their owners, and bartered tins of corned beef for eggs, camembert, cider or, better still, calvados! Sergeant John Hooper, RASC, expert on rations, recalled:

The dehydrated forty-eight hour rations were eaten without relish. Unfamiliar with the dehydrated porridge, minced meat, etc., most people used too little water when cooking them on the solid fuel Tommy cookers, producing severe constipation. The seven varieties A to G of fourteen man/day compo packs offered a wide range of tinned food including M & V (meat and veg), corned beef, Spam, tinned bacon, salmon, peaches, other tinned fruit salad, currant duff, treacle pudding, biscuits, butter, jam, chocolate bars, ninety-eight cigarettes, four sheets of toilet paper per man. The favourite was F pack, containing M & V plus tinned pineapple.

But many apparently untouched packs with wire binding intact were 'missing' their cigarette quotas!

Rifleman Jefferson notes:

For the next ten days we were static and did no fighting and we began to wonder whether we had been forgotten. The thunder of war was ever present in the distance. The whistle of huge shells fired from the battleships out at sea (*Warspite* and *Rodney*) could be heard above us as they fired over our heads into the German positions around Caen. Many of us had all our hair cut off in case of lice infestation. We looked pretty gruesome with no hair.

All tanks, half tracks, SP guns and carriers were carefully de-waterproofed and then re-loaded for battle. Noel Bell discovered 'there was much more room in the vehicles and although we were well crowded we at least could sit in them and get ourselves *under* the level of the armour plating – *a problem to which all of us gave much thought!*'

The Rifle Brigade engaged in various activities. Michael Lane blazed away at a hostile plane with his bren gun. Of course it turned out to be a Spitfire. Rifleman Gobbett drew the Derby winner, Ocean Swell, in the regimental draw and won 730 francs. A sports day was arranged with prizes awarded by a strange (but curiously familiar) 'Duchess of Cully'. There were church services, swimming jaunts in rivers, walks, much 'active service' washing of clothes, and culinary experiments galore, but, most importantly, there were many practical conferences between 8 RB 'management' and 3 RTR for mutual protection drills in the bocage country. This produced valuable dividends in the months to come. Another dividend was the day when 3 RTR handed over dozens of superfluous .50 Brownings from their Sherman tanks (equipped with BESAS), which 8 RB mounted on carriers, trucks, and even on some scout cars.

And so 11th Armoured Division finally, irrevocably, went to war.

CHAPTER SIX

'Cry Havoc – and Let Slip the Dogs of War'

Many of the young soldiers now in action for the first time had had some experience of battle camps and firing exercises in their training in the UK. Derrières hugging the ground as 'boot' sergeants fired live ammo a foot above is one thing, but the first salvoes in earnest from the other side of the hill can be quite startling. Here are comments from the 'sharp end' leaders.

The 23rd Hussars' historian wrote: 'Those who witnessed it will always remember the shock of seeing for the first time one of the Regiment's tanks go up in flames. One moment an impregnable monster, with perhaps a crew containing some of one's best friends forging irresistibly towards the enemy; the next, a crack of terrific impact, a sheet of flame – and then, where there had been a tank, nothing but a helpless, roaring inferno.'

Sergeant Frank Moppett, 2 Company 1st Herefords, talked about his first action with his carrier section:

At the start of Epsom my carrier was leading down a narrow lane on the edge of Cheux. Suddenly we were in chaos. Shots flying everywhere. Numerous dead Scotsmen were lying everywhere, one corporal lying over a branch of a tree twenty foot above the ground. A torso without arms or legs. Six 17-pounder anti-tank guns still attached to their quads all burning furiously. A group of dead Scots soldiers lying on their blankets. A Tiger tank knocked out on its side still burning.

To his driver Moppett said: 'If this is war, mate, we're really in it.'

Noel Bell records his feelings on his first day of action. He noticed the details of the ruined villages – gaily coloured advertisements for Byrrh and Cinzano painted on the sides of houses, enamelled signs displayed *Boulangerie* and *Boucherie-Charcuterie*, knocked-out German SP guns, Canadian Bren-carriers, and the surrounding cornfields littered with Canadian dead: 'All-pervading was the sweet, sickly repulsive smell of death. Dead cattle blown and stinking lay round the smouldering farms. Truly the four horsemen of the Apocalypse were riding through Normandy.' But the next morning his No. 10 platoon supporting 3rd RTR patrolled through St Mauvieu village and then Cheux:

We rolled down the slope. Suddenly a gun spoke, once, twice and again. Some sparks seemed to fly off one of the leading tanks and the air was filled with a sound like that of a racing car passing at great speed – a rushing, whirring note. A moment's pause and the tank burst into a mass of flames. Micky said 'Eighty-eights'. We were too green to be scared for we failed to recognize the significance of it all. It had not yet registered on our minds that we were in the enemy gunner's sights and at that moment another armour-piercing shell was being loaded into the breach. It was our first taste of direct enemy action and it seemed coincidental that the shells were coming our way. We had yet to learn to be afraid. We had yet to learn to respect the German 88 mm.

Lieutenant Steel Brownlie noted:

At dawn in a steady drizzle that soaked everyone to the skin, we motored (Shermans of 2nd Fife and Forfarshire) through the gun area, through gaps in the minefields and past German trenches, empty except for bodies. A few shells dropped close. We had gone about 300 yards when two armour piercing shots came from the high ground on the right, sending up showers of earth and killing two infantrymen. I wheeled the troop right and saw the turrets of three Germans tanks nicely positioned hull-down about 1,800 yards away. AP was no use at that range so I did an HE shoot on them. They brewed up a half track nearby (you could see their solid shot whirling down in our general direction) but after a few minutes they withdrew. Encouraging. . . . That night, after our first day in action, I don't think that anyone slept. The petrol and ammo took three hours to reach us. The enemy were only a few hundred yards away, and everybody was shattered by the day's events. Long afterwards you thought about Cheux as just about the worst and anything else seemed an improvement. You also thought about Cully, a tiny hamlet, as a sort of haven of peace.

Stretcher-Bearer Corporal Ron Cookson, 4th KSLI, took part in the action to clear Baron and wrote:

I well remember my baptism of action and the Battalion's first two casualties, when we moved up that evening to Baron, B Company together with A. We waded across the River Odon and I remember how warm the water was at that time – up to waist level. All was peaceful until we approached the higher wooded ground, then all hell let loose with 'moaning minnies', shelling and airbursts above us. Our first casualty was Private Askey who was killed. Then Private Jones had his leg shattered. I went to Askey first but I could see he was already dead with a great big piece of shrapnel in the middle of his back which had smashed his vertebrae.

'Later that dreadful day', recalled Geoffrey Bishop, 23rd Hussars, on his first day in action near Modrainville, 'I was to learn that poor young Peter Halyar's tank had been hit just before Bob's and that young Peter was mortally wounded and his operator killed. Three out of Bob's four tanks knocked out and two out of four officers killed within twenty minutes. I went on firing at the anti-tank gun in the hedge 1,500 yards ahead.'

Trooper Ernie Hamilton, 15/19th Hussars, described his first day in action west of Argentan: 'The same feeling as being on a scheme in England until a loud explosion – a German panzerfaust – and the green young crew said in unison 'What the bloody hell was that?' Through his 2-in telescope Ernie spotted a hull-down Panther in a sunken road: 'Why was my commander not giving me the order to fire? I expect fate stepped in here; we found this particular tank had been abandoned.' In Argentan, Ernie noted through his telescope, American GIs were throwing the bodies of their buddies into Dodge trucks: 'We were now in a real war.'

During Operation Epsom on Hill 112 young Lance-Corporal Reg Worton, in the carrier platoon of S Company, 1st Herefords, was ordered to take No. 2 section up the hill, left of a copse, and dig in round E Troop 75 A/Tank SP guns. 'Right oh lads, up we went; when I got up there I was on my own. As soon as I showed my face, the mortars came down, twice I tried it.' He and his section then sheltered behind the SPs, 'but we could not move for the mortaring. My first taste of war. Captain Barnaby, our platoon commander, said to me, 'You will be OK when you have shot your first Boche, Worton.' He was killed the next day. I soon came to the conclusion I was not to last long.'

CHAPTER SEVEN

Operation Epsom

Day One – 26 June

Monty was determined to make a third effort to take Caen, with a massive flanking attack by VIII Corps supported by XXX Corps and I Corps. The start line was a 4-mile front between Rauray and Carpiquet, respectively 8 and 4 miles due west of Caen, just north of the Caen–Bayeux road. The main objective was a crossing of the rivers Odon and Orne with their thickly wooded banks, some 3 or 4 miles due south. VIII Corps consisted of 15th Scottish, 11th Armoured and 43rd Wessex Division plus 4 Armoured Brigade. The Corps was commanded by Lieutenant-General Sir Richard O'Connor, a superb leader in the earlier African campaigns, who more recently had spent two years as a POW in Italy. VIII Corps had 60,000 men with 600 tanks and almost 1,000 guns in support. 12 SS Panzer Division and specifically battle groups of 1 and 11 SS Panzer Corps, a detachment of Tigers and a Luftwaffe battery of 88-mm dual-purpose guns was to bear the brunt of the main attack.

At 0730 hrs on 26 June, preceded by an Army Group Royal Artillery barrage, 15th Scottish advanced and captured their first two objectives, the villages of St Manvieu and Cheux. Major General 'Pip' Roberts wrote: 'About 1230 hrs I got orders to send 2nd Northants Yeomanry on their dash for the Odon bridges, to be followed by 23rd Hussars, 2nd Fife and Forfarshire Yeomanry and supported by 3 RTR. But unfortunately no close infantry/tank mutual support for which the Division had trained for many years.' Initially 23rd Hussars were on the left, 2nd Fife and Forfarshire on the right and 3 RTR in reserve. The REs had cleared minefields, bulldozed and laid special tank tracks and the CMPs had signposted the routes very well – all three vital services rather taken for granted. The cartography did not always make for accurate map reading!

Tim Ellis, 4 KSLI, wrote in his diary: 'It rained all night and in short sharp bursts all day as well – it couldn't have been bloodier.' Cheux itself had been wrecked by the artillery barrage, the roads blocked, and progress by our Cromwells and Shermans was very slow despite use of flame-throwers. The Hitler Jugend fought as usual like demons, with panzerfausts and magnetic mines, supported by dozens of nebelwerfers.

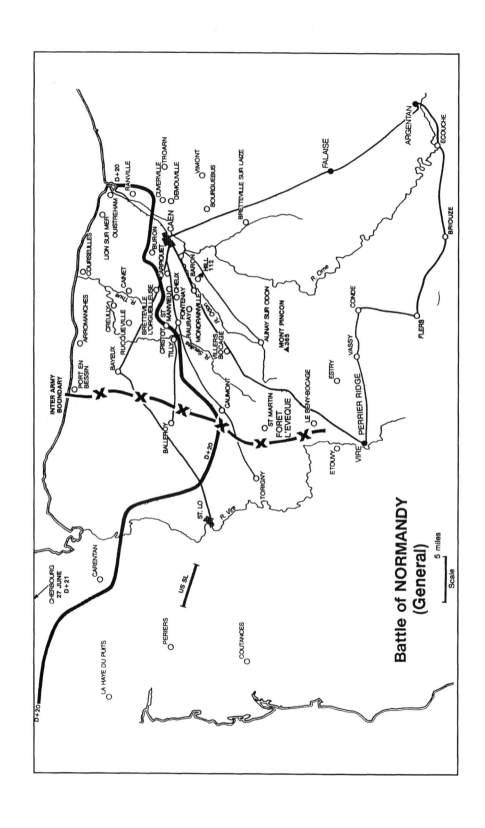

Battle of NORMANDY (General)

Scale
5 miles

Tiger tanks on the Rauray spur just south-west of Cheux dominated the western flank of the 29 Armed Brigade advance. Lieutenant Steel Brownlie, 2nd Fife and Forfarshire recounts:

The regiment formed up 1,000 yards short of Cheux alongside a regiment of Churchills of 31 Tank Brigade and an assault was made on the village. C squadron went straight in. We went left but were stopped by tank ditches and sunken lanes, so were switched to the right. Don Hall took his troop round the edge of a wood, myself following. Two of his tanks went up in flames and he came roaring back, laying smoke. I took cover but could not see anything because of the trees and smoke from the burning tanks. Two APs came just over my head so I too laid smoke and got out.

On the left flank the pride of Scotland – Seaforths, Gordons, Cameronians and Argyles – were taking a terrible beating. Our two leading armoured regiments had a difficult time. 23rd Hussars were ordered to bypass Cheux to the east through typical bocage country with thick hedges growing on steep banks, which made excellent tank obstacles. C squadron arrived at La Bijude on the high ground east and slightly south of Cheux overlooking the Caen–Villers railway and Carpiquet aerodrome. Soon four tanks were brewed up with casualties, but they had helped the infantry push into Colleville. 2nd Northants Yeomanry had one squadron knocked out and 2nd Fife and Forfarshire lost nine tanks.

Lieutenant Keith Jones, 2nd Northants Yeomanry, praised his Humber scout car driver Nobby Clark. In Cheux he saw 'abandoned bazookas, cylindrical gas mask containers, several knocked-out Churchill and Cromwell tanks and everywhere the sweet and sour stench of defecation and death'. During the charge for the Odon bridge the divisional history noted: '2nd Northants Yeomanry withstood the fiercest counter attacks of the operation and repelled them, though sustaining heavy losses especially on the first day.'

At Cheux Sergeant Brettle in his M–10 SP engaged a Mk IV tank brewing up 2nd Northants Yeomanry tanks. In a cornfield he spotted it lurking behind a house, fired AP and ordered his driver to start up ready to move. Muzzle smoke was a dead give-away. Brettle saw a return fire AP cutting through the top of the corn crop and reversed smartly. The wireless operator could see through his periscope as the enemy AP sizzed past: 'Curly, that was bloody close!'

13 RHA and the Ayrshire Yeomanry regiments fired another huge defensive fire programme in front of 29 Armoured Brigade, mainly around Haut du Bosq south-west of Cheux. Roland Jefferson, 8 RB, recalls:

We moved through the blasted ruins of Cheux and for the first time encountered being shelled ourselves. There was German sniper action and we had to seek these out and eliminate them. Perhaps for the first time I then realized that there was a vast difference between the text book soldiering when we were winning the battles on the Yorkshire moors and the real thing we were now experiencing.

So far it was a badly planned battle. 15th Scottish, 11th Armoured and 31st Churchill Tank Brigade were fighting over the same ground – everybody got in each other's way. Noel Bell, 8 RB, wrote:

> Around us was the litter of men's kit, water bottles and respirators, a rifle or two, steel helmets and sets of equipment. . . . We drove down a grassy slope between woods on either side. The slope ran down a little hollow where there were many 25-pounders. We halted there and made a brew and received new orders. A dead horse lay by the hedge. The 25-pounders were firing for all they were worth and their muzzle flashes made quick stabs in the fast-falling darkness. Most of us slept in our vehicles where we sat, for it had been a long day.

A frustrating first day in action for 11th Armoured. The Odon had not been reached and the enemy still occupied the high ground to the west. Rommel was sufficiently alarmed to order a significant battle group from the American front with two brigades of minnenwerfers to tackle our advance. The General wrote: 'It was almost dark before the situation was stabilized. During the day John Currie, CO 4th Armoured Brigade, was killed and Mike Carver took over.'

Day Two – 27 June

Co-operation between 15th Scottish and 11th Armoured was regrettably, in the General's words, 'not very close; they rather went their separate ways' – although later on 23rd Hussars helped the Gordon Highlanders down to the banks of the River Odon. Lieutenant Steel Brownlie reported:

> At dawn we moved again to the east of Cheux where the infantry had made progress during the night and some of the anti-tank ditches bridged. Churchill tanks were to take the woods south-east of Cheux when we would pass through and take the ground beyond. There was great confusion while their attack went in and four Panthers came into the village, scattering the infantry and getting to within 200 yards of us before being knocked out. I saw the commander of one of them blown out of his turret, 20 feet in the air in the middle of a huge smoke ring!

The 2nd Fife and Forfarshire took casualties but fought their way towards Grainville, where, despite heavy fire plans and attacks by 15th Scottish supported by Churchill tanks, the German defences held firm. 119 Battery

75 A/Tank claimed one Tiger and five Panthers, put out of action round Cheux for the loss of Sergeant Hancock's M–10. At Norrey-en-Bessin 118 Battery had a troop under command of 4 KSLI, 1st Herefords and 3rd Mons. On the left (east) the 23rd Hussars battled their way on. Two Honeys were knocked out by a single AP shot near Cheux and another by an SP gun from Mouen down on the railway. B squadron pushed through Mouen to a position north-west of Mondrainville and picked off targets on the far side of their objective, the River Odon. Their Belgian major, Henri Le Grand, DSO, was killed in action when four 23rd Hussar tanks were brewed up by 88s east of Mouen. Mondrainville was like a wasps' nest full of Panthers and snipers, and was then only partially 'smoked out'. The main Caen–Villers road was straight and well covered by 88s and German tanks. 'Mondrainville was a blackened mass of ruin,' wrote Rifleman Norman Habertin. 'Burning tanks were poking out of doorways, enemy guns were overturned; in fact it was like most of the other villages in Normandy.' When the depleted Argyll and Sutherland Highlanders seized an unblown bridge over the River Odon at Tourmauville, C squadron swept through and crossed the river at about 1730 hrs. By 1900 hrs two squadrons of 23rd Hussars were across the river and H Company 8 RB were guarding the precious Odon bridge. But on the west bank the German counter-attack towards Mondrainville took its toll, and half a dozen tanks were lost. During the 27th, 23rd Hussars lost twenty-four killed, twenty-four wounded and five, including two officers, were taken prisoner. It had been a tough and dangerous day.

The divisional artillery fired 'Uncle' targets against Tiger tanks on the east side of the river. Later on 2nd Fife and Forfarshire Yeomanry crossed, followed by the infantry of the Herefords and 4 KSLI. Unfortunately 3rd Mons set off in the dark, wandered offline and found themselves in the village of Mouen, south-east of Cheux. Leaving C Company to hold Mouen, 3rd Mons moved south, took Colleville and Mondrainville and arrived on the north bank of the River Odon by dawn. The Germans counter-attacked at Mouen and captured or killed all but fourteen of C Company. Despite a chaotic briefing by the 159 Infantry Brigade CO, 4 KSLI made their way from Odon, missed the covering artillery barrage, marched cross country through the night, crossed the River Odon, captured their objective, Baron, and were well dug in by dawn. A superb effort.

Major Tim Ellis, OC B Company, noted:

It was very dark among the trees and the maps were a trifle suspect. However, we crossed the river intact and just in time to meet the 'moaning minnies' for the first time. B Company was sorting itself out in a field when these things arrived with their quite horrendous noise. The stonk seemed to fall around us – the ground seemed to bounce up and down but nobody was hit.

However, Ned Thornburn, OC D Company wrote: 'I looked at my map – one of the outstanding successes of the campaign was the quite superlative 1–inch Ordnance Survey maps with which we were provided.' Map reading is a vital art on a modern battlefield.

The KSLI found a small ornamental (unmapped) bridge across the River Odon north-west of Baron. The General wrote:

> I could see the route leading from the bridge to Hill 112 and I was delighted to see the tanks of 23rd Hussars winding their way up the hill. The Herefords and KSLI had to enlarge their bridgehead in the dark and were subjected to both mortar and artillery fire. The Mons held and protected the bridge on the north side.

Thus ended day two of Epsom. Despite muddled planning and tough defences 11th Armoured had their small bridgehead over the River Odon, on the slopes of Hill 112.

The first duty of Padre Christopher Mackonochie, RACHD, on Hill 112, was to recover the body of the Hereford's first casualty, Private F. Ward. Just before dark the padre set off in his jeep. The inevitable challenged passwords were 'Snow' and 'White'. Wailing banshee noises of 'moaning minnies' were heard and jeep and body were abandoned temporarily for the safety of a slit trench. 'The funeral next day was the first I'd had to conduct in Normandy. We prepared a grave in the corner of a field and the service was quiet and simple. Attached to the cross was the following verse:

> He has laid aside his weapon
> And he is parted from our sight
> He has entered into Heaven
> And he has entered into light.'

Day Three – 28 June

Hill 112 dominated the Normandy battlefield. A wayside calvary near the road at the crest gave the hill another name, 'Calvary Hill', as many of the division were to die there. To the north-east lay ruined Caen, to the north Carpiquet airfield; both still held by 12 SS and 1 SS Divisions. The Colombelles factory and steel mill chimneys could be seen to the east of Caen, and to the south lovely vistas of the bocage countryside and the River Orne valley. The Germans now fought bitterly to regain Hill 112, where 8 RB were dug in on the top. Roland Jefferson commented: 'Hill 112 will always be remembered as our initiation into the real hatefulness of war. We found ourselves in a cornfield protecting the flanks overlooking the valley leading to Esquay.' Noel Bell, 8 RB, recounted: 'All day long we had waited with every nerve alert for the expected counter-attack while shells and 'minnies' rained down on us,' The bridgehead was 1,000 yards long, from

Gavrus to the south-west and Baron to the west of Hill 112. Half a dozen Tiger tanks were skilfully dug in on the southern wooded slopes around Esquay, and 23rd Hussars and a company of 8 RB had to deal with them. 'All that day we fought on that ground [Hill 112] and in the late afternoon,' described Geoffrey Bishop, 23rd Hussars, 'Tigers were reported to our north and the position looked very tricky. Calmly under perfect orders from the CO we withdrew to our original positions. About nine at night we got back into harbour, unshaven, tired out and hungry. With just a short break I had been in my tank constantly for more than twenty-seven hours – it seemed like twenty-seven days.' Meanwhile the General was not happy. The brigadier of 159 Infantry Brigade was relieved and replaced by Lieutenant-Colonel Jack Churcher, CO 1st Herefords. Unfortunately the two brigadiers of 159 and 29 brigades could not get on with each other and the General frequently had to act as mediator!

Major Ned Thornburn described Hill 112 as a very broad, flat-topped feature, relatively easy for tanks to take but much more difficult to hold without plenty of infantry. Some observers noted the apparent success of rocket-firing Typhoons.

The infantry battalions dug in around Hill 112 were under enemy observation OPs from Carpiquet aerodrome in the north, Rauray hill to the north-west and 88 mm from Tiger tanks to the south. Occasionally the Luftwaffe joined in too and FW 190s machine-gunned 4 KSLI. 'By the side of a small copse on the side of Hill 112, in the morning we were shelled,' remembered Corporal Reg Worton, 1 Herefords, 'from near Esquay where we had spent the night and Bell and Evans were killed in their weapon pit on my right. I had to pull them out of the trench in bits mixed into each other when we buried them.'

Meanwhile 4th Armoured Brigade sent 44 RTR across the Odon in the direction of Hill 113 and Esquay to the south. That gloomy afternoon 3 RTR travelled through Cheux which was littered with dead Canadians, through the 'Scottish' corridor littered with dead Highlanders, up to the top of Hill 112 where they spent the night. They were protected by 8 RB who had taken over from 23rd Hussars, who had lost tanks and had fifteen casualties. 2nd Fife and Forfarshire stayed firm in the bridgehead. As Rifleman Jefferson observed: 'The stench of death was all around us. Corpses, both German and British, were everywhere and nothing could be done to bury them. They had to remain there for several weeks.'

4 KSLI were under shell and mortar fire in the village of Baron and took many casualties. The worst was when the ration trucks arrived shortly before dusk to supply the first meal for forty-two hours. Rowley Tipton, CQMS D Company, recalls: 'We reached Baron after dark and issued rations under some difficulties. Then we had our first experience of heavy shelling and showers of 'moaning minnie' mortar bombs, which continued throughout the night without respite. With no slit trenches for cover we lay face down on the open ground.' The accuracy of enemy fire, according to

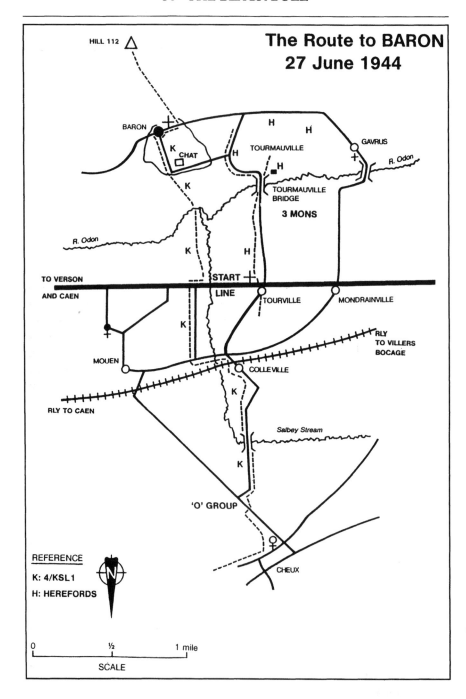

The Route to BARON
27 June 1944

REFERENCE

K: 4/KSL1
H: HEREFORDS

0   ½   1 mile

SCALE

Major Ned Thornburn, 'was due to a French civilian wandering round the village with a wireless transmitter and communicating with the Germans. He made his getaway. The slowness of our reactions must be laid at the door of inexperience in the hard realities of war.'

> The storm broke. The enemy had been watching us settle down [remembers Rifleman Norman Habertin, 8 RB], and before a single trench had been dug, down came those dreaded 'moaning minnies'. There was nothing to do but lie down and bite the earth. A half track a few yards away went up in flames and when finally the mortaring stopped the complete battalion was in a state of utter chaos – all the company vehicles were mixed up, no one knew where their section or platoon was, wounded men were yelling for help and nobody in authority could get any orders carried out.

During the afternoon in view of the casualties being taken, lost guns and half tracks, 8 RB were ordered to withdraw down from Hill 112. German infantry were seen advancing from the west and 25-pounder stonks were showered on them. Under the cover of darkness 8 RB withdrew. Noel Bell noted: 'We made laager and attempted to find order out of chaos. Spirits were low and a great feeling of depression and failure swept through us. There were only two officers left in G Company. The task of re-organization went on through the hours of darkness. Few had more than a wink of sleep that night, some none at all.'

Day Four – 29 June

The morning started inauspiciously for 8 RB. 'As soon as it was light again we set about digging in. We dug with a will and by 9 a.m. had trenches of a reasonable depth that would protect us from all but a direct hit,' was Noel Bell's recollection:

> A party was detailed to return to the hill to recover the half track and two guns which had been ditched the day before. We prepared breakfast. The first shells came over and fell among us. Then like a bolt from the blue came the order that the Company would return to 112. A man nearby said softly 'Oh Christ'. It reflected the feelings of us all. [At the top] all day a continual barrage came down varying in pitch from time to time. Several times the carriers were blown bodily off the ground by the blast. Typhoons again attacked the wood on the right. G and H Company mortars put down a steady stream of fire on the enemy position on the forward slope of the hill.

3 RTR were in action most of the day with 13 RHA FOOs bringing down divisional barrages and Typhoon fire on Tigers dug into the woods.

Captain Philip Kinnersley, 13 RHA, brought down fire on his own OP since the tanks were so close. His tank was hit, mortar bombs rained down on him, his wireless set was smashed, all his crew including himself wounded, so he crawled to a hilltop with another wireless to continue bringing down 'Uncle' targets. Captain Nicoll, Ayrshire Yeomanry FOO, engaged four enemy tanks with his OP Sherman and lived to tell the tale. Over 300 enemy tanks were now attacking the salient from three sides, and fifty Nebelwerfers rained down their noisy mortar bombs incessantly. Sergeant Buck Kite of 3 RTR reported: 'The first thing we get at daybreak are the 'moaning minnies'. Jerry knew the range to a T and the bombs were stroking the top of the hill as they went over. HQ got the worst of it and we lost four NCOs who'd been caught outside their tanks. One a good chum, Dick Brill, who'd been right through the desert.' At Baron 4 KSLI had stood to at 0430 hrs and were getting quite blasé about snipers and 'moaning minnies'. Lieutenant 'Jenny' Wren noted: 'We did no patrolling, so just had to sit in our slit-trenches all day which was very demoralizing.' Their CO, 'Mossy' Miles, was relieved, 'a classic case of battle exhaustion', and replaced by Major Max Robinson. The 2 i/c Major Ned Thornburn complained bitterly of a shell fragment which passed through his shaving kit, but nevertheless 4 KSLI passed a relatively peaceful day.

During the day 2nd Fife and Forfarshire tanks were in action near Mondrainville where Lieutenant Steel Brownlie reported:

A terrific flap was in progress. Support troops were hurriedly digging in, tanks taking up position, shells coming over from Carpiquet aerodrome. When I turned right at the crossroads in the village I was met by three German tanks (Tigers? Everything looked like a Tiger in those days) and some half tracks coming in the opposition direction. The leading tank fired and the shot went over my head. We moved so fast that he had no time for another shot. This would be one of the many counter-attacks that were being mounted to nip off the corridor.

The 23rd Hussars' role was to protect the right flank of the bridgehead. The forward squadrons soon engaged the enemy and almost at once the CO had his tank hit. Geoffrey Bishop thought his Colonel was a great commander: 'keeps a firm hand on the tactical situation, at the same time giving direction and encouragement to his squadron leaders. Monkey and Chris prove themselves first rate leaders and handle their squadrons with great confidence after such short experience under fire'.

In the afternoon the General visited Hill 112 where he was pleased to see that '8 RB supported by 3 RTR had attacked and captured a small wood on the southern slopes of Hill 112. 2nd Fife and Forfars had advanced slightly on the left or north-east shoulder of PT112. And on the right (i.e. south) 44 RTR of 4 Armoured Bd had made a slight advance. In fact everyone in 29

Armoured Bd seemed rather pleased with themselves – and rightly so!' And the Herefords beat off a counter-attack in the Odon valley from the south. At Gavrus 119 Battery 75 A/Tank destroyed five tanks including one Tiger, lost two of their M–10s and two officers were killed, a third on the 30th. At 1800 hrs the expected major counter-attacks started coming to cut the Villers-Bocage–Caen road and the road from Noyers to Cheux. On Hill 112 Noel Bell saw:

At last light some eight tanks reported as Tigers together with about 150 infantry advancing from the west. Very lights were going up and machine gunning broke out. Artillery support was enlisted – time was urgent – and a devastating barrage was brought to bear on the advancing infantry. The gunners succeeded in wreaking complete havoc on the enemy on the ground. The tanks finding their ground support virtually liquidated . . . withdrew. With darkness now complete we awaited our next call to action.

'We were more concerned about survival on Hill 112 than the Orne bridges,' remarked Bill Close, 3 RTR. 'We knew there was only a narrow corridor behind us back to the Odon and were afraid of being cut off or attacked in the rear. . . . We lost about a dozen tanks in all . . . five from my squadron.'

9th and 10th SS Panzer Divisions had hurled themselves against the south-west salient so the orders came down. From General Dempsey to General O'Connor to General 'Pip' Roberts to Brigadier Roscoe Harvey, CO 29th Armoured Brigade, 'Call it a day' was the message.

It was no consolation to learn subsequently that Colonel-General Friedrick, the GOC of German Seventh Army, was so stressed by the apparent success of 15th Scottish and 11th Armoured's bridgehead over the River Odon, that he died of a heart attack (suicide was another possibility). General 'Pip' commented: 'It became clear on the 29th we were out on a limb. On the right 30 Corps had not kept up with 8 Corps and on the left flank, the Canadian attack on Carpiquet airfield had been postponed.' The Corps Commander then ordered no further advances over the River Orne. The General continued:

Since dawn air reports had been coming in showing large-scale enemy movements towards our front from Flers, Argentan and Vire. We would have to go over to the defensive but present positions would be maintained. The bridgehead over the River Odon must continue to be held (by 159 Infantry brigade). The move by 29th Armoured Brigade was carried out between 2300 hrs and 0400 hrs, not a very easy task but generally very well done.

Before dawn Geoffrey Bishop recorded:

We move slowly up to the crest. Suddenly there is a flash on my left and an 88 whistles in front of my tank. We swing round and fire at him. Meanwhile Tiger tanks are reported advancing on our position. They are engaged, orders to withdraw to our new position are given, and last but one my troop is told to go. The little stone bridge over the Odon has stood, thank God, and with my corporal towing a broken down tank in front we rumble over.

8 RB came down from Hill 112 and Noel Bell wrote:

Just over an hour before dawn we were again ordered to withdraw. With most of the vehicles already gone, it was once more a case of climbing on to anything that moved. Through the night we made our way back to an area south-west of Norrey-en-Bessin (6 miles north of the Odon bridge). Even God never knew how good it was for us to see the sun again.

Nevertheless the General replaced the 8 RB CO with Tony Hunter from the KRRC. However, close working relationships had been formed. 'We knew we could rely on 8 RB to protect us in close country when we were at our most vulnerable and in attacks on villages', remarked Bill Close, 3 RTR. 'I worked on Hill 112 with G Company under Noel Bell, in whom I had tremendous faith. We knew most of the company commanders personally which helped us immensely when engaged in joint operations.'

2nd Northants Yeomanry had been ordered to guard the west flank during the move, and Corporal Reg Spittles wrote sadly about their ill-fated night march between Bretteville and Rauray via Haut du Bosq and Cheux. Within two hours 11th Panzer Corps destroyed many of A and C squadron Cromwells who suffered over fifty casualties. Corporal Spittles remembers that Captain Raynsford issued each tank of A squadron with a half pint of rum during the 'crisis'!

At the end of Operation Epsom VIII Corps had 4,020 casualties. 15th Scottish suffered most with 2,331, and 11th Armoured and 43rd Division lost 1,256. During 'Epsom' the KIA (killed in action) losses were 2nd Northants Yeomanry 38, 8th Bn Rifle Brigade 36, 23rd Hussars 36, 4 KSLI 34, 3rd Mons 30, 2nd Fife and Forfarshire Yeomanry 27, 3rd RTR 15, 1st Herefords 12, and the three gunner regiments 29.

It certainly did not appear to be victory to the troops on the ground. Caen had not been outflanked and taken. Monty estimated that on 30 June 725 enemy tanks of seven Panzer divisions were clustered around the Epsom salient compared with only 140 on the American front. And Hitler sacked von Rundstedt from his post as Commander in Chief West, to be replaced by von Kluge. By 5 July a million soldiers had disembarked in Normandy.

'But what good came of it at last? Quoth little Peterkin,
"Why that I cannot tell" said he, "But 'twas a famous victory."'

Certainly Cheux, Hill 112 and Odon rank among the famous regimental battle honours in the British Army.

Epsom Bridgehead: 30 June – 6 July

The General wrote:

> 159 Brigade were not relieved from the Odon bridgehead until 6 July, and during the whole of this time they had been subjected to constant shelling, mortaring and sniping and to frequent attacks from vicious probing of their defences to full-scale tank and infantry assaults. The brigade had stood firm and resolute under very trying and tiring conditions and had established tactical dominance over the SS formations facing it. Brigadier Jack Churcher did a fine job in command.

However, the Germans retook Hill 112 and Gavrus. So 4 KSLI, 3rd Mons and 1st Herefords had a really nasty week, supported by 2nd Fife and Forfarshire Yeomanry Shermans and all the might of twelve artillery regiments of 8 Corps AGRA. (3 RTR had been lent to 32 Guards Brigade against the Germans esconced at Carpiquet aerodrome, west of Caen.) The three defensive fire artillery barrages were quaintly named 'Dorothy', 'Dainty' and 'Duchess'. Major J.J. How, then a platoon commander of 3rd Mons, described their effect: 'Near the Tourmainville bridge at 2200 hrs on 30 June the 10th SS Panzer Grenadiers moved into the attack and regiment after regiment of guns, field, medium and heavy, was switched in to thicken up the barrage. The 10th SS Grenadiers and assault guns withered away under the weight of over 15,000 shells.' FOOs of 151 Regiment Field (Ayrshire Yeomanry) under their CO, Lieutenant-Colonel Phillips, were with every infantry battalion. And Major Ellis, 4 KSLI, recorded in his diary: 'Just as the rations arrived in the evening of the 30th, they started to stonk us in no uncertain terms. The noise was terrific, and even at Dunkirk I had never known such shelling. At the same time an attack was put in against the Herefords on one night, including our C Company. Our DF fire came down like a blanket and caused havoc. It must have killed hundreds of them.' Sergeant Frank Moppett, 1st Herefords, noted of the DF fire: 'It went on for hours and we suffered mentally as much as the Germans – the constant scream of shells overhead, the crash of German shells exploding amongst us.'

The 3rd Mons were on the high ground on the west bank of the River Odon. Joe How noted:

> A night of bangs and crashes and flashing light. In the bridgehead across the river the Herefords and Shropshires were getting a pasting. Explosive flashes darted rapidly about in the valley below – strings of tracer curved

slowly and gracefully away into extinction – flames flickered in the darkness and Very lights hung seemingly motionless over the valley. The noise was deafening. How I wondered, could anyone survive down there.

The Royal Navy 16-inch guns were plastering Hill 112 from 21 miles away! Afterwards Brigadier Churcher calculated that 8 AGRA fired 38,000 shells during the night of 30/31st to see off this major counter-attack.

Tim Ellis saw that the 'Boche had brought masses of kit. The German dead belong to the Hitler Youth. They are all between eighteen and twenty completely fanatical and judging by their photographs taken off the bodies, mainly homosexual.'

2 July was a bad day for 4 KSLI with thirteen casualties including RSM Wall, and CSMs Lewis and Carter, but Tim Ellis noted that the night of 3rd–4th was 'a hell of a bad night from enemy mortars and artillery. The devil of it is that *we* get shelled from the Germans in the Carpiquet area (almost directly behind us in the Salient). As our guns are also firing on the same line (from south of Cheux) it always seems as if they are firing short'. Ned Thornburn 'held the wireless set microphone of the 19 set in my hand with its almost instant response to the call "Duchess Now"'. The Herefords on Hill 112 had nine days of constant shelling and mortaring, mainly from Carpiquet. On 30 June a determined counter-attack, in Frank Moppett's words, 'was only held off by our divisional artillery, who were superb. Their DF fire saved us'. On the next day he was ordered: 'No fighting, Moppett, just a recce, but no one had told the Germans.' He took his carrier gingerly up to the top of the hill which gave a good view over Esquay and found six to eight knocked-out tanks and eight or ten wounded Germans. As his company CO, Captain Barnaby, arrived in a second carrier, Moppett spied enemy helmets peeping above the high yellow corn and the Herefords were immediately swamped with fire. Captain Barnaby was hit, and died later, and Corporal Curtis, the smallest man in the regiment, was killed on the spot. A mortar bomb then fell on top and wounded four more men. Moppett related: 'I had a moment of panic. How long would we last?' At the end of the Hill 112 attack and counter-attack, he was a 'much wiser man'.

13 RHA at St Manvieu and 151 Field Regiment (Ayrshire Yeomanry) near Cheux remained permanently in action every day and most nights. They supported the bridgehead DF plans and had very heavy fire plans on Caen to support I Corps attack on 8 July and 43 Division on 10 July on the west bank of the River Orne. Fire plans of 400 rounds per gun were fired in each instance and on some desperate days, 1,000 rounds. 13 RHA moved gun positions eight times in fourteen days to get closer to their target areas. Both regiments often received counter-battery fire from Carpiquet aerodrome, which made them unpopular with their neighbours. The 'Q' side was magnificent. Come stifling heat or solid rainstorms, huge dumps of 25-pounder shell were carted up at night to the gun positions. And quite often hot meals and mail!

118 Battery 75 A/Tank helped 4 KSLI and 1st Herefords fend off enemy tank attacks until the night of 6 July. Several guns were over-run, quads destroyed and casualties taken, mainly by J, K and L Troops. They reported: 'Violent enemy infantry attack reached its peak about 0200 hrs on the 1st. A terrific barrage by our own artillery inflicted heavy casualties in breaking up the attack. When Corporal Reg Worton, aged twenty-three, came off Hill 112 after eleven days' fighting with hardly any sleep, he was in a coma for many hours.

Within Epsom week 159 Infantry Brigade had three masters, initially 11th Armoured, then 15th Scottish, and next 53rd Welsh Division, before marching back to Cheux on 6 July.

CHAPTER EIGHT

Interlude

For the twelve days after Epsom the Division was at rest based around Brécy. Reinforcements of men and replacements of tanks lost in Epsom arrived. 'I have a queer mixed bag of memories of those days,' wrote the Revd J. du B. Lance, Inns of Court chaplain.

> Perhaps they give a true picture of the mixture of gravity and gaiety which made up our experience. Tending the wounded, both British and German; many contacts with the French, who had mixed feelings; hunting for missing men; pinching strawberries from a chateau garden with the RSM; burying the dead; a fierce argument with the CO, who wanted me to carry a gun contrary to the Geneva Convention; visiting the wounded in the very first hospital still being set up; going to bed in my boots; my first and last surgical operation in removing a man's leg; exhuming a man buried by the Germans in order to identify him; drinking perry in a French farmhouse.

8 RB and 3 RTR licked their wounds at Norrey-en-Bessin. Noel Bell noted:

> We had lost a great amount of kit on Hill 112 and we were to learn later that the more seasoned a campaigner one becomes, the less kit one loses. Our area had been heavily fought over and a few dead Germans were found in some of the many slit trenches and dugouts. By far the most unpleasant thing though was the presence of dead cattle and the appalling stench of them.

Bulldozers of 3 RTR buried dozens of animals daily. Trucks were sent to Bayeux to buy butter, camembert, fresh milk and cream. Mail came in and a great deal went out; the junior officers censored thirty letters every night. Home-made showers of perforated petrol jerricans, suspended from a bar, then pulled by string, worked rather well. The riflemen and tank crews fired at every plane that flew near them, including Spitfires, without doing much damage. PIATS were put into practice use against the many knocked-out tanks but 4 KSLI spent a peaceful, well-deserved rest at Rucqueville, with eleven days out of contact.

The 23rd Hussars were visited at Putot-en-Bessin by Brigadier Roscoe Harvey on the 4th and the General on the 5th. 'Again the men are all talked to and congratulated, so we begin to feel that we are quite important. I am sure,' noted Geoffrey Bishop, 'every man feels proud to be in the regiment.' On the night of the 7th the bombing of Caen took place:

> Literally as far as the range of my binoculars the sky is filled with bombers coming on in a slow relentless stream like something from a Wellsian dream, or one of the early war films of the sky filled with the Luftwaffe, but now there is not a single German plane in sight. High above, our bombers, Spitfires and Lightnings are weaving about like little silver minnows in a great inverted fish bowl. Great vibrations shake the ground as their loads of bombs crash down.

Between 10 and 16 July 13 RHA and Ayrshire Yeomanry gunners were blasting away at targets at Maltot, Estreville and around our old friend Hill 112, in support of 43 Division and 3 Canadian Division. The fighting was perhaps even more ferocious as Panzer Group West was determined to contain the Odon bridgehead, come what may. Both sides suffered over 3,000 casualties but the Tiger tanks stayed on Hill 112 until 22 July.

Operation Charnwood was a large-scale operation from 7 to 10 July to take Caen, which had been wrecked on the night of the 7th by 267 RAF heavy bombers. By the 10th all of Caen north of the Orne river and Carpiquet aerodrome had been taken with enormous infantry losses.

Reg Spittles with 2nd Northants Yeomanry maintained his Cromwell tank. His favourite meals were pre-cooked bacon, with local eggs, porridge 'tablets' and tinned biscuits lavishly topped with Normandy butter and ration jam. Bully beef was popular, but Reg was worried about a more serious subject: 'They never seemed to put enough of the 4 inch by 4 inch Crown paper pieces in our compo packs. We were pleased when we started to receive newspapers.' The official ration was 2½ sheets per man per day.

'Sandy' Saunders' squadron adopted a cow named Miserable Pastry by the troops after Le Mesnil-Patry, where she had been 'liberated'. She lived a life of great luxury with daily grooming till her skin shone. In return the pampered animal kept the squadron supplied with several gallons of creamy Normandy milk per day. A cider factory had been discovered nearby, located by its alcoholic aroma. Every water jerrican was rounded up and despite a number of extremely drunk Canadians, 2nd Northants Yeomanry obtained enough cider to keep them happy for several days.

Rifleman Jefferson, 8 RB, had a quiet few days interrupted by tip-and-run raids made by enemy fighter planes in flights of three. Writing letters home was popular, and the Army bakery produced fresh white bread with the rations.

2nd Fife and Forfarshire Yeomanry were in action from 10 to 14 July around Baron, then Mondrainville and finally Fresny-Camilly. On the 12th Steel Brownlie and his squadron leader, John Powell, made a recce on foot to the top of Hill 112 from Baron: 'We crawled for about half a mile and got to the crest when a furious 'minny' stonk came down on the tanks behind us,' which inflicted damage on gunner Buchanan, their slit trench and Steel's tunic and beret which – it was a hot day – he had fortuitously left behind. In Mondrainville the tank crews had showers under a pump and alfresco meals in an orchard where they had a sing-song round a piano.

Trooper Tony Matza, 23rd Hussars, liked camembert cheese. Unfortunately, left by mistake in a bedroll on top of a warmed-up Sherman engine, camembert produced a pungent, revolting, unpopular smell. But mobile bath units and visits to a cinema were both well attended, although a sports day was rudely interrupted by two German divebombers. C squadron tested their guns at Rauray against knocked-out Panthers, with depressing results. The 75-mm gun made no impression on the front at all! Vats of cider and bottles of calvados were sometimes 'liberated' but unripe apples bombarded tank commanders in the orchards and mosquitoes bit everyone at night. Indeed, the General's ADC was out of action one day with savage bites! Barter trade was rife. One trooper swapped his second pair of boots for a large chicken! Jimmy Carson, 2 i/c CREME, recovered a Panther from an orchard in Cheux 'which the Huns objected to rather emphatically. Fortunately I had attended the enemy AFV course at Furde at Chobham so we could cope with demolition, charges and the rewiring of the burned-out V8 Maybach engines' ignition.' Jimmy proudly showed the working model to General 'Pip' before it was shipped back to England.

But the General was not at all happy. His division had been split asunder, the armour loaned to other brigades, the infantry still in the Odon bridgehead and the gunner regiments with 8 AGRA. 'I fear,' he said to Bobbie Erskine, GOC 7th Armoured Division, in a similar situation, 'that the outlook for armoured divisions doesn't look good.' Moreover General 'Pip' had just 'retired' one brigadier and two regimental COs, which was not good for anyone's morale.

However, on 16 July the Black Bull shook itself and was off to bloody war again.

CHAPTER NINE

Operation Goodwood

The Plan

Monty had to keep up the pressure around Caen, to continue the war of attrition and 'write down' the opposition, thus allowing the future American breakout from the western flank. As the Duke of Wellington once said: 'Hard pounding, Gentlemen', and that was the way it turned out. 'I had decided that the time had come to have a real "showdown" on the eastern flank and to loose a corps of three armoured divisions into the open country about the Caen–Falaise road' were Monty's words. With a million armed men in the constricted bridgehead, huge supplies of tanks and munitions, a grand scale operation was needed. Planned initially as Operation Jupiter, it was renamed Operation Goodwood. Monty and his generals hoped for a breakout to Falaise and this message was passed all the way down the line.

Since infantry losses in the first six weeks had been very high – almost on a First World War scale – Monty decided to husband his manpower resources. Behind a massive air bombardment, and equally devastating creeping artillery barrage, the 750 tanks of VIII Corps under Lieutenant-General Richard O'Connor would thrust into the open spaces south-east of Caen. Flanks would be protected by the Canadians in the eastern Caen suburbs and 3rd British and 51st Highland Divisions on the left (eastern) flank.

To reduce the risk of infantry casualties the order went down to General 'Pip' Roberts, GOC 11th Armoured Division, via his Corps Commander, that 29th Armoured Brigade and 159 Infantry Brigade would fight parallel actions. Despite Roberts' strong protests that combined armour/infantry tactics were needed to take out the score of nearby fortified villages, he was told 'take it or leave it', in other words, another armoured division would lead instead. 7th Armoured and Guards Armoured would come through on 11th Armoured's immediate flanks for the second stage attack. Monty's orders were specific. 11th was to take Bras, Hubert-Folie, Verrières and Fontenay; 7th Four and Garcelles-Secqueville; and Guards Cagny and Vimont.

There were many other serious problems which, perhaps fortunately, the 'sharp-end' soldiers knew little about:

1. Lack of surprise. The British salient – a small sector 3 by 5 miles on the east side of the Orne – the launch pad for Goodwood, was under constant German observation from their strongpoints in the Colombelles, Mondeville

and Cormelles factory areas in the eastern suburbs of Caen. The noise and confusion of three armoured divisions moving up at night with thousands of support vehicles could not be concealed from General Deitrich, the Panzer Corps Commander.

2. Rommel had caused the twenty Norman villages to be strongly fortified to a depth of 15 km in three lines of defence – immediately in the path of Goodwood attack.

3. The six bridges over the River Orne/Canal de Caen were insufficient to feed the huge amount of armoured traffic through quickly. Immense traffic jams built up which in due course were bombed and shelled.

4. The main Allied artillery formations were west of the River Orne and the barrage of 1¼ million shells would cover the armoured formations up to the first barrier – the Caen/Mezidon/Lisieux railway embankment 5 miles from the start lines between Ste Honorine and Escoville. After that line had been crossed the two divisional artillery regiments would be firing non-stop with occasional long-range medium support.

5. The only RAF Forward Air control post to deploy Typhoon support was knocked out almost immediately. There was no back up, no RAF close support. When later on 23rd Hussars needed a Typhoon attack, G Battery, 13 RHA wireless sent a message back on BBC frequency to be relayed to RAF HQ.

6. General Roberts was unhappy about orders to take the heavily defended village of Cagny on the left flank. O'Connor allowed a compromise by which a 'masking' was undertaken. It still remained a thorn in the side, as will be seen.

7. Rommel had strongly fortified and reinforced the vital heights of the Bourguébus ridge (aptly christened Buggers Bus) which lay south-west of the second embankment of the Caen/Vimont railway. There were seventy-eight 88-mm guns dug in, and although American Flying Fortresses bombed the area to some effect, the surviving three regiments of III Anti-Aircraft Corps inflicted severe damage later.

8. By deliberately choosing 'ideal' open tank warfare country with few hedges and rolling cornfields, Monty had provided an excellent killing ground for Tigers, Panthers, Mk IVs and the dual purpose 88 mms. And so it turned out.

The Order of Battle

Behind the rolling barrage of 192 field and 64 medium guns, covering 5 miles to the hour, 15 yards per minute, the lead regiments were moving across the start line between Escoville and Ste Honorine-la-Chardonnerette at 0745 hrs. The artillery barrage was to be 2,000 yards wide, initially 4,300 yards south-east, then a further 2,000 yards south-west. Leading was a borrowed squadron of Westminster Dragoons equipped with Churchill flail

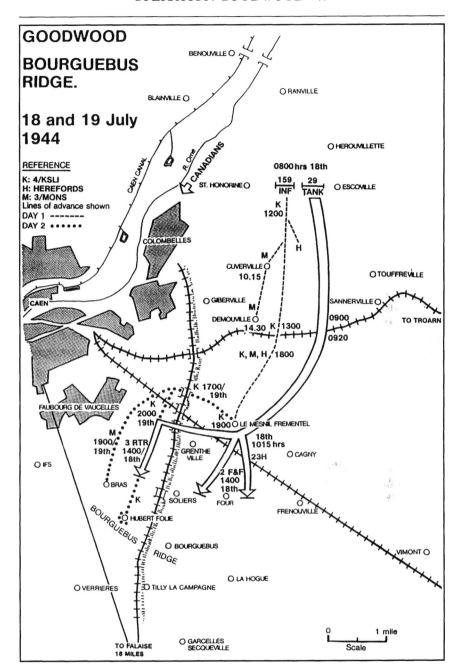

GOODWOOD

BOURGUEBUS RIDGE.

18 and 19 July 1944

REFERENCE

K: 4/KSLI
H: HEREFORDS
M: 3/MONS
Lines of advance shown
DAY 1 -------
DAY 2 ••••••

tanks. Later on they performed nobly as gun tanks. 3 RTR with H Battery 13 RHA and G Company 8 RB were in the van, followed by Brigadier Roscoe Harvey and Lieutenant-Colonel Bob Daniell, CO 13 RHA. Then came 2nd Fife and Forfarshire Yeomanry with I Battery 13 RHA, 23rd

Hussars with G Battery RHA. Then 2nd Fife and Forfarshire would move to the left, 3 RTR to the right, with 23rd Hussars in reserve. The front was so narrow that the Shermans would be only 30 yards apart. A mass of vehicles crammed together – a marvellous target for Panthers and 88s. The best open tank country was the area east of the two villages of Cuverville and Démouville. Their clearance was entrusted to 159 Infantry Brigade with the Cromwells of 2nd Northants Yeomanry in support. The guns of Ayrshire Yeomanry were dug in at Blainville, north-east of Caen, with FOOs out – two with 2nd Northants Yeomanry, one with each of the three infantry battalions.

The Air Bombardment

1,700 Allied, mainly USAAF, bombers would take out selected villages on the Caen plain. Then medium bombers from 9th USAAF plus Flying Fortresses would saturate an area 6,000 yards long and 2,000 yards wide.

Every British and Canadian soldier gaped, amazed at this awful, astonishing bombardment. However, a Marauder bombed 23rd Hussars and killed several men. The immediate effect was horrific, as these German accounts show.

Captain Freimerk von Rosen, aged nineteen, was acting CO of 3 Company, 503 Heavy Tank Battalion. Early in the morning of 18 July he reported:

> My own tanks [twelve Tiger tanks] were combat ready, well placed, camouflaged and dispersed in the park of Manneville [between Troarn and Mondeville, 5 km east of Caen]. We had dug foxholes under each of them in which were sleeping part of the crew. I was awakened early in the morning by engine noise and saw the first bomber waves approaching. From this moment on our concentration zone was subject to air bombardment by heavy bombs which lasted for 2½ hours without interruption. We were located in the very middle of this bombardment, which was like HELL and I am still astonished to have survived it. I was unconscious for a while after a bomb had exploded just in front of my tank almost burying me alive. Another tank 30 metres away received a direct hit which set it on fire instantly. A third tank was turned upside down by the air pressure, a Tiger at the weight of 58 tons, which shows you in just what a hell we found ourselves. This was followed by fire of heavy guns. All tanks were completely covered with earth. The engines were full of sand. Weapons were thrown out of adjustment. Fifty men of my company were dead, two soldiers committed suicide. Another soldier went insane. When we withdrew in the early afternoon to the Cagny area the entire battalion had only six to eight tanks left [out of forty-two].

At 0545 the RAF Lancasters and Halifaxes came first, followed at 0700 by the 402 Mitchell Marauders and Havocs and the 539 Flying Fortresses with their small fragmentation bombs. Ted Jones, 4 KSLI, thought 'the sight of those bombers filled everyone with pride'. Altogether 7,200 tons of bombs were dropped plus powerful naval salvoes from HMS *Mauritius*, *Enterprise* and *Roberts*, anchored off Juno beach.

The Opposition

Before he was seriously wounded on 17 July Field Marshal Rommel had fortified a total of forty-five villages. These included Cuverville, Démouville, Cagny, Emiéville and, in the area south-west of Caen, Fours, Ifs, Soliers, Bras, Bourguébus and Hubert-Folie. Each strongpoint centred round a strongly built hamlet of stone farmhouses amid dense apple orchards and extended 15 km in depth. In front of 3rd British Division between Troarn and Emiéville were 21 Panzer Division; between Emiéville and Cagny 12 SS Panzer Division; and in front of 11th Armoured was 1 SS Panzer Division with forty-six tanks plus twenty SP guns, and parts of 272 Infantry Division. British Intelligence estimated there were 100 German tanks and 194 field guns in position, plus seventy-eight deadly 88-mm dual purpose guns, twelve heavy flak guns and no less than 272 'moaning minny' nebelwerfers. It was anticipated that most of this weaponry would be taken out by air bombardment and the rolling saturation artillery barrage.

German Morale

At the time of Goodwood General von Luttwitz, who commanded 2nd Panzer Division at Villers-Bocage and Caumont, sent a secret document to the GOC Infantry Division relieving him:

The incredibly heavy artillery and mortar fire of the enemy is something new both for the seasoned veterans of the Eastern front and the new arrivals from reinforcement units. Whereas the inexperienced reinforcements require several days to do so after which they become acclimatized. The average rate of fire on the divisional sector is 4,000 artillery rounds and 5,000 mortar rounds per day. This is multiplied many times before an enemy attack, *however small*. For instance on one occasion when the British made an attack on sector of only two companies they expended 3,500 rounds in two hours. The Allies are waging war regardless of expense. In addition to this, the enemy have complete mastery of the air. They bomb and strafe every movement, even single vehicles and individuals. They reconnoitre our area constantly and direct their artillery fire. Against all this the Luftwaffe is conspicuous by its complete absence. . . . Our soldiers enter the battle in low spirits at the thought of the enemy's enormous material superiority.

Forming Up for Goodwood

2nd Fife and Forfarshire tanks set off on 16 July 'in a light rain that mingled with the fine dust. Everything was coated with a film of sticky mud, making goggles useless and life miserable', noted Lieutenant Steel Brownlie. The regiment eventually formed up in the fields by Bénouville, where scores of crashed 6th Airborne gliders were still lying. During the night his Sherman was refuelled with a jerrycan of water, so that it was a non-runner. He changed tanks and everyone was tormented by swarms of mosquitoes. John Thorpe received his mail from the Fife and Forfarshire ration truck and one FREE bottle of Whitbread's beer from the NAAFI, a fresh white loaf to each tank crew and a tuppenny bar of Cadbury's milk chocolate per man. 'Coo! What have they got lined up for us? Why are we being buttered up like this?'

Much the same happened at 8 RB. The colour sergeant brought up the supplies of war, NAAFI rations and a bottle of English beer. 'Most of the latter,' Noel Bell recounted, 'was consumed hastily, many being unwilling to take a chance on their bottles, or themselves coming through the battle, and English beer by no means grew on trees in Normandy. Cider had been all that we could get to drink, which upset most people's stomachs.' 8 RB concentrated just north of Ranville. Roland Jefferson felt that 'there could be no stopping a force so powerful – three full armoured divisions – and we were all cock-a-hoop that this massive drive was going to be the big breakthrough.'

For 13 RHA it was a nightmare march to the start line. The dust clouds covering the battlefield settled in the dew, making a paste that covered men and vehicles, penetrating even the inside of their tanks and SP guns.

4 KSLI moved from Rucqueville on a road newly made by the Pioneer Corps, to the canal and river at Bénouville after a tiresome journey in their TCVs. They dug themselves in by Ranville church in swampy, smelly land plagued by mosquitoes. Jack Clayton mentioned: 'Baron was nothing to this. They died in their millions but still they came.'

On the morning of the 16th, 23rd Hussars held a church service in the orchard by RHQ near Cully; then there were open-air hot baths in the afternoon. At eleven at night the regiment moved on roads thick with dust. 'This was to be a nightmare drive,' said Geoffrey Bishop. 'There was no vestige of moonlight and by midnight it was just a pitch black, cold, dusty hell. We passed through Douvres still smouldering from its bloody taking by the Canadians a few hours before.' His driver said on the intercom: 'This place stinks of death.' 'The twin spires of the town church looked like great black arms crying to heaven for mercy. God! It was a desolate shambles.'

The following day the 23rd Hussars reached the pontoon bridges over the double estuary of the Orne and the Canal de Caen, and passed through a field littered with 6th Airborne gliders – over 200 of them – large enough for two or three Shermans to park under one wing. Crews slept fitfully, fending off swarms of mosquitoes.

'It seemed to me that 3 RTR reached its concentration area as much by luck as good judgement,' noted Bill Close, after a nose-to-tail night march with dust reminiscent of North Africa. 'We camouflaged our tanks amid [6 Airborne] wrecked and burned-out gliders.'

The Tank Battle: Day One – 18 July

At first it all went according to plan. The first Germans encountered were dazed and hundreds surrendered. The 51st Highland Division minefields had been efficiently cleared. The Inns of Court armoured cars under command for the first time reported chirpily back that all was clear. Captain Lemon with 3 RTR recce troop 'rather enjoyed the first few minutes as I think most of us did'. The sun came out:

> There was very little opposition and one had a wonderful feeling of superiority as many Germans, shaken by the preliminary bombing and shelling, gave themselves up. As time passed though, they grew more aggressive . . . targets kept appearing in the hedgerows and beyond the villages of Cuverville and Démouville there were a couple of embankments to cross which proved awkward obstacles.

The ripening cornfields, 3 feet high, provided good cover for enemy snipers and panzerfaust-operators from slit trenches. Rifleman Roland Jefferson noted that 8 RB:

> took at least 200 prisoners and sent them back with their hands on their heads. We were still in high spirits and occupied the trenches which the Germans had vacated. We learned just how comfortable a trench could be, as they had left behind some superb specimens. The high chimneys of the factories at Colombelles could be seen clearly and we were finding it difficult to keep up with the tanks which were forging ahead. Our carrier was bouncing about and lurching from side to side as the driver made all the speed that he could. This was fantastic – we were in the thick of everything. 17-pounder self-propelled guns, flail tanks, flame-throwing tanks spurting fire into suspected enemy pockets.

This was a borrowed squadron of Westminster Dragoons from Hobart's 79th Armoured 'Funnies' who had Churchill flail tanks to strip minefields. Geoffrey Bishop noted in his diary:

6th Airborne glider near Caen   German Mark IV tank in flames, Normandy

The dawn of the big attack! The whole regiment (23rd Hussars) was spread out on a fairly open plain, sloping forward; our objective a high ridge of land in front of us and to the right about five miles away. We had advanced about four miles [behind 3 RTR and 2nd Fife and Forfarshire] without much trouble and reached the line of the main railway. So far so good! But now we had no air support and the artillery barrage had ceased.

'Shells and mortars were still exploding all over the place,' recalled Rifleman Habertin, 8 RB. 'An SS officer properly dressed and wearing a peaked hat, was slowly and deliberately walking back through all this with his hands up, neither running nor ducking. Arrogant and cocksure, maybe, but every inch a soldier, and the sort of enemy we were up against.'

At 0945 3 RTR/8 RB had reached the first hurdle of the Caen–Troarn railway line where the very deep ditches slowed down the advance of 3 RTR. Jim Caswell reported that 'the artillery barrage was now too far ahead. Soon the right flank of my squadron was threatened by three camouflaged Tigers concealed in a wood to our left on Bourguébus Ridge. Most of our twenty tanks were hit in a matter of minutes. We were on the right of our regiment so I ordered the driver to make a left turn so that we could get into a good position from which to fire back.' Noel Bell with 8 RB observed that 'the Germans had by now obviously collected their wits together after the first colossal onslaught and things rapidly became very unpleasant for us. Armour-piercing shells began coming in from all directions and tanks of 3 RTR began brewing up. Then on our left Panthers appeared and the fun really began.'

The 23rd Hussars historian described the confused tank battle early in the day in front of them: 'We could see some of the leading tanks on fire and sad little parties began to come back on foot. They were the survivors of the leading crews. All looked smoke grimed and the black-skinned figures of badly burned men staggered along with the help of the more active.'

Meanwhile 2nd Fife and Forfarshire Yeomanry were also in trouble. Trooper John Brown was driving one of the rare 17-pounder Sherman Fireflies and noted:

It was not long after the earlier euphoria that we realized what was in store for us – thirteen tanks, one of our squadrons knocked out, some burning and what remained of their crews either walking or crawling back from the front. Our tanks reached the Caen–Vimont railway [the second main obstacle] close beside a level crossing in the Cagny area. From our position we knocked out two, probably three German tanks, but it was difficult to recognize this in the carnage.

Brown's Firefly was knocked out but the crew made their way safely back to rear echelon in the glider fields near Ranville.

The 23rd Hussars, still in reserve, could see that the ground beyond the second railway line en route for Soliers and Four 'was completely open and lay in a cup dominated by the high ground on which Bourgébus stood. As the Fifes advanced across this open country, they were subjected to withering crossfire from hidden Germans tanks and in their mass formation fell easy victims. The lines of Shermans were raked and shattered by hidden Panthers and so easy was the mark,' wrote the 23rd Hussars historian, 'that had the German gunners been able to load their guns quickly enough, barely one of the Fifes would have escaped.'

John Thorpe, 2nd Fife and Forfarshire, recited the twenty-third psalm to himself:

'The Lord is my shepherd. . . . Yea though I walk through the valley of the shadow of death I fear no evil'. . . . I see palls of smoke and tanks brewing up with flames belching forth from their turrets. I see men climbing out on fire like torches, rolling on the ground to try and douse the flames but we are in ripe corn and the straw takes fire. Soon what with the burning tanks and the burning men and the burning cornfields plus smoke shells and smoke mortar shells from one tank, visibility is being shut out.

Captain Lemon was now less confident: 'We did not hit the crust of the enemy, the 21st and 12th SS Panzer divisions – it was just as the leading tanks were level with Hubert-Folie when the fun began. I saw Sherman after Sherman go up in flames and it got to such a pitch that I thought that in another few minutes there would be nothing left of the Regiment.' This was 3rd RTR, the most experienced tank regiment in the British Army!

Major Bill Close, OC A squadron, wrote:

[I saw] several anti-tank guns among the trees . . . the gunners frantically swinging their guns round towards us. In the cornfield around us were many multi-barrel mortar positions which were already firing over our heads. They were quickly dealt with in some cases by simply running over them with the tank. But the SP anti-tank guns [of Major Becker's Battery 3, 503 Heavy Tank Battalion] were a different matter. Opening fire at almost point-blank range they hit three of my tanks out of the nineteen in action, which burst into flames and I could see that the 3 RTR squadron on my left also had several tanks blazing furiously. My orders were to pass on and bypass the village.

So 3 RTR charged through one of the tunnels of the 20-yard tall Caen–Vimont railway embankment to keep moving towards the villages of Bras and Hubert-Folie.

Sergeant Jim Caswell takes up the story:

Three Tiger tanks suddenly opened up from some trees on the left. Within minutes most of our tanks were hit. I swung the tank around to a better fighting position. I saw an 88-mm gun pointing right at us – a bright muzzle flash – a missile screamed past just overhead. 'Reverse', I shouted, 'Reverse'. Back we went – but we were hit. The gunner was killed instantly. The wireless operator had collapsed badly wounded to the turret floor.

Caswell eventually baled out and carried his seriously wounded operator, Trooper Stanley Duckworth, three miles back on foot to the RAP. 8 RB found themselves on the outskirts of Hubert-Folie 'stuck out in front with no one upon either flank', noted Noel Bell. 'Shelling became rather unpleasant owing to our being in full observation of the enemy. It was no use moving because the shells just kept on following us around.' Three RB carriers hurtled through and back to declare (mistakenly) that Hubert-Folie was clear. His company was involved when 3 RTR was taking a beating from Major Becker's SP guns from 200th Assault Gun Battalion. Their very long, dangerous guns were often mistaken for Tigers. G Company 8RB wisely took shelter from view behind a thick hedgerow, but their carrier platoon suffered heavy casualties. Noel Bell produced a bottle of gin, which unfortunately lowered everybody's spirits even further. Then 2nd Northants Yeomanry Cromwells appeared 'but they did not appear to be in the picture and suffered disastrous losses . . .'. 88s firing from Bras brewed up many tanks and 'moaning minnies' thundered down too close to be pleasant.

The General's Tac HQ followed 29 Armoured Brigade route across the first railway embankment. He noted:

There was some firing on our left and we caught up with (Brigadier) Roscoe Harvey in a wooded area facing a little hamlet called Le Mesnil-Frémentel, about 1,000 yards west of Cagny. The area was being heavily mortared, the flail tanks of the Westminster Dragoons were firing at the hamlet and on the left some 300 yards nearer Cagny were a whole squadron of the Fife and Forfarshire Yeomanry all knocked out and some burning. It wasn't quite so bad as it looked. 3rd RTR had gone on in a south-westerly direction and were now putting a squadron the other side of a high railway embankment which ran from north to south. The Fife and Forfarshire had gone on south leaving Le Mesnil-Frémentel on their right and had now halted because of the decimation of their rear squadron. The 23rd Hussars were well back on the left as some German tanks had come to life in that area.

The General now made a rare mistake. He felt that Cagny must be firmly held since strong fire from there had wrecked the Fife and Forfarshire. So he ordered a 8 RB attack on the village to be cancelled and for the 23rd Hussars to 'mask' Cagny without getting knocked out. Theoretically if they kept further west – near Le Mesnil – they would be safer.

So Brigadier Roscoe Harvey ordered 23rd Hussars forward to the Fife's assistance. B squadron's first troop was hit and blazing within seconds. The squadron was in full view of the Panthers and completely outranged by their guns; nearly all their Fireflies were knocked out and the 75s were virtually useless at long range. C squadron on B's left was now within 300 yards of Four ahead of them. They took out a Tiger and a Panther outside Cagny on the left but suddenly without warning the whole squadron was hit by a terrible concentration of fire from Four virtually at point-blank range. Everywhere wounded and burning figures ran or struggled painfully for cover while a remorseless rain of AP riddled the already helpless Shermans. There were many acts of bravery. Captain Peter Walter was wounded, supervised a collection of wounded, then took over a surviving Firefly, organized the remnants of his squadron and personally destroyed a Panther. He was awarded the DSO and as Ted Harte said afterwards: 'He was recommended for a VC. It was a magnificent performance.' Captain Mitchell, RMO, at one stage had seventy badly wounded men lying in his RAP, and that day 23rd Hussars had twenty-five killed and thirty-two wounded.

This is one of the oddest tales during the 'Overlord' Normandy campaign, as related by the hero (or the villain) of the story:

On the morning of 18 July, after returning from leave in Paris I moved by HQ tank to Cagny [related Colonel Hans von Luck, CO of a Battle Group behind 16 Luftwaffe Field Division], where I saw to my surprise at least thirty to forty British tanks crossing the road Caen–Cagny, west of Cagny. Not knowing that 1 SS Panzer Division had been withdrawn the night before, I assumed that a breakthrough would be attempted. To prevent that I intended (and it was my task) to make immediate counter-attacks with all tanks in order to hit the British tanks in their east flank. But I got shortly afterwards the message about the heavy bombing on both tank battalions. Much to our fortune I saw 88 Flak battery [with dual purpose 88-mm guns] and ordered the Company Commander to act in a anti-tank role, with the result that more than twenty British tanks were knocked out in a short time. Additionally I employed my HQ company in the gap between Cagny and 2nd Battalion to protect my left flank.

Von Luck in fact threatened the luckless AA Commander with his revolver, and told him: 'Either you will move and shoot those tanks and get a medal or I will shoot you.' The 88-mm guns with a *total crew of eight men*, well concealed by the very high corn in the field, destroyed the reserve squadron of the Fife and Forfarshire Yeomanry before breakfast. To add insult to injury von Luck also deployed two Sherman tanks, captured by the Germans in June, to good effect in Operation Goodwood.

Unwittingly, General Roberts then advised Alan Adair, GOC Guards Armoured Division, that Cagny must be fairly strongly held! Moreover, 7th Armoured Division seemed reluctant to get into action, and only appeared about 1700 hrs, much to 'Pip' Roberts' disgust. To be fair there was an enormous traffic jam, caused by minefields and crowded roads, so that both support Armoured Divisions were very late in arriving and the Guards took until 1600 hrs to capture Cagny. The RAF had dropped 650 tons of bombs on the village but von Luck's battle group defended indomitably.

By early afternoon the 29th Armoured Brigade was in trouble from flank attacks and suffered heavy tank losses. It was at Cagny that the three Armoured Divisions would split off in different directions. At 1445 hrs Panther tanks counter-attacked from the Four–Frénouville area, halfway between Cagny and Bourguébus. Although six Panthers were knocked out, the wretched 2nd Fife and Forfarshires took terrible punishment. John Thorpe's tank was one of the few survivors:

Explosions are taking place inside the burning tanks as the ammunition burns and in the almost still air of this hot sunny day, the gases passing through the round turret hatches form huge smoke rings rising high in the windless sky. Cliff orders Best to fire off more smoke shells and tells Robby to reverse and we go backwards zig-zagging 'right stick, left stick, Gunner keep on target and keep firing. . .' and so on as he guides us back to the railway embankment. We have lost radio contact with the rest of the Regiment. We cannot raise our Troop Leader, nor Squadron Leader or the CO. There is no reply as there is no one to answer.

That day 2nd Fife and Forfarshire had four officers and thirty-seven other ranks killed, six officers and sixty-eight other ranks wounded.

During the night the German bombers caused a great disturbance. As Bill Close noted: 'They didn't miss us by much and we got hardly any sleep.' But they did not miss 2nd Fife and Forfarshires, who took many casualties back at their echelon, tank crews and fitter staff.

I Battery 13 RHA Sexton 25-pounders were in action all the day with two troops of the 2nd Fife and Forfarshire just south of the railway line, firing stonks on Cagny and Bourguébus, under fire themselves from AP, HE and snipers in the cornfield. H Battery 13 RHA were in action with 3 RTR, took seventy-five prisoners, and one FOO was killed, another wounded. G Battery with 23rd Hussars also took casualties and the RMO, Captain Cree, handled over eighty wounded during the day, mostly tank crews. BSM 'Pedro' Powdrill was awarded an (unusual) MC for his brave rescue work taking wounded tank men back to RAP under fire.

The 23rd Hussars, who came through the stricken Fife and Forfarshires, who now had only sixteen tanks left, themselves started to take heavy tank losses. They were attacked by Tiger tanks, survivors from the von Luck group from Manneville, now commanded by Lieutenant von Rosen. Two of their eight Tigers went up in flames, shot clean through their armour plate in front as they advanced towards Le Prieuré. British tanks were simply unable to pierce the Tigers' frontal armour, so it was the Cagny 88-mm anti-aircraft crews, unfamiliar with tank recognition, who had mistaken Tigers for Shermans. The morale of the other Tiger crews suffered and their counter-attack petered out.

Between Frénouville and Four, south of Cagny, 2nd Fife and Forfarshire were caught by flanking Panther fire and both CO and 2 i/c were hit and wounded. So 23rd Hussars in reserve were sent to help, but despite destroying several Panthers they met the same fate, and twenty Shermans were brewed by 88 mm and Panthers in Four. The fields south of the Caen–Vimont–Paris railway embankment were strewn with knocked-out tanks from 3 RTR, 2nd Fife and Forfarshire and 23rd Hussars. Ambulances and stretcher bearers arrived at dusk to search, find and succour the survivors. It was a disaster area.

Advancing towards Four, Geoffrey Bishop saw:

Peter Robson's tank hit by an 88 and went up in smoke. The rest of the squadron moved on and I could hear Jock Addison reporting a Panther on the outskirts of the village, which he was trying to engage. This was almost the last coherent message to be heard from the rest of C squadron. They were all brought under heavy and accurate fire and within a matter of minutes about five tanks were on fire and another three out of action.

Bishop told his CO his was the only surviving squadron and was curtly told to command it and hold the railway line to the last man and the last round!

By the afternoon 119 Battery 75 A/Tank were in action at Grentheville where G Troop M–10s destroyed two Panthers and a captured 'decoy' Sherman!

At 1720 hrs the General saw this situation:

2 Northants Yeo west of the railway embankment facing west and north-west linking up with 3 RTR who were facing south towards Bras and Hubert-Folie. 23rd Hussars were in Grentheville-le-Poirier and Four. 2nd Fife and Forfarshire were re-organizing in reserve 1,500 yards north at Grentheville. At 1800 hrs 7th Armoured started to arrive at La Hogue, south of Four and 5th Guards Armoured Bd made a belated but welcome appearance on the left flank taking Cagny, advancing towards Vimont.

21 Panzer and 16 Luftwaffe Field were positioned to meet VIII Corps when they attacked east of Caen. Brigadeführer Wisch, commander of 1 SS Panzer Division (Adolf Hitler) sent his eighty remaining tanks to help hold up 11th Armoured Division. He wrote:

When the British attacked south of Caen my division was immediately sent into battle once more. My Panther tanks became heavily involved around Frénouville, while my lighter tanks had not yet advanced past Roquancourt. I was on a reconnaissance trip on the evening of 18 July when one of those things happened which occurs to a soldier once in a lifetime. Approximately a hundred British tanks, having completed their job for the day had chosen an exposed part of the countryside in which to camp for the night. This mass of armour was lying only a stone's throw from where my own tanks were assembled. I immediately ordered my Panthers to attack from the east and my light tanks from the west. The range was perfect. From my point of view the manoeuvre was highly successful. With my own eyes I saw forty tanks go up in flames during the evening engagement. At dawn of the next morning [19th] we went into action again and we must have destroyed another forty tanks. My own losses were twelve Panthers and one light tank.

The 23rd Hussars harboured a quarter of a mile back and Bishop recorded sadly:

The sky was lit by the flames from our own blazing tanks and the whole battlefield seemed to be littered with burnt-out Shermans. It was a sorry sight. A heavy barrage of artillery fire then seemed to land on top of us and Chris Seymour was seriously wounded. So ended a disastrous day which came to be heralded as the greatest tank battle of the war . . . we were convinced nothing could have been a greater failure and everyone had seen the last of some of his best friends.

By nightfall the Armoured Brigade held a line overlooking, but not occupying, Bras, Hubert-Folie and Soliers. Tank losses had been very heavy: 50 per cent of the Division's armour was out of action. 2nd Fife and Forfarshire lost forty-three, 3 RTR forty-one, 23rd Hussars twenty-six and 2nd Northants Yeomanry sixteen. Total casualties for the day were 336 killed and wounded. The Guards had 137 and 7th Armoured 48 casualties on Goodwood Day One.

The Infantry Battle: Day One – 18 July

On the Corps Commander's orders Goodwood, in effect, became two separate battles. The trials and tribulations of 29th Armoured Brigade have been described on the left (eastern) flank. But parallel on their right on the western flank, a separate attack started with 159 Infantry Brigade, with Cromwells of 2nd Northants Yeomanry in support. The start line was Ste Honorine and their task was to take the village of Cuverville, 1½ miles south, and east of the Colombelles factory area east of Caen, which despite intensive bombing was still aggressively defended. The next objective was Démouville, a further mile south of Cuverville. The 1st Herefords were left flanking, taking the orchards and woods between 159 Brigade and 29 Brigade. Early in the morning the Herefords quickly took thirty POWs, dazed from the air bombardment, but 'moaning minnies' took their toll, killing two men, wounding others. Frank Moppett's carrier platoon harboured that night near Démouville surrounded by friendly tanks. He ordered a 25 per cent stand-to at dawn assuming that the tanks were manned, but discovered they had all been knocked out the day before. 'That was a rude shock.' Frank's carrier platoon stayed under fire, in action until 21 July when they were relieved by Canadians. The 4 KSLI were in reserve and 3rd Mons were leading. Cuverville was reached by 0900 hrs and cleared by 1015 hrs, but the opposition in Démouville was more determined and was not cleared until 1430 hrs.

On their way to Démouville Major Joe How, 3rd Mons, reported:

Machine guns opened up as we approached the village, but the fight had been taken out of the enemy. Many ran back through the standing corn to disappear over a slight rise in the ground. Beyond we could just see the tower of Démouville church. We were collecting up prisoners when a faint screech, a crescendo, a shout of 'Take cover', and we dropped to the ground among the shattered walls as great bangs and crashes and flying debris and dust filled the air. The Germans were doing what they always did: having seen our success they had brought down the already arranged mortar bombardment. Nearby a corporal lay screaming; one leg was hanging on by a few shreds of skin. It was ten o'clock. The sun burned down from a cloudless blue sky.

At 1100 hrs Cuverville was so heavily mortared and shelled that Brigadier Churcher delayed relief by the 7th Battalion Argyle and Sutherland Highlanders (51 Division), allowing 3rd Mons to continue the advance to Démouville. During the day the Ayrshire Yeomanry 25-pounders were dug in near Blainville, north-east of Caen, beside the scores of Airborne gliders undisturbed since D-Day. They fired three supporting barrages during the day and at 1600 hrs crossed over 'London' bridge, but not until six hours later – because of the horrendous traffic jams – could bring their guns into action south of Démouville.

At 1200 hrs 4 KSLI moved forward 2½ miles level with Démouville and just short of the Caen/Troarn railway embankment. Ned Thornburn, CO D Company, relates how 'the battalion advanced in open order down a gentle slope in full view of the enemy's guns through a curtain of German defensive fire, dropping on their faces between each salvo of shells, reminiscent of the famous advance by 4 KSLI on Bligny Hill in 1918'. Casualties inevitably were heavy.

Gunner/Wireless operator, W.R. Moseley, with B squadron 2nd Northants Yeomanry, watched the early crossing over Pegasus Bridge, waited for first light and then set off in his Cromwell in support of 159 Infantry Brigade. Minefields destroyed four of their tanks around the start line:

> It was a beautiful summer day and we advanced through cornfields as far as the eye could see – towards Bras and Hubert-Folie. Very little resistance except for isolated pockets which were soon mopped up by the infantry which accompanied us. Things became tougher, however, as the day wore on and we came upon a field thick with blazing and brewed up tanks, the remains of the Polish Armoured Brigade which, according to rumour, had cavalry charging over a ridge and had been decimated by well dug-in 88s.

In late afternoon his tank was brewed by AP shot. The survivors made their way to Sergeant Tite's tank and climbed on the back. Shortly afterwards that tank too was hit and put out of action. On their way back to echelon: 'we were mortared and sniped at for most of the way, eventually arriving at the crossroads 1 km north of Grentheville as darkness was falling, where we sat a sorry, weary and crestfallen bunch of Yeomen, amid the lurid flames from burning tanks and that revolting smell of burning bodies, not to mention the regular stonks by mortar bombs on the crossroads'.

Captain Jack Clayton, CO B Company 4 KSLI, adds his account: 'The picture was changing [in the Démouville area]. Lots of tanks were now stationary and I said to Dick Mullock: "The Armour is doing us proud. They are going to shoot us into Cagny." But we soon found that the stationary tanks had been knocked out. It was then that we realized what a tough party the Armoured chaps were having.'

About 1800 hrs the whole 159 Infantry Brigade moved 3,000 yards across the railway line to the hamlet of Le Mesnil-Frementel, 1,200 yards north-west of Cagny. Jack Clayton continues his story: 'We ourselves dug in and watched a number of small but determined German counter-attacks being repelled by small groups of our tanks. It was quite grim for us to watch German and British tanks stalking each other round the houses in Grentheville [just south-west], tank after tank eventually brewing up – all too often our own.' Ned Thornburn had cannily arranged to keep a crate of 100 tins of corned beef in the back of his jeep, which Sergeant-Major Eddie Hughes issued that night. The shelling and mortaring continued through the night. During the night Lieutenant-Colonel Ivor Reeves took over command of 4 KSLI from Major Robinson, the 2 i/c. Although the battalion was mainly in reserve that day they took thirty-eight casualties.

★ ★ ★

The division was exhausted and depressed. The 2nd Fife and Forfarshire laager initially consisted of nine tanks out of the sixty that had started out in the morning. Gradually others came in. 'Nobody said very much, except things like "You know so-and-so's had it." The surviving reserve crews brought up spare tanks and the whole night was spent replenishing, re-organizing, repairing and getting set for the next day. Once more, sleep did not figure on the programme,' Steel Brownlie commented.

That same night, by the light of flares, the Luftwaffe bombed the 29 Armoured Brigade echelons, causing yet more numerous casualties. 151 Field Regiment Ayrshire Yeomanry moved their guns up to Démouville for evening DF targets, while 13 RHA batteries were still ensconced with the remains of the armoured regiments. As Noel Bell, 8 RB, put it: 'So ended a day of thrills and disappointments. Our company losses might have been a great deal higher. We had netted a good haul of prisoners.'

Day Two – 19 July

3 RTR had received eleven replacement tanks during the night, so the badly depleted regiment now had three squadrons, each with ten Shermans. At first light, 0430 hrs, after being bombed during the night and having lost two squadron leaders and many tank commanders, 3 RTR pushed out from the railway embankment – once again into 'Tank Alley'. As they reached the lines of derelict tanks that 29 Brigade had lost the day before, even heavier fire came down from artillery on Bourgébus ridge and enemy tanks and 88 mms, between the day's two targets – Bras and Hubert-Folie. An AP shell went through the turret of Bill Close's Sherman and his gunner and wireless operator were killed. Sergeant Kite, however, managed to brew up two SP guns and a Panther from the western corner of Bras. 'We were completely

Captured Wehrmacht,
Normandy

unable to advance. The whole brigade was pinned down,' reported Bill
Close. Again they licked their wounds.

At dawn 8 RB moved to a big open field near the railway embankment
next to the remaining seventeen tanks left to 3 RTR out of their original
sixty. Noel Bell records: 'Here we were lucky as the rest of this field which
was packed with vehicles came in for some very heavy shelling, our part
being left fairly well alone.' Because of the division's heavy tank losses,
General O'Connor now assigned it the limited objectives of taking Bras,
some 4 miles west-south-west of the overnight harbour, and Hubert-Folie,
some 3 miles south-west. 7th Armoured were to attack Soliers and
Bourguébus, and Guards Armoured was pitted against Cagny to the east
and Four to the south. General 'Pip' Roberts had his O group at 1400 hrs.
His plan was for 2nd Northants Yeomanry to support 8 RB into Bras
starting at 1600 hrs and then 3rd Mons would clear the village. Then 8 RB
would advance from Bras to Hubert-Folie supported by 3 RTR, and 4
KSLI would clear the village. There was one outstanding problem in that
the 3,000 yards from start line to the two villages was a completely open
area! When 3 RTR had tried to cross it the previous afternoon they had
been torn to pieces. A secondary problem was that artillery support would
be limited, since AGRA were still west of the Orne, so 13 RHA and Ayrshire
Yeomanry were in action most of the day. 2nd Fife and Forfarshire deployed
out of laager about dawn, A squadron was shelled and John Powell, the

squadron leader, was killed. John Thorpe's breakfast of MacConochie's stew and vegetables was hit by shell debris, and his tank sergeant had a nervous breakdown and was taken away by the RMO. 23rd Hussars, sadly depleted, were in reserve and were attacked by twenty Messerschmidts.

2nd Northants Yeomanry sent their Cromwells against Bras, but by mistake they veered too far west and immediately lost five tanks to dug-in 88 mms from the village of Ifs, 2,000 yards away. So 3 RTR took over the attack with 8 RB against 88s and panzerfausts of the 1st SS Adolf Hitler Panzer Grenadier Regiment. General 'Pip' Roberts wrote: 'Such was the dash of 3 RTR and the effective mopping up of 8 RB that almost the whole garrison was either killed or taken prisoner. At 1730 hrs 3rd Mons followed up and took over from 8 RB.' 'The artillery was as good as its word and at 5 p.m. fire came down and an excellent smokescreen enabled us to move up the slope rapidly and properly,' said Bill Close, 'troop by troop, giving each other supporting fire.' By 6 p.m. seventy PZ grenadiers had been killed and 300 captured.

Ted Jones of KSLI and his mates spent most of the morning in their slit trenches. He thought Hubert-Folie, their objective, was an English-sounding name. 'When one was a private soldier one was not always aware of what was happening especially on your right and left, although our officers and NCOs tried to keep us in the picture as much as possible.' Ned Thornburn was impressed with their new CO's order group: 'Colonel Reeves proceeded to deliver the most copybook set of orders I have ever heard, unhurried and clear.' However, when Company Commander Jack Clayton asked for 3-inch mortar support, it was refused. A bad decision since artillery support was obviously limited.

Roland Jefferson, 8 RB, bayoneted a 'taller and thicker' German in Bras and then felt rather guilty about it! 'At last we were relieved by 3rd Mons and three of us escorted about fifty prisoners across the field to where our carrier was. There were more prisoners there and we left them and thankfully made our way back into cover. It was pitiful to see so many burned out tanks. Bodies of the tank crews were lying around and charred bodies were hanging from some of the tank escape hatches. There were far more dead British than Germans.' A dozen enemy SP guns were put out of action or captured in Bras.

Meanwhile H Battery 13 RHA, was putting down a smokescreen to shield 3 RTR, and G Battery FOO had a hotline to the far distant medium 5.5s across the Orne, brought down fire and knocked out two Panther tanks. I Battery supported 2nd Northants Yeomanry as best they could – 13 RHA had 3 FOOs killed during Goodwood. Noel Bell mentioned that F and H companies successfully cleared Bras: 'We went on to begin our attack on Hubert-Folie. A very effective smokescreen was put down by our 2-inch mortars. The village had been previously shelled and the tanks were pumping stuff into it.' There were two 'rogue' Shermans captured by the Germans the day before but its machine guns were now deployed against their previous owners. 'We later had the satisfaction of seeing the "German" brewed up in no uncertain manner.' Unfortunately a false rumour that Hubert-Folie had already been captured caused a needless delay during which 2nd Northants Yeomanry quickly lost a further five tanks.

By the end of the day the unhappy 2nd Northants Yeomanry had lost a total of thirty-seven tanks in addition to the sixteen on the first day. The General now decided that 13 RHA and Ayrshire Yeomanry should fire a heavy barrage on Hubert-Folie for ten minutes to shield 2nd Fife and Forfarshire Yeomanry's attack. Steel Brownlie's diary noted:

> We moved to the west side of the railway running south from Caen and stood by while 23rd Hussars and 3 RTR took Bras. In the afternoon we passed through them and took Hubert-Folie behind a barrage. We lost only one tank and the infantry took over at dusk. We hoisted a young wounded German private on to the back of the tank and I fed him with grapes.

4 KSLI advancing in open order towards the village ran into German mortar fire DFs and Captain Clayton reported: 'Without warning we were enfiladed from our left by machine-gun fire from the high embankment. In a matter of seconds the swishing bullets through the corn had accounted for almost a third of my weakened company'. They badly needed 3-in. mortar support. Then Colonel Reeves was wounded with thirty-six fragments from an 88-mm airburst. 2-in. mortars fired smoke but for a time 4 KSLI were in grave trouble. Lieutenant Hank Henry, the Canadian Carrier platoon commander, dislodged the 1st SS PZ Grenadiers along the embankment and inflicted heavy casualties on them. Lieutenant Mike Sayer revealed:

> The advance on Hubert-Folie was an infantryman's nightmare. There we were in a huge open field of corn dominated by high ground ahead and the railway embankment on the flank, from which the enemy machine gunners and artillery FOOs had us in full view. The squadron of tanks ahead in battle formation had all been knocked out on the previous day.

By 2115 hrs 4 KSLI had taken the village and Ned Thornburn recalled: 'Within fifteen minutes the Germans were shelling and mortaring us fiercely and accurately.' He and S/M Eddie Hughes had to dig their own slit trench – most unusual: 'I don't think I have ever been in such a flat spin as I was then in our first few minutes in Hubert-Folie.'

A battle group of 4 KSLI, 3rd Mons and 23rd Hussars then held Hubert-Folie throughout a noisy night when shells and Nebelwerfers rained down. The weather had been very hot and sultry, and everyone was very thirsty.

During the day the division achieved its two objectives, again at a heavy cost. Another sixty-five tanks were written off (2nd Northants Yeomanry 37, 3 RTR 16, 2nd Fife & Forfarshire 8 and 23rd Hussars 4) and casualties were 399. 3rd Mons lost 66, 4 KSLI 54, 1st Herefords 32, 3 RTR 31, 8 RB 41 and 2nd Northants Yeomanry 40. The German command had reacted quickly to the massive threat posed by Goodwood. 21 Panzer Division were now on the eastern flank, 1 Panzer to the south, part of 12 SS Panzer and 272 Infantry Division to the south-west and 116 Panzer came down from Amiens as a reserve. 7th Armoured took Four and the Guards Le Poirier, but Goodwood was now contained.

On the following day heavy rain reduced the battlefield to a sea of mud and 2 Canadian Corps relieved 11th Armoured, who moved back across the River Orne by 22 July and concentrated once more north of the Caen–Bayeux road. But the infantry brigade stayed on for a further forty-eight hours under command of 7th Armoured and then 51 Highland Division!

Meanwhile, due to the heavy losses in 29 Armoured Brigade of relatively experienced squadron and troop leaders, a crisis quickly developed, as Geoffrey Bishop reported:

All squadron leaders were hastily summoned to the Colonel's bivvy (on Thursday 20 July p.m.), where they were told that immediate plans had been made to organize the remnants of the regiment. The position was so critical that the Colonels of the three Armoured regiments had been told that either they would re-organize their regiments and get immediate reinforcements to be ready to go back into battle in full strength within five days, or else the whole brigade would be taken out of the line and be completely re-equipped, which would take about six weeks. There would be no guarantee that we should fight again, either as individual regiments or as a brigade. The Colonels had instantly decided on the former course and there were some very glum looks from the troopers when they were told about this, as morale was at its lowest possible ebb and the prospects of several weeks out of the line had a very strong appeal.

So the AA Troop was absorbed by the Sabre squadrons and Bishop was given the job of training new drivers in his squadron. He was in an exhausted state, soaked to the skin and tired beyond belief, but the QM arrived with a bottle of whisky under one arm, a bottle of gin under the other, so 'the awfulness of the situation slightly lessened'.

Although 30 square miles of Normandy cornfields had been expensively and painfully captured, it is interesting to read comments from three experts after 11th Armoured Division had lost 191 tanks and suffered 735 casualties. Colonel Brian Wyldbore-Smith, GSO1 of the Division, argues convincingly that it was a great mistake to launch the attack with massed tanks. 'One squadron per infantry battalion would have been ample. More than that simply confused the issue.' Colonel von Luck, a highly experienced German Battle Group commander, made these comments about Goodwood: 'The British failure to capture the Bourguébus ridge was because the British tank advance was too slow and no British infantry was advancing in close contact with tanks to break any kind of resistance. Also a strong British night attack south-east on the 18th could have probably opened the way for further advance on the 19th.' He admitted to one stroke of luck in that the great Allied air bombing had not reached the two anti-tank/anti-aircraft battalions on Bourguébus ridge. If German troops trained on the Russian front had been entrusted with the attacking role in Goodwood 'the attack would have been made very early in the morning with one infantry division in front assisted by armoured assault guns to break through the first resistance followed at once by armoured divisions to break through'. General 'Pip' Roberts would have agreed. General O'Connor would have disagreed.

The Army commander, General Miles Dempsey, told Chester Wilmot after Goodwood had finished:

> The attack we put in on 18 July was not a very good operation of war tactically, but strategically it was a great success, *even though we did get a bloody nose. I didn't mind about that, I was prepared to lose a couple of hundred tanks.* So long as I didn't lose men. We could afford the tanks because they had begun to pile up in the bridgehead [500 or more Shermans lying idle]. Our tanks losses were severe but our casualties in men were very light. If I had tried to achieve the same result with a conventional infantry attack I hate to think what the casualties would have been.'

Dempsey made it clear that attracting enemy armour to the eastern flank (away from the American front), wearing down his strength by attrition, expanding the bridgehead, and capturing Caen and its airfield were the priorities of Goodwood.

Bill Close, 3 RTR, had no doubts at all about the tactics forced on 11th Armoured Division: 'Goodwood was a shambles, but only because the method of advance was forced upon us without infantry to clear up the villages. Certainly the fact that 159 Infantry Brigade were divorced from 29 Brigade for practically the whole of the first day had a great effect on the conduct of the battle.'

'Into the valley of death', wrote Alfred, Lord Tennyson, 'rode the six hundred,' and that is the way it was on 18–19 July 1944; and 'cannon to right of them, cannon to left of them, cannon in front of them – volley'd and thunder'd'. In all, the Goodwood operation cost 6,100 casualties. The KIA for the division during Goodwood were 2nd Fife and Forfarshire 39, 3 RTR 29, 23rd Hussars 26, 2nd Northants Yeomanry 25, 3 Mons 24, 4 KSLI 23, 8 RB 13, 1st Herefords 13 and two artillery regiments 18.

CHAPTER TEN

Another Interlude

Immediately after Goodwood Jimmy Carson, 2 i/c CREME, looked over 115 tanks and other AVs. Brew ups were left behind, but all 2nd or 3rd line repairs were recovered, often at night, and brought back to a 'crook' park in a 'safe' area. 29 or 129 Brigade workshops hauled them back for repair using teams of a Sherman 1 ARV plus Scammell tractor. 'The Boche sometimes thought we were burial parties as we had to climb on and into turrets and open engine hatches.' Once they caught on, a barrage of Nebelwefer was quickly let loose. Because of battlegroups with mixed infantry and armour, both brigade workshops were able to repair a wide range of vehicles. Shermans Mark 2 and 5 were considered easier to repair than Cromwells.

For ten days between 20 and 29th July most of the division was out of action. A violent thunderstorm had produced torrential rain on the 20th, filling up gun pits, slit trenches, shell craters and making the roads a misery. While Ayrshire Yeomanry were firing at targets the gunners wore bathing trunks, and between targets bathed in rain-filled craters, before moving back to Vieux Cairon across the Orne. There fresh denim overalls were issued and the regimental band gave a concert. 4 KSLI moved back through a sea of mud to Buron, 4 miles north-west of Caen. Major Ned Thornburn thought little of Buron: 'It had been heavily fought over and exuded the amosphere of destruction with a number of unexploded shells as an added hazard.' 8 RB ended up at Cussy, 2 miles north-west of Caen, where they spent a week. A NAAFI mobile van appeared. Liberty trucks were run into Bayeux. Swimming parties were organized. Roland Jefferson noted that reinforcements from the Rifle Brigade's sister regiment, Kings Royal Rifle Corps, were reluctant to exchange their badges. New Bren gun carriers appeared:

[They were] miraculously painted with our Black Bull division and formation signs. Our carriers and other vehicles took on the appearance of tinkers' carts. Pots and pans and biscuit tins hung on the backs of vehicles. The best way to make a cup of tea was to put some sandy soil in one biscuit tin and pour in liberal quantities of petrol. Fill another biscuit tin with water, place this on top and put a lighted match to the petrol. These field stoves didn't take long to boil up sufficient water for a 'tea powder' mashing. Then we would pierce holes in tins of stewed steak, or soya links and put them in water for a hot meal. Also we bartered fried or boiled eggs and boiled potatoes. Any water left over produced a warm, luxurious shave!

Every regiment took it for granted that supplies of jerricans of water and petrol, compo rations and ammo would appear on time in the right place. Quite a few of 23rd Hussars went back to the Corps rest camp to see the film *Jane Eyre*, but would have preferred to see Betty Grable! Their ack-ack troop was disbanded, the recce troop reduced to three tanks and reinforcements arrived from Royal Gloucestershire Hussars.

When 13 RHA pulled out of Goodwood on 21–22 July it had been in action for twenty-seven days out of the previous four weeks, so a few days out of the line was a welcome relief, with exchanges of clothing from a mobile laundry, visits to mobile showers, even an ENSA concert. The mobile cinema had a limited repertoire, usually showing *Four Jills in a Jeep*. Patrick Delaforce, who had recently joined 13 RHA as troop leader, quickly found that a modest blurring of the 21 set would produce non-stop Glenn Miller on the US Army forces network. His favourite rations were tinned marmalade pudding and soya bangers. Steel Brownlie, 2nd Fife and Forfarshire, retrieved his battered Sherman tank, No. 829, which still had a lot of valuable and personal kit in it, from workshops in Mondeville. REME workshops repaired about eighty of the tanks 'lost' in Goodwood, but nearly fifty were total write-offs. 'The regiment harboured at the Abbaye des Ardennes, a ruined monastery in a great walled orchard, green and inviting. The rain stopped, the sun shone, the war was out of earshot and the only reminder was a burnt-out Panther among the trees. Heaven.' He visited the rest camp near Courseulles where nude bathing was the order of the day. There he bathed, strolled and gloomily worked out the average life expectancy of a troop leader. But he had fun trying out his French on a waitress.

Four desert veterans – tank sergeants – lined up to Major Bill Close, 3 RTR, after Goodwood and protested that they no longer felt able to command tank crews in action. They were persuaded to stay. 3 RTR had more battle trained (and battle weary) troops than any other regiment in the division. A large number of 23rd Hussars squadron and troop leaders, their best NCOs and men had gone. They refitted at St Germain in low spirits. The Battle of Caen was a costly affair.

Many of the troops were allowed briefly on pass into Bayeux, where food and drink were the main interest. Church services were held, ENSA parties arrived, NAAFI supplies were readily available, and there were swimming parties to St-Aubin-sur-Mer. Jack Lockyer, Sapper officer, and Geoffrey Bishop, 23rd Hussars, swam in 'La Manche' even though it was rather choppy and dirty. Repainting of vehicles, tank maintenance and weapon cleaning continued every day.

Corporal Alastair Tait, RASC/3rd Mons, was having his left eye treated and cleared of sand at the Medical Officer's wagon near 159 Brigade HQ. In the field was a company of SS POWs in their black uniforms awaiting their orders to march back to the beaches. A keen-eyed RAF fighter pilot saw them, though he was over enemy territory and machine-gunned them. The medical orderly treating Alastair's eye was killed outright by this 'friendly fire'.

4 KSLI had suffered a hundred casualties in Goodwood. Jack Clayton, CO B Company, recalls: 'We had three days to train our intake – this meant getting forty men fit, graded, allotted and converted into infanteers from coastal artillery.' This was happening throughout the Division. Nearly 800 replacements had to be welcomed, absorbed and trained quickly, ready for the last final thrust through the bocage – a richly wooded countryside, a mass of small rolling hills and valleys, numerous small rivers, with winding sunken roads protected by high banks, small fields and thick hedges. A beautiful country ideal for defence with hidden strongpoints and gun emplacements, that made *conventional* armoured warfare almost an impossibility.

Few people knew of the 20 July plot to kill Hitler, or that Monty's job was in the balance, or that no fewer than six SS divisions were now fighting in Normandy. Nor was it known at the time that British and Canadian casualties had reached 49,000 out of 591,000 troops in Normandy, but that the US forces had suffered 73,000 casualties out of 770,000 Americans ashore. It was thought that the Caen battlefields were the anvil of the campaign, but we little realized the extent of the American losses in the western sector. Nor did we know of their massive offensive named Cobra, which started on 25 July. But at that date the Germans still had 645 operational tanks containing the British/Canadian front, compared with 190 against the Americans. The proportion of 88-mm guns was the same. So Cobra was successful, Coutances was captured on 28 July and Avranches on the 30th. Patton's 3rd Army was on the point of a dramatic breakout but US 1st Army and British 2nd Army had to keep up ever-increasing pressure on the eastern sector. This was Operation Bluecoat.

CHAPTER ELEVEN

Operation Bluecoat

Day One – 30 July

General Roberts received his orders on 28 July that VIII Corps and XXX Corps with their six divisions would launch a major offensive south from Caumont. As Monty put it: 'Step on the gas for Vire.' VIII Corps consisted of 11th Armoured, Guards Armoured and 15th Scottish. XXX Corps on their left were two infantry divisions, 43rd Wessex and 50th Northumbrian, plus 7th Armoured Division. VIII Corps targets were St Martin-des-Besaces, Forêt l'Evêque, Le Bény Bocage and Vire, while XXX Corps were heading for Villers-Bocage, Aunay-sur-Odon and the vital Mont Pinçon. The regrouping was difficult, but achieved on time. From north-west of Caen 11th Armoured, followed by Guards Armoured, had to move right across the British sector and the supply lines of 12 Corps and 30 Corps to get into position near Caumont. The distance was 21 miles on heavily cut up, congested, dusty roads. Major Ned Thornburn's 4 KSLI company travelled in TCVs and noted how Corps Pioneers had cut out new roads. As usual the Military Police achieved wonders in keeping the traffic moving during the night of 28–29 July, and in the right direction. 4 KSLI started Bluecoat from La Vacquerie with the Division forming up between Balleroy and Caumont-L'Eventé.

General Roberts was told that the first thrust would be by 15th Scottish supported by 6th Guards Tank Brigade in their Churchill tanks. Their principal objective was Point 309, some 2,000 yards east of St Martin-des-Besaces (patron saint of beggars!). 11th Armoured would protect the Guards' right flank and in turn keep in touch with the American 5th Infantry Division's left flank. 2nd Household Cavalry armoured cars led the Division, but for the first time General Roberts was allowed to plan his own battles. Four battle groups were formed – 23rd Hussars (Colonel Perry Harding) with 3rd Monmouthshires (Colonel Hubert Orr); 2nd Fife and Forfarshire (Colonel Alec Scott) with 4 KSLI (Colonel Max Robinson); 3 RTR (Colonel David Silvertop) with 1st Herefords (Colonel Turner Cain); and 2nd Northants Yeomanry (Colonel D. Cooke) with 8 RB (Colonel J.A. Hunter).

The left-hand centre-line was from La Vallée to the south-west of Caumont bypassing Sept-Vents, then east of Dampierre towards St

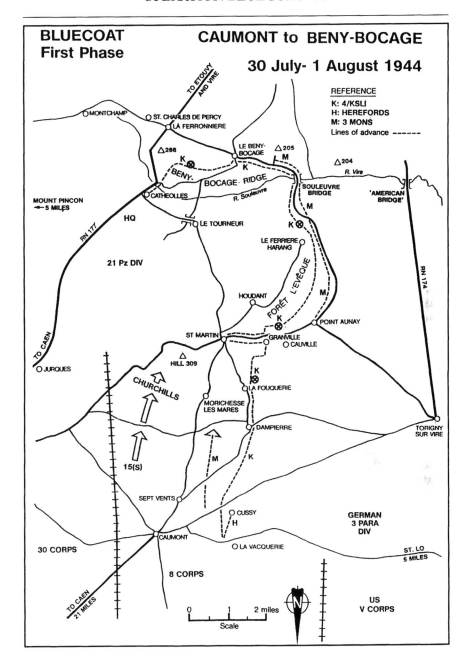

Martin-des-Besaces. The right-hand centre-line attack was to be via Cussy, La Baisselière, then Dampierre converging on St Martin-des-Besaces. The left-hand group was 23rd Hussars/3rd Mons and the right, 2nd Fife and Forfarshire/4 KSLI.

The division had little experience of fighting in the bocage country. This countryside is always difficult for infantry, unpromising for tanks and makes it hard for gunners to pinpoint their fleeting targets efficiently. The RAF could not find their targets, tucked away in valleys or woods. The only advantage to the attacks was that the German tank and 88-mm superiority was reduced by the inevitable short range targets – unlike the long range massacre of Goodwood. But the bocage was a paradise for the sniper, bazookaman, the minelayers and the aggressive German infantry.

Major Ned Thornburn, 4 KSLI, noted: 'We had a pleasant time doing what I can only describe as the "Bocage Bound". Tanks brew the next hedge [with HE and BESA]. Infantry trot briskly across the open space. Tanks join 'em . . . repeat ad infinitum.' German infantry rarely crossed *open* fields, preferring to advance in small groups using the natural cover of copses, hedges and covered lanes in order to infiltrate the defences, pick off and panic the defenders.

Ernst Streng, commander of a Tiger tank with 9th SS Division, wrote:

The bocage was a cruel area. Every road, every little field and meadow, was surrounded by thick hedges two or three metres in height. It was full of frightening opportunities for tanks and anti-tank guns to hide in ambush. The fighting was confused and difficult: each crew member had to react in a flash to any threat of danger. Tank clashes at short range, sometimes only a few metres, were not unusual.

Nevertheless, in the bocage country, on both British and American fronts, the German armies suffered their final and fatal defeats. German aircraft bombed 8 RB before dawn, then a church service was held in the apple orchards before breakfast. Noel Bell felt that 'the orchards of Normandy will remain for ever in our memories as cool restful places in which our most peaceful hours were spent . . . during these difficult times religion undoubtedly played a bigger part in our lives than it had ever done before'. The Ayrshire Yeomanry gun positions were near Béziers, 2,000 yards behind the front line. Their FOOs supported the three infantry battalions and 2nd Fife and Forfarshire. 13 RHA FOOs supported 3 RTR, 23rd Hussars, 2nd Northants Yeomanry and 8 RB. The first divisional barrage was fired at 0655 hrs and Bluecoat started five minutes later, on an overcast and cloudy morning. The RAF bombed up in front and 15th Scottish with 6th Guards Brigade headed for Sept-Vents. The division attacked on a 2-mile front. Immediately both the Mons and Herefords took heavy casualties from American-laid mines and very heavy mortar and shell fire on the Caumont road, before they crossed the start lines. It was a disastrous day for the Herefords, known to them as 'Black Sunday'. 'That day', recalls Ken Crockford, 'the Herefords suffered 129 casualties, twenty-five being killed on the day or dying later of wounds. This from a total of about 680 who had set out that morning.' The Herefords were to be in action continuously from 2 to 14 August – fighting hard every day.

'The American minefields had not been cleared, the ground was hard and we took a terrible pasting on Black Sunday,' wrote Sergeant Frank Moppett, 1st Herefords. 4 August was his fourth wedding anniversary; he looked at his wife's photograph and wondered if he would ever see her again. The Herefords at La Vacquerie put thick sandbags at the bottom of their carriers and used them, rather dangerously, to run round large fields checking for mines, although for known minefields 'potato picking' was the usual method of clearance. 'We heard a hell of a blast. I dashed back', wrote Reg Worton, 'to see Geoff Farmer, driver of the first carrier, over in the field with his backside all blown off.' He died twelve days later.

Steel Brownlie, 2nd Fife and Forfarshire, reported: 'Trouble started at once. The Herefords were heavily mortared on the start line and suffered casualties before even seeing the enemy. They captured their first objective, a low ridge covered with orchards, which had been a line of lightly held enemy posts. The ground was rock covered by an inch or so of soil.' Captain Wardman, 1st Herefords, wrote:

Lucky were those who found an abandoned German trench. Most tried to get what shelter they could along a narrow sunken lane. A lot were killed and wounded there. The enemy had us under direct observation. They knew the exact range; they brought everything down on us with extreme accuracy. The sky was filled with the wail of 'moaning minnies' (fired electronically in sticks of five or six, united in a spine-chilling inharmonious high pitched screech). Stretcher cases and walking wounded filtered sadly to the rear, pushing past the KSLI. For hours the Herefords waited hugging the ground, watching as comrades were killed or wounded, waiting for the RAF bombing programme delayed by fog. It was midday when the bombers at last arrived. The Herefords rose and advanced towards the clouds of billowing smoke and dust and found the area strewn haphazardly with schumines.

The fields were baked by the late summer sun and digging slit trenches was almost impossible, so infantry casualties were very high. Major Ellis, 2 i/c 4 KSLI, noted: 'It was bad for morale waiting to go up and seeing rather mangled Hereford wounded coming back through us on jeeps. Our artillery was absolutely first class and we had more of it than the Boche, whose fire started to slacken about 1500 hrs.'

Major Joe How noted:

The guns opened up behind us. We rose from the trampled corn to move forward. The field was filled with the high pitched scream of falling shells, a mild accelerating whistle that finished in a succession of blinding flashes and explosions. We threw ourselves down, pressing against the corn and we would have burrowed down into the protecting comfort of the earth beneath had we been able. Earth and stones rained down on our backs and legs, dust and smoke rose in the air and shrapnel whined away into the distance. It came so unexpectedly that our concussed minds couldn't work out what had happened. Some of those hit lay still and lifeless, others lay struggling for breath, dimly aware that something had happened to them and wondering why they could not feel their arms and legs. The dust settled. Silence weighed after the din of the explosions. The air filled with the sweet sickly smell of explosive. We had lost seventeen men before moving off the start line. It wasn't a good start.

The enemy opposition intensified as Major Joe How relates. In a park-like area with tall trees west of Caumont, 3rd Mons were mortared and shelled heavily:

There was the sound of machine-gun fire not far ahead. Word went round that we were waiting for the 15th Scottish. They were held up in the village of Sept-Vents. At midday two Sherman tanks came down the slope and joined us. One was hit on the engine casing by a falling shell. The crew threw themselves out of the hatches as flames billowed up. A great mushroom of smoke rose in the air.

They were tanks of 23rd Hussars. The apple orchards showered hard, unripe apples on the tank crews. And everywhere there were mines, German, British and American, and tanks were immobilized with tracks blown off. Captain E. Campbell, 3rd Mons, remembered one tragedy: 'There was a detonation and a cry, "My God! my guts. Mummy, Mummy, Mummy." The man had let his rifle fall as he clutched at his stomach.'

On the left flank the Mons later reached their first objective of Sept-Vents village. 'In a long single file,' wrote How, 'we moved along the main street of Sept-Vents past two in the afternoon, past the debris of the houses and the litter of battle. There was no living soul to be seen, just a few dead bodies.'

Geoffrey Bishop, troop leader with 23rd Hussars, helped take the village of Sept-Vents.

Seven Winds, although not a breath of air . . . eventually the village is cleared with the assistance of flails. This is the first time I have seen these extraordinary looking monsters in action. They are just ordinary Shermans with a large contraption on the front, projecting about 10 feet in front of the tracks and consisting of a large iron roller about 4 feet above the ground with chains fixed to it, which revolves and explodes any mines immediately in front of the tank as it moves slowly forward.

But at 1400 hrs 'Badger' divisional fire plan in front of the Herefords allowed them to take Cussy and 4 KSLI then passed through them with 2nd Fife and Forfarshire. Fireplan 'Buffalo' was fired at 1600 hrs on Dampierre, plus red smoke for RAF medium bombers. Although 2nd Fife and Forfarshire lost several tanks from mines at the start line their co-ordination with 4 KSLI was excellent as Ned Thornburn recollects.

The enemy we came upon were disorganized and scared – no fanatics from the Hitler Youth here. Provided they were met by us with obvious toughness they capitulated. Our Fife and Forfarshire tanks were at our shoulders spreading destruction in all directions and within half a mile we knew we were on top – the only place to be where Germans were concerned. Our gunners gave us their usual wholehearted support on the standard 11th Armoured basis of 'ten rounds back for every one round fired at us'. The advance continued from Dampierre to La Fouquerie and took 150 prisoners from 326 Infantry Division (with 70 per cent non Germans). A successful advance of 5 miles in the day – unheard of! It had been a tremendously exciting day. For the first time in the campaign we had felt that we were really making the running, forcing the enemy back instead of knocking our heads against a brick wall.

Steel Brownlie with 2nd Fife and Forfarshire was having an exciting day too:

Several tank commanders were killed or wounded by the mortar fire. In theory we should have had the Sherman hatches closed, and looked through periscopes which were useless. *The only way to see where you were going, to spot targets and to control your troop was to put your head out.* The crust of the German defences broke and we were told to move and move fast. We called it 'baffing'. No more creeping through hedges and grinding about in first gear, but doing what we had to been trained to do: move. A Squadron went first and I was leading troop. It was a case of motoring flat out, 35 mph on the straight, for the faster you went the harder you were to hit. There were Germans all over the place, running and scampering. We fired wildly at them, overtook them and left them far behind. There were targets at every turn of the road. It was exhilarating.

Shortly afterwards by dusk. Brownlie's tank was hit by a Panzerschreck (heavy bazooka). 'I rolled out down over the engine and into the ditch, really frightened, my tank halfway through the hedge at a crazy angle.' La Baisselière was then captured by 2nd Fife and Forfarshire and 4 KSLI.

The indomitable 3rd Mons and 23rd Hussars then fought their way south to St Jean-des-Essartiers where the Germans sent in a battalion of infantry supported by assault guns. There Major How found only devastation, deep craters, trees swept bare of all foliage and thick dust everywhere, a target of air bombardment:

There was a last spasm of enemy mortar fire as we moved in a long file past the tanks of 23rd Hussars at the village entrance. The flickering flames of the burned buildings grew brighter as darkness descended. Exhausted after fifteen hours of battle we started to dig in. We were hungry. Would food get up to us? It was doubtful. The company was to move forward after midnight and maintain contact with 8 RB 2 miles further on. 'What did I tell you, boyo? Can't make their bloody minds up.' The tired men picked up their rifles, their picks and shovels and trudged wearily into the dark night.

They linked up with 23rd Hussars and then took the hamlet of Saint-Ouen-des-Besaces. 'On this occasion', noted Geoffrey Bishop, 'the entire Second Army advance is being led by our two squadrons, and in each case Ted Harte and I are the leading troop leaders. This is a most nerve-racking operation as the road twists and turns.' Mines in the road, covered by branches, blew off tank tracks. Bishop watched the sappers hastily summoned forward. 'The expert discovers a few more mines in a side track which would undoubtedly have blown my tank up had I gone forward, and keeping well out of his way I observe him rendering the rest useless without getting himself blown to bits.' Other sappers from 612 Field Squadron RE with mine detectors swept the grass verges and road ahead.

During the night H Company of 8 RB pushed on again to reach the Caumont St Martin road, and by early morning was established north and east of St Martin-des-Besaces.

At dusk the General noted:

Progress was slow but it had been made. After a very tiring approach march, and little sleep, and then a hard day's fighting there was a natural tendency to call it a day as soon as the sun went down but firm orders came from the Corps Commander that we could not relax. The main village in front of us was St Martin-des-Besaces; it was an important cross-roads; one main road ran east–west and the other north–south. We could hold it in front and attack from the west.

Colonel Max Robinson, new CO of 4 KSLI, called Ned Thornburn on the blower late that evening and said: 'Better call it a day, Ned.' It was not to be. Although 15th Scottish held the high ground north-east of St Martin-des-Besaces, 4 KSLI started at 0400 hrs and marched 5,000 yards in the pitch black night in single file. Captain Jack Clayton, OC B Company led, and 'dawn saw us astride the road and railway 1,000 yards west of our objective, tired but triumphant'. The General wrote later: 'It was a magnificent effort of 4 KSLI'.

Day Two – 31 July

4 KSLI were ordered to attack St Martin at 0930 hrs from the right flank, supported by a squadron of 2nd Fife and Forfars. Steel Brownlie wrote:

'The infantry were under heavy Spandau fire. We pushed forward slowly through outhouses and orchards and Corporal Newman's tank was brewed up by a Mark IV. We laid smoke and crossed safely.' By 1100 hrs the town was cleared but 8 RB had to cross a high railway embankment on the north side of the village and lost nine killed and twenty-one wounded in half an hour. Noel Bell reported that 3 RTR Shermans could not get across the embankment and 10 and 11 platoons came under heavy fire, were pinned down and suffered heavy casualties. 8 RB licked their wounds and moved on through the Forêt l'Evêque to La Ferrière. In the forest they marched parallel to American infantry and fed them UK army ration biscuits 'for which they appeared most grateful'. Some AVREs, modified Churchill tanks with a vast short-barrelled mortar, were also involved in this action. Before midday the town was handed over to the Cameronians of 15th Scottish.

2nd Northants Yeomanry were involved in a mêlée near St Martin, lost tanks and took fifteen casualties.

The advance continued – in an amazing way. 2nd Household Cavalry had been probing every road and track ahead of the division. Two scout cars had pushed 1,500 yards south to Houdant and run into a hornets' nest of the advancing 21st Panzer Division. But north of Canville, a mile to the west, Lieutenant Dickie Powle in another armoured car and scout car nipped across the main road St Lô–Bény Bocage, into the Forêt l'Evêque and drove down an undefended track for 2 miles to find ahead of them an unguarded bridge over the River Souleuvre. The boundary line between the defending German 3 Para Division and 326 Infantry Division was in dispute – and each claimed it was the other's responsibility. Powle nipped across the bridge, camouflaged the two cars and radioed back. 'At 1030 hrs the bridge at 637436 has been captured intact.' The General knew that:

[This] was wonderful news: it needed a real 'thruster' to get to this bridge five miles away. The 23rd Hussars/3rd Mons group was comparatively fresh, and Perry Harding, CO 23rd Hussars, was certainly 'a thruster', but 2nd Northants Yeomanry with 4 KSLI were the nearest, as flank protection west of St Martin. They did well and after one or two vicissitudes [they met two German SP guns guarding La Ferrière-Harang] reached the bridge about 1400 hrs, much to the relief of the [intrepid] Dickie Powle and Corporal Bland of the 2nd Household Cavalry.

This group held the bridge until the 23rd Hussars/3rd Mons arrived later. The main opposition had been the American V Corps, whose map reading persuaded them that their boundary was 2 miles further west than originally agreed.

8 RB were holding La Ferrière-Harang and 4 KSLI were in the Forêt l'Evêque eating their first hot meal for some time. General O'Connor now instructed General 'Pip' Roberts 'to capture the high ground round Point

Aunay tonight so that the advance to Etouvy can proceed rapidly tomorrow. You should occupy tonight Point 204, Point 205 and the high ground east of Le Bény Bocage about Point 266. 2 Household Cavalry will tonight patrol south with the utmost vigour in the direction of Vire'. So 23rd Hussars and 3rd Mons pushed up the wooded slopes that night for a mile, despite mines and defensive fire, and dug in for the night.

The second day of Bluecoat had gone remarkably well thanks to the two Household Cavalry heroes and the quick, forceful follow-up. In La Ferrière-Harang the division encountered its first enthusiastic Liberation welcome with pretty girls, flowers, cider, calvados and kisses. It helped, of course, that this was the first unflattened village in the path of the Black Bull!

Day Three – 1 August

The General ordered 23rd Hussars and 3rd Mons to establish themselves on the high ground overlooking Le Bény Bocage. The division had to push south with 29th Armoured Brigade on the left and 159 Infantry Brigade on the right, while 2nd Household Cavalry reconnoitred towards Vire. This important crossroads town was practically unoccupied but it was technically within the American boundary, so could not be captured. Moreover the division, restricted to a narrow road of advance, was almost stationary. It took the Household Cavalry three hours to cover the 3 miles between Point Aunay and the Souleuvre bridge. Sergeant Sears of 23rd Hussars first reached the outskirts of Le Bény Bocage with 8 RB, 4 KSLI and 3 RTR beside and behind. By lunchtime Major Ellis, 2 i/c 4 KSLI, set up Battalion HQ in the main square. The welcome was overwhelming. Rifleman Kingsmill, 8 RB, described in a letter home:

> I have never before seen people go so absolutely mad with joy. Everybody was either shouting, waving, cheering, clapping, kissing one another, singing the 'Marseillaise' or doing the whole lot at once. The market-place was a fairish sized rectangle about 80 by 20 yards. At one end a Jerry Mk VI tank, charred and blackened, still pours forth smoke. At the other end a party is going on in a hotel.

Kingsmill was given champagne, cool and bubbly. A gendarme was running up and down the square waving a huge tricolour. Fresh 'Cross of Lorraine' armbands appeared on young proud Frenchmen. Flowers were thrown, wine was offered and in turn sweets, bars of chocolate and cigarettes were handed out. 'People are rushing here and there, to and fro – they're still kissing each other – mother and child, husband and wife, soldier and girl. Elation? Ecstasy? It's difficult to find a word that aptly describes it. It's a tremendous sight – and no one who witnessed it could ever forget.' The hospitable villagers plied the Hussars with a drink described as 'whisky' but which turned out to be calvados, an extremely potent liquid distilled from apples – but the advance continued!

4 KSLI were ordered to bear left and seize Point 266, north-east of Le Bény Bocage, and push down the Souleuvre valley, two companies on the ridge, two in the valley, supported by 3 RTR. The ridge was taken by midday with Private Eardley earning the MM by knocking out an MG post. 4 KSLI advanced quickly along the valley, captured the important road bridge across the Souleuvre and pressed on to seize the village of Cathéoles. Here they enjoyed themselves enormously. Major Ned Thornburn wrote: 'Four roads ran into the village and Jerries came from all directions not knowing we were there. It was an amazing bag. Men and vehicles of all descriptions and types kept coming along. We kept firing at 'em. This ended another good day with a fine bit of progress.' Eighty prisoners were captured at a cost of six KSLI wounded. Since the start of Bluecoat the KSLI had captured 250 Germans, killed as many more and suffered fewer than twenty-five casualties altogether.

I was the Recce officer with 119 Bty 75 A/Tk and my BC Mike Harris sent me to take two SPs [M–10s] to support 4 KSLI at the Cathéoles bridge. We drove along a track in single file through Forêt de l'Evêque, tanks, SPs, halftracks and carriers [recalls David Swiney], churning up clouds of red dust which covered everyone. Walking alongside our vehicles were American infantry, silent, tight-trousered, chewing gum and looking as surprised to see us as we were to see them.

Meanwhile 8 RB and a squadron of 3 RTR continued south-east and soon reached St Charles de Percy, thus cutting the main Caen/Vire road. They settled down astride the crossroads strengthened by SP 17-pounders from 75th A/Tank Regiment RA and prepared for a counter-attack. The third road was the responsibility of 159 Brigade led by 2nd Fife and Forfarshires with 1st Herefords following up in lorries. 'Beyond the Souleuvre the country was even rougher. Our objective', Steel Brownlie reported, 'was a hill commanding the country for miles around from which Jimmy Samson exchanged shots with two or three tanks on a nearby feature.'

In the afternoon 23rd Hussars and 8 RB, a new partnership, moved off south from Le Bény Bocage towards Le Désert, up to Point 218, down the valley through Presles, up again to the high ground of Le Bas and Le Haut Perrier, on to Chênedollé to their objective, the main Vassy–Vire road. 2nd Fife and Forfarshires were on the right, but the left flank was wide open. Divisional HQ was in Le Reculey, 1½ miles south-west of Le Bény Bocage. The General described the terrain: 'Looking south from Bény Bocage there were clearly two ridges running north-east to south-west, the first one 4 miles from Bény Bocage and the second one 1½ miles further on and higher than the first. From either of them they must command all the ground northwards up to Bény Bocage and either side of it.' The main objective remained the cutting of the Vire–Vassy main road east of Vire. The divisional artillery targets were designated Coventry, Warwick and Rugby, and they were the three roads leading north-east and east out of Vire.

Day Four – 2 August

'August 2nd was going to be an exciting day', the General wrote. 'We were clearly going to be out on our own as on both flanks there appeared to be more opposition than in front of us, but on the right the Germans seemed to have reinforced Vire.' It was a very hot day with a clear blue sky and 2nd Northants Yeomanry were sent off to Etouvy 2 miles north of Vire. They probed into the outskirts of Vire supported by a squadron of sappers, as the infantry battalions were deployed across three vital roads. By the evening 8 RB and 23rd Hussars had taken up a position beyond Presles, on high ground at Bas Perrier. Digging slit trenches was difficult but essential. 2nd Fife and Forfarshire with 3rd Mons pushed tanks and infantry down to the Vire–Vassy road and 8 RB moved southwards through the village of Beaulieu towards Presles. Noel Bell recounts that they took prisoner 'one of the most enormous blond Aryans I have ever seen – a 9th Div. SS Panzer Grenadier'. And Rifleman Jefferson noted:

> The narrow road towards Le Bas Perrier ridge caused several delays. Almost half-way up we came to a stop and we dismounted and took up covering positions. To our left we could see German infantry crossing the field towards us. Hedgerows gave us some cover . . . they came forward across the open meadow as if they were on an exercise. An uncomfortable 20 or 30 yards away we opened fire and many fell dead or wounded.

3rd RTR followed by 4 KSLI in their TCVs travelled from Cathéoles and the ridge, passing St Charles-de-Percy and Aigneaux towards point 218 just short of Presles. For some time then there were three centre-lines more or less parallel, running due north/south. Near St Charles-de-Percy 4 KSLI and 3 RTR clashed with German tanks and infantry and took twelve prisoners. The advance slowed down, enemy pockets holding out and fighting for every yard of ground. Each one had to be eliminated separately as they slogged their way slowly south over Hill 176, one of those little-known rises in the ground that become important when battles develop on them, so the resistance toughened. They were up against the 1/19th Battalion of the 9th SS Hohenstanfen regiment assembled at Montchamp, 1 mile north-east. 4 KSLI eventually reached Point 218 and dug in for the night but Major Ned Thornburn set off at 2030 hrs eastwards towards Le Grand Bonfait, a small hamlet. He spotted three Panther tanks advancing on the unsuspecting 3 RTR Shermans in the dusk. Fortunately over a 38 set he

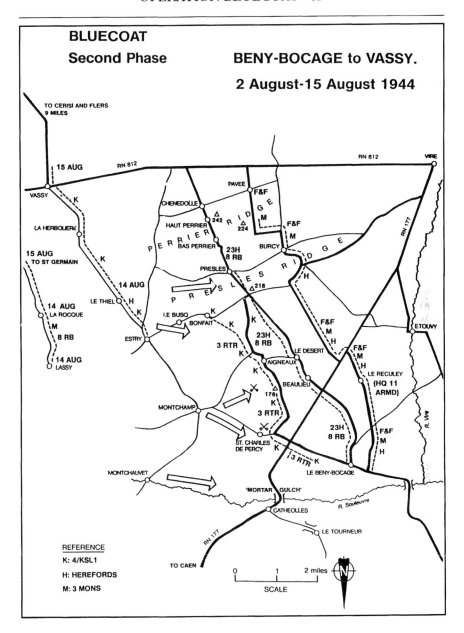

BLUECOAT

Second Phase   BENY-BOCAGE to VASSY.

2 August-15 August 1944

REFERENCE
K: 4/KSL1
H: HEREFORDS
M: 3 MONS

was able to warn them in time. CSM Harrison, however, destroyed a Panther by stalking it with a Piat, although the first bomb hit at 70 yards and bounced off harmlessly. The other Panthers withdrew to Le Busq 1,000 yards to the east.

Meanwhile 2nd Fife and Forfarshire had taken Burcy, where they had a genuine 'Liberation' welcome. They then pushed south to cut, and if possible hold, the vital Vire–Vassy main road, codenamed Rugby. 'Short of the road,' Steel Brownlie remembered, 'I put on a German helmet and took a German rifle, crawled the last 30 yards. The road was quite empty for two miles in both directions.' His squadron assembled but: 'Shots began to arrive from Panthers coming down the road from Vassy [near Chênedollé]. On the road we were sitting ducks. Off the road you could see little for the trees and hedges. We therefore called for LIMEJUICE, the codename for rocket-firing Typhoons guided by red smoke to their target fired by the Gunners. The Tiffies were effective.' But American Thunderbolts arrived on the scene and attacked 2nd Fife and Forfarshire for ten minutes with cannon-fire despite canisters of yellow smoke [friendly signals]. During the day a local farmer appeared with bottle and glasses on a tray to greet his liberators, offering the tank crews a refreshing drink. The calvados had more effect on 2nd Fife and Forfarshire than the enemy – for a short while! Aided by a platoon of 3rd Mons, Steel Brownlie and his squadron held their little 'bridgehead' all night, although PZ patrols were swarming over the area in half tracks. The rest of 3rd Mons and 2nd Fife and Forfarshire took up a defensive position for the night around Pavée. Meanwhile on the middle centre-line 23rd Hussars were attacked near Le Moulin and A Squadron was cut to pieces in a few minutes and the four survivors limped back to Le Bas-Perrier to rejoin the regiment. Five men were killed and a dozen wounded in this short, sharp engagement as Geoffrey Bishop reported:

News now starts to come in from A squadron who have been silent until now, and they appear to have run into an enemy troop and they are being engaged at short range by enemy armour. It sounds absolutely appalling; half their tanks have been hit and are on fire. The squadron leader has been badly wounded, two troops are missing and it seems as though the whole squadron is going to be annihilated. Geoffrey Taylor is trying to get things under control and withdraw the remains of the squadron. They are out of sight of our position and there are a great many wounded.

Panthers and SP guns from the open left flank caused havoc with the 23rd Hussars' Shermans between Presles and Le Bas Perrier, although four Panthers were destroyed – so it was prudent to withdraw their B squadron back from Chênedollé which lay in a hollow before a rise up to the Vassy–Vire road. The regiment harboured on the high ground above Le Bas Perrier.

North of Le Desert, Fox Troop 13 RHA was trundling briskly at about 25 mph along a flat dusty road towards the forward area gun positions. Patrick Delaforce recalls: 'Suddenly three AP shell whizzed through the line of three half tracks and four Ram-Sextons. Probably a Mark IV or SP from the woods on the right about 500 yards away. A sudden sharp acceleration ensued'.

13 RHA arrived at Le Desert on the Presles road and though they did not realize it, were to spend a week there firing almost non-stop amid PZ

Shermans at Le Desert
during Operation Bluecoat

infiltration, nebelwerfers and snipers. Ayrshire Yeomanry engaged targets in
a large wood, noted huge ammunition explosions and christened the feature
'Dump Wood'.

'Sandy' Saunders noted that 2nd Northants Yeomanry were spread out in
a rough triangle, B squadron on the outskirts of Vire, RHQ at La Bistière
and his A squadron west of Burcy:

> Suddenly in the middle of the afternoon some German Tiger tanks and
> infantry appeared mysteriously from the outskirts of Vire and advanced
> slowly and ponderously up the road behind B squadron towards RHQ.
> There was little our Cromwells could do to stop them, and due to some
> confusion between the gunners and rocket-firing aircraft they got within
> striking distance of RHQ, who withdrew losing lives and soft vehicles. As
> the night turned foggy, enemy infantry proceeded to stalk our tanks on
> foot with bazookas and a number were lost and crews captured.

By the evening the division had cut the Vire–Vassy main road at two
points and held the Presles–Burcy ridge, plus Bonfait on the western flank –
a front of 3 miles. It had advanced 7 miles during the day at a cost of thirty-
one tanks against stiffening opposition. Because of the narrow roads,
supplies of petrol and ammunition would soon become short. But the
General had three alternatives: capture Vire, 'and we could have done that',

but Monty had firmly allocated its capture to the Americans; advance and 'thrash around in his rear areas inflicting enormous chaos'; or continue 'to hold these two very dominating ridges and then the Germans can attack us. Within range of the corps artillery we could inflict very heavy casualties. In retrospect the gap ahead in the German front was too narrow and our administrative tail could have been shot to pieces'. The Corps Commander visited Divisional HQ at Le Reculey and was very heavily shelled. He agreed with General 'Pip' Roberts' plan and loaned 185 Brigade from 3 Division to help fend off the savage counter-attacks due to appear. Von Kluge realized he must at all costs stop the British Bluecoat attack or his whole front would collapse. So he committed 21 Panzer, 9 SS, 10 SS and a Tiger Tank battalion of twenty tanks to close the gap 11th Armoured had opened between his two armies. In the first four days of Bluecoat, 200 tanks were destroyed, but two-thirds of them were British.

Meanwhile Guards Armoured were making very heavy weather of their advance around Le Tourneur and Cathéoles, north-east of Le Bény Bocage, and 7th Armoured were having difficulties on their way to Aunay-sur-Odon, 5 miles south of Villers-Bocage. Monty fired Lieutenant-General Bucknall, GOC XXX Corps, Major-General Erskine, GOC, and Brigadier Hinde of 7th Armoured, but this did not produce a significant improvement in performance.

Day Five – 3 August

Various German counter-attacks were building up and the General anticipated 9th SS Panzer would exert strong pressure from Montchamp and Estry. If the Estry and Perrier ridges fell then the whole of VIII Corps would go rolling back the 7 miles to Le Bény Bocage. Quite soon Presles, a small village in the valley between the two ridges, was recaptured by the Germans. A glorious hot day now brought heavy attacks all along the thin red line. On the left flank 4 KSLI and 3 RTR held – just – Le Grand Bonfait position against determined tank and infantry attacks from Le Busq. Ned Thornburn, 4 KSLI, recalled: 'In the middle of the day we were attacked by a dozen or more Panthers in open order and a few infantry, on the northern edge of Presles and towards Point 218.' Then followed a bombardment of the position where 3 RTR had unwisely parked their fifteen Shermans in close formation in laager-style inside an orchard:

> The attack burst with an unnerving shriek of falling missiles. The flash of exploding shells and mortar bombs darted erratically about the branches of the trees. Detonations shattered the air. Earth and stones fountained up, showers of leaves fluttered down. The 3 RTR tank crews were caught outside their tanks. With so much metal flying about they could only hug the earth. Several tanks burst into flames, including that of the Ayrshire

Yeomanry FOO Peter Garrett. For fifteen minutes the bombardment rained down. Then the din stopped as suddenly as it had started. Stretcher bearers ran half crouched through the trees to answer calls for help.

Four Panthers and a Tiger had attacked the Grand Bonfait position. Sergeant 'Buck' Kite of 3 RTR noted:

The field was suddenly full of exploding shells and mortar bombs. We jumped up on the tank and climbed in. We were immediately in battle with an enemy tank that was advancing behind a hedge. It was less than 200 yards away. Over in the field beyond, the outline of two Panther tanks appeared. The wheat had grown high and was almost ripe. Each time the German tanks fired, the shell cut a narrow furrow through the ears of corn. There was a flash. I saw the corn bending down along the flight of the shell. It was going to hit us. Death coming at full speed.

Sergeant Kite was one of 3 RTR's twenty casualties. He was awarded his third Military Medal, the only British soldier in the Second World War to receive so many. Strong DF targets from Ayrshire Yeomanry and 13 RHA persuaded the Germans to call off their attack.

The rest of 4 KSLI were in a tight box in their reverse slope position just behind the ridge overlooking Presles. They were attacked all day and took many casualties including fifteen killed, but their line held. The Herefords held a similar reverse slope a mile further west (to the right) overlooking Burcy but were later sent to support 3rd Mons. 13 RHA guns were just behind near Le Desert, and Ayrshire Yeomanry behind Pavée. Further to the west 3rd Mons, with 2nd Fife and Forfarshire, were dug in around the village of Pavée. Steel Brownlie noted that Panthers were coming down the road from Vassy with the sun behind them:

All kinds of things were flying about, so I put down smoke and belted along the road to join the Squadron. This was no safe haven. There were enemy infantry everywhere, ours had been overrun, Jimmy had been knocked out. Bill Hotblack got a grenade in his turret and more casualties were coming every minute. We fired a lot of smoke and ran for positions half a mile back astride the road leading north to Burcy.

The General was concerned because 8 RB and 23rd Hussars were cut off for twenty-four hours. A Panther appeared in Presles, 2,000 yards behind them, and 23rd Hussars fitters and an 8 RB ambulance were ambushed causing casualties. Presles was reoccupied by 9th SS Panzer grenadiers, but on their hill 23rd Hussars had refitted with ammunition and food. Only the evacuation of wounded would become a problem. In a heavy mist 23rd Hussars moved into their squadron positions at 0530 hrs and troop leader

Geoffrey Bishop, with a large 8 RB sergeant as bodyguard, went for a recce on foot 1,000 yards ahead to check possible enemy tank cover: 'It is quite exciting stalking along the hedges in No Man's Land, but probably rather a foolish thing to do.' Later on: 'There is a good deal of chatter going on through the wireless and it now seems that our supply route from the rear has been cut out by the enemy, which means that we are isolated on our small hilltop. . . . This is rather tricky.' A long range tank duel started with 9th SS Panthers, but only the nine remaining 17-pounder Fireflies could catch them. The little hill on the Perrier ridge was a fireworks display: sparks and wisps of smoke shot up into the air as shells and bombs exploded. 23rd Hussars lost four tanks (Major Wigan had two brewed up under him in twenty minutes) and 8 RB also suffered casualties, as Noel Bell reported:

> German infantry could be seen streaming back into Presles, thus cutting our centre line and tanks and SP guns, most concealed in sunken roads, opened up from all sides. 'Moaning minnies' added to the fun and soon tanks began brewing up and casualties began to mount. Morale dropped. Magnificent work was done by Michael Wilcox and Captain Mitchell, the RMO of the 23rd Hussars. At no time were wounded or dead left unattended for more than a few seconds. No praise can be too high for their work, all of which had to be done under heavy fire: due to the cut centre-line no casualties could be evacuated.

8 RB had four half tracks and a carrier hit and took twenty casualties. Rifleman Roland Jefferson was impressed with the RAF Typhoon support: 'More often than not when they appeared they would score for us.' But an American Thunderbolt discharged all its rockets at the hilltop RAP.

On the very far right flank 2nd Northants Yeomanry were patrolling vigorously. One squadron passed through Montisanger and reached the Paris–Granville railway line; another headed towards Etouvy and the third towards Vire via N 177 which appeared to be empty of Germans *and* Americans. But by early afternoon Tiger tanks supported by infantry caught and savagely mauled the regiment around La Bistière, north of Vire, and at La Papillonière road junction, 2 miles away from Vire. Here three tanks were destroyed by Unterscharführer Ernst Steng and his three Tigers under command. That evening the 2nd Warwicks of 3rd British Division were brought into action and behind a barrage and smoke screen retook Presles, thus allowing ambulances to collect the wounded and dead of 8 RB and 23rd Hussars. It had been a long hot day all along the divisional front line with 4 KSLI stoutly holding their corner, but 3 RTR and 2nd Northants Yeomanry suffering heavy losses of tanks and men. The Inns of Court had a rough time around Cathéoles and had a dozen casualties and brewed-up scout cars. During the night 3–4 August Panzergrenadiers infiltrated the 2nd Northants Yeomanry laager and destroyed eight more Cromwell tanks with their panzerfaust. After adding these losses to the one-sided battle earlier on, the Yeomanry casualties were fourteen crew killed, sixteen wounded and thirty-eight missing. Demoralized after their heavy losses and the poor performance of their Cromwells, crews had dismounted and were patrolling *on foot* towards the Vire road. 'They could at least stalk the brutes,' but these foot patrols were also shot up and suffered casualties.

Day Six – 4 August

On their hilltop 23rd Hussars moved out of close laager at 0515 hrs in a heavy mist. In the eerie silence Geoffrey Bishop had bacon and beans on biscuits fried in the bacon fat: 'what a sumptuous affair'. By 0900 hrs the divisional artillery was in action putting defensive fire down several hundred yards ahead. A shower of 'minnies' descended on Geoffrey in the middle of performing a private function and he had to dive for cover beneath the nearest tank, where six other Hussars were already sheltering. The modern phrase is 'friendly fire'. American Thunderbolts were notoriously trigger-happy. They swarmed over the thin red line of the British defences and bombed everyone in sight despite the orange phosphorescent panels displayed on the top of the Fife and Forfar Shermans at Pavée and the yellow smoke emitted by special smoke generators. Nearby at La Biste, Corporal Reg Worton of 1st Herefords remembers: 'Our carriers were parked all round the sides of a field when a Yankee Thunderbolt came snooping round at hedge height and you could see the pilot. A Jerry gun shot at him which scared him and he sliced right down my section and hit [Private] Wilf Finnikin, one of my drivers, who died in my arms.' Another Thunderbolt attacked an 8 RB First Aid Post at Presles, which had a plainly visible Red Cross, and discharged all its rockets. Fortunately only the trucks were hit.

After 2nd Warwicks had cleared Presles, 2,000 yards behind, the corridor was reopened and fifteen ambulances sped up to the 23rd Hussars/8 RB hilltop to collect the wounded. 8 RB padre, Jeff Taylor, held a service for the dead. Two companies of 8 RB went back to Presles, where Roland Jefferson reported: 'We camouflaged the vehicles as best possible in orchards and gardens, dug a little, but the Warwicks had left some good trenches. We were under almost constant mortar and shellfire but we kept our heads down.' For a further four days 8 RB stayed in Presles. Each time carriers passed through to collect food, fuel and water, mortars rained down. 'Dust means Death', and signs were put up stating just that.

The 8 RB company on the hill sent Piat gangs into Chênedollé looking for enemy tanks, but at 1500 hrs the expected counter-attacks came in from the woods to the south. Besides the 23rd Hussars were two companies of 2nd Warwicks and G Company 8 RB. A heavy ten-minute mortar stonk ensued causing casualties. Colonel Hunter, CO 8 RB, rallied his mixed command; 23rd Hussars poured HE shells into the woods and 13 RHA/Ayrshire Yeomanry fired defensive fire targets. The Germans fell back but remained in Le Bas Perrier village. Another counter-attack in the evening with a heavy bombardment was also beaten off.

> Then as the afternoon wears on comes greater tragedy [wrote Geoffrey Bishop with 23rd Hussars on their lonely hilltop], tragedy of gallant lives lost in vain endeavour. One of our mobile supporting guns [75 Anti-tank Regiment RA] about two hundred yards behind me, moves to another position and is immediately hit by a shell from a German Panther hidden in the woods somewhere in front of our position. The crew bale out but the vehicle is on fire and smoking furiously. A Warwicks officer, recently decorated for gallantry, leaps on and starts to throw out the live ammo. Two of his sergeants and Peter Robson, our young troop leader, go to his assistance and get a lot of shells out of the burning hulk . . . then in a flash there are two blinding reports. Flames pour from the wrecked gun. Peter, the Warwicks major and the two sergeants are no longer. The smell of a burnt offering to the God of war.

At one stage the 23rd Hussars were again isolated and the divisional supply route was broken by four Tigers and thirty Panzergrenadiers, who threatened a long supply column of ammunition. The convoy took the wrong route but arrived safely.

Communications were very difficult, a nightmare for signallers as lines and wireless leads were being continually broken by shell fire. For 2nd Fife and Forfarshire it was almost peaceful. Steel Brownlie was stonked in Burcy and liberated some calvados:

> A German patrol came cautiously towards us, within Panzerfaust range. I opened up and they ducked for cover. I did some fancy shooting, like putting two or three HE on delay through a haystack but the infantry were not impressed. They said they would have bagged the lot had the patrol been allowed to come closer. And firing of tank guns might bring down shells. Point taken!

Chênedollé, the obvious concentration point for the German counter-attack, was shelled by 13 RHA and Ayrshire Yeomanry and the latter had two FOOs wounded in confused fighting near Burcy, which was taken and retaken. 4 August was the third sweltering day in a row and the defensive boxes on Perrier ridge were still cut off. 4 KSLI were having a relatively peaceful day. Tim Ellis was angry when he heard on the BBC 8 am news that the Guards Armoured were the 'spearhead of this party'. 'This is a bloody disgrace – they are miles behind us and did not start until three days after we did'. Ned Thornburn, carrying his batman's rifle with his shoulder titles reversed, heard a stonk approaching and walked calmly to a slit trench. The 'minnies' came and stopped. The KSLI private in the trench said: 'Cor, you're a cool cuss', not realizing he was addressing his company commander.

But on the right flank it was rather different. 119 Battery 75 A/Tank at Forgues were under command of 3 RTR and in a day of heavy shelling and mortaring had a successful offensive operation, destroying two Panthers, one Tiger and a SP gun.

On the far right flank the Americans had pushed south through Etouvy towards Vire, and on the far left the Guards Armoured had reached the village of La Marvindière, north-west of Estry. This German strongpoint was destined to be held tenaciously by 9 SS Panzer for another week.

Day Seven – 5 August

9 SS Panzer Division had surveyed the 11th Armoured salient, and maps captured from them showed how accurately the British positions had been charted. On the left 4 KSLI and 3 RTR had an 'average' day with the forward infantry companies around Bonfait changed over for relief. Ned Thornburn wrote: 'We were unlucky with our casualties having no fewer than five killed during the day.' Enemy patrols had reoccupied Burcy cutting off the Pavée box, so Steel Brownlie's 2nd Fife and Forfarshire troop was sent to Burcy: 'I was getting to know this village rather well. We were stonked as my tanks were getting into defensive positions. We liberated some bottles of calvados from a house. One use for this was to fill cigarette lighters – it burned with a clear blue flame and no smoke, unlike petrol.' During the day a strong attack on 3rd Mons and 2nd Fife and Forfarshire in the Pavée box was repulsed by massive Corps artillery defensive fire programmes. 3rd Mons held their ridge and inflicted heavy casualties, but a patrol sent to La Botterie never returned. Since two Ayrshire Yeomanry FOOs were wounded, Major Mitchell was left alone to serve 3rd Mons and 2nd Fife and Forfarshire. The Mons had been in action for a week and most platoons were at half strength. During the day 23rd Hussars sustained and beat back three counter-attacks originating from Chênedollé. Distinguished visitors from Brigade, including Roscoe Harvey, visited the Bas Perrier hill and accepted the hospitality of a large trench under the CO's tank during the frequent stonks. The Quartermaster, Captain Garcia, was left outside on one occasion. When the shelling stopped he was still there waving a NAAFI cheque awaiting signature and saying plaintively: 'Isn't there any room for me?' The gallant MO, Captain Mitchell, crossing an open field to attend to some wounded, was badly hit in the chest and was replaced by Captain McBeath. Geoffrey Bishop noted:

Fox Troop, I Battery, 13th Regiment (HAC) RHA

The afternoon wears on. On our right flank two more of our tanks are knocked out . . . several killed and an officer badly wounded – a leg blown off. That night as we move to the corner of our shell-torn field another tank is hit high up in the turret, another young officer mortally wounded. Now of the five officers, tank crews and nineteen tanks left to defend this position, Len and I are the only officer survivors and only eleven tanks are fit for battle. There is a feeling we have been left here to die. Black night settles over our grim little battlefield.

Ted Harte of B squadron destroyed a 75-mm gun which the German PZ had manhandled into position in the trees, then went with a platoon of Warwicks into Le Bas Perrier village where they were surrounded by enemy infantry. A difficult time with a Tiger being hit three times at close range and one Sherman being brewed, but the British patrols retired in fairly good order. Echelon sent up supply columns between Presles and Le Bas Perrier Hill, running the gauntlet of PZ patrols and 88 airburst but usually getting through. In the darkness A and B squadrons withdrew to La Barbière leaving C and RHQ on the hill with 2nd Warwicks.

75 A/Tank 117 Battery was in action most of the day at Burcy, Hill 218 and Le Bas Perrier, losing guns and again taking heavy casualties supporting 3 RTR, 2 Warwicks and 2 KSLI (both of 185 Brigade under command). At Sourdeval 338 Battery had their heaviest shelling of the Normandy campaign, suffering sixteen casualties, losing four gun quads, two guns and a carrier.

The historian of the 23rd Hussars described Bas Perrier hill on 5 August:

An extraordinary picture with the peaceful fields disfigured by the ugly shape of tanks, pitted with shell holes and torn up by tracks. Burnt and blackened vehicles dotted the hedgerows and besides many of them were a few rough crosses made of two twigs with a beret or a rifleman's steel helmet resting upon each of them. Spoil from slit trenches was heaped between the tanks and below ground crouched the riflemen not on look-out duties, together with the small number of echelon personnel who travelled with the tanks. The tank crews were tired but still full of fight. Most of them had not spent more than thirty minutes outside their tanks for forty-eight hours and were destined to do the same for another two days. Many tanks had been stationary and camouflaged for five days – a very considerable strain. No one doubted that the Germans meant to take Bas Perrier hill.

General Roberts admitted: 'There is no doubt that we remained in a highly precarious situation for several days.' Guards Armoured on the left and the Americans on the right were slow and well behind their planned timetable. It took them both four days to catch up. The General sent a message to all troops: 'I wish all ranks to know that during the present period of operation, tremendous demands will be made on their powers of endurance . . . I will only call upon troops to do the almost impossible but not the completely impossible. The stakes are high and the prize great.' It was the calm before the storm.

The Storm: Day Eight – 6 August

11th Armoured Division's deep salient into the heart of the German defence line was to be sorely tested. 10th SS Panzer Division was sent south-west from Mont Pinçon to launch a full scale attack on the two defensive boxes at Le Bas Perrier and Pavée. A German general described the salient as 'a festering abcess'. He was right.

General Roberts noted:

The reconnaissance unit of 9 Panzer Division had been surveying the area of our breakthrough: captured maps showed that they had performed their mission thoroughly and accurately. But when the attack came it was head on against the well-defended apex, not against the vulnerable flanks. The main attack was by 10 SS Panzer Division who had moved south-west from Mont Pinçon, plus a battalion of Tiger tanks from 110 Panzer Division, a battalion of engineers fighting as infantry, most of 363 Division newly arrived from Denmark, and a mixed force of Tigers and SP guns from 2 SS Panzer Corps Heavy Tank battalion.

The main attack started at 1800 hrs just as 185th Infantry Brigade from 3 Division was about to take over complete responsibility for the sector. So the General ordered the 29th Armoured Brigade plus the 2nd Warwicks to hold the left, and 159 Infantry Brigade plus the 1st Norfolks to hold the right.

At Le Bas Perrier 23rd Hussars and 2nd Warwicks were soon attacked by Tiger tanks which had infiltrated into the woods during the night. Geoffrey Bishop lined up his remaining 'babies' (code name for tanks) behind a small bank and hedge immediately in the rear of the field 23rd Hussars had been holding for four days. Throughout the long day he and the eleven lonely tanks guarded their hill 'with a few dug-in infantry on this shell-torn hilltop'. He sent back targets to the gunners behind and eventually at 2200 hrs after seventeen hours of vigil his squadron were ordered back into laager. The regimental historian noted: 'The enemy began to creep round the left flank. As darkness was falling they reached the top of the hill and began to bazooka the tanks. This serious situation was overcome largely by the bravery of Lieutenant Bishop commanding the left-hand troop, quite unshakeable, whose coolness put fresh heart into the Warwicks.' During Bluecoat, 1–7 August, 23rd Hussars had seventy-four casualties, of whom twenty-one were killed.

Heavy shelling and nebelwerfer mortar bombs battered the Warwicks, causing many casualties. Ken Thorpe, 2nd Warwicks, stated: 'It was the worst shelling and mortaring in a short time since we landed on D-Day. We were crowded together in a small area and I wondered that even more were not being killed and wounded'. The battle raged for several hours and the Corps artillery firing non-stop almost certainly saved the day. The Warwicks were due to relieve 8 RB and this was only achieved at 2000 hrs.

It was a close run thing. During the late afternoon on the left flank the Panzergrenadiers in the thick wood attacked again and again with great determination. The Warwicks took many more casualties and by dusk SS infantry had reached the crest of the ridge and picked off the 23rd Hussars tanks one by one with bazookas. The historian of the 23rd Hussars related:

Our [13 RHA FOO] Major Gaunt incessantly gave instructions to his guns for more and more support, a call nobly answered. The OP on the hill went off the air so Major Hagger, 23rd Hussars, passed the fire orders back and forth. 'East 200 yards – No. North 100. That's exactly right, well done!' The Germans were creeping up to the crest of the hill in the fading light. The roar of the guns was accompanied now by flickering red flashes as they fired. It grew dark. The defenders, Warwicks and Hussars were withdrawn into a tight ring, infantry and tanks together, all very tired. Voices now had a slight irritation and strain but Hill 224 was not lost and was not going to be. General Eberbach had reported to von Kluge that 10th SS Panzer had captured Hill 224 – not true!

The artillery FOOs performed nobly. Captain Davidge, 13 RHA, was with 23rd Hussars near Le Bas Perrier using his No. 18 wireless set as remote control. His OP was shelled, the set destroyed. He went back to his tank, ran a telephone line back to his OP and for five hours under intense and continuous shell and mortar fire, directed the divisional artillery on DF targets. The gun crew No. 1s of both artillery regiments dared not leave their guns loaded as the pieces were so hot. Both 13 RHA and Ayrshire Yeomanry fired 250 rounds per gun during that long, hot afternoon and night. Major Mitchell, Ayrshire Yeomanry FOO with the 2nd Fife and Forfarshire and 3rd Mons, under constant fire brought down defensive fire with devastating effect. A wireless set damaged, two of his tank crew killed, he kept his OP going despite Tiger tanks plunging about among the defenders.

3rd Mons and 2nd Fife and Forfarshire tanks at Pavée were at the sharpest point of the salient, 1,000 yards from the Vire–Vassy road. Major How, 3rd Mons, recalled: 'It was not safe to keep one's head above ground for very long. We were being continuously shelled from the south – the 'moaning minnies' were bad and there were many casualties. Sweat saves blood: better a deep slit trench than a shallow grave!' The already overburdened infantryman gladly humped a pick or shovel: it could be a matter of life or death. For two days the Mons cooks' trucks had failed to get through, so hard biscuits were the only food available. How painted the life of the 'sharp-end' infantryman vividly:

Worst of all was the feeling of tiredness: for days we had had no more than two consecutive hours of sleep. The drain of casualties had made the burden of guard duty and patrols heavy for those who remained. We just couldn't catch up with lost sleep. Dusty, begrimed, sore-eyed, we could doze off at odd times only to be wrenched back to sweaty consciousness by the woof and crump of another bombardment.

Supporting 3rd Mons and the relieving 1st Norfolks around Sourdeval on the right flank were 2nd Fife and Forfarshire Yeomanry. Steel Brownlie's troop was watching Dump Wood:

There was much shelling which rose to a climax till suddenly in the afternoon Don Bulley's and Corporal Newman's tanks burst into flames and we heard the whine of AP shot. Tanks, SP guns and infantry came towards us from Dump Wood and C Squadron on our left reported being attacked by Tigers. Our infantry were rolling back in confusion. Pinkie Hutchinson got a Mark IV and I got an SP while we killed many of the advancing infantry. The squadron, already depleted, lost four more tanks. Shelling continued till dark, when we were ordered back a few hundred yards to a regimental harbour. I squeezed as many of the worst wounded into my tank as possible and motored round the base of the Pavée feature, fires burning everywhere. We were reduced from three squadrons to two.

Seven men were killed and two wounded that day. Sergeant Hedley Bunce, 3rd Mons, noted: 'Between bouts of heavy shelling and mortaring, a steady stream of wounded was moving into the barn behind me. I had a trench facing back towards the valley. We were told that German tanks were moving up the road towards us from Burcy. God, did I have a funny feeling in the stomach.' Captain Carrick and his medical orderlies were exhausted. Essential medical supplies had run out. Some of the seriously wounded were placed, for their protection, in great cider casks with the ends knocked out.

The German attacks were coming in from Chênedollé in the east and along the road over the ridge to Pavée from the south.

The handover plan was proceeding at Pavée and at 1500 hrs the strong point was being held with two Norfolk companies forward and two of 3rd Mons behind them. One company of the Mons had left and another was preparing to leave when the main German attack came in. Lieutenant Tommy Aplin, 3rd Mons, the sole surviving officer of his company, noted:

My company had just been relieved from the foward positions on the right. It was hell. We all scattered. I had seen it all the day before and knew what to expect. I shouted to the men. They were to try to get back to the positions they had just handed over. There was only one small trench not occupied by the Norfolks. We all managed to get in – God knows how! Enemy infantry and tanks advancing towards the eastern perimeter from Chênedollé.

Then the Norfolks and Mons were bombed and machine-gunned by American Thunderbolts. Corporal Sidney Bates of the Norfolks bravely kept a Bren going, was wounded three times, died of his wounds and was posthumously awarded the Victoria Cross. Eighty men of the Norfolks and Mons who died in the battle around Pavée were temporarily buried there and the field is still known as Le Champ des Morts. Lieutenant Aplin continued:

The Norfolks who had taken over our company HQ were getting out of their trenches. They were slaughtered. As far as I knew every one of them was killed. We crawled out of the trench and through the dead bodies of the Norfolks. They were lying everywhere. I wondered why the German infantry had not put in an appearance to take advantage of the havoc caused by the Tiger tanks.

By 9 p.m. the Ayrshire Yeomanry's 25-pounders' ammunition stocks were almost exhausted, but in the nick of time thirty RASC trucks were seen driving hard up the road. The Yeoman cheered and the guns continued firing for two more hours.

About 160 of the Pavée defenders had been killed, wounded or were missing. Most were infantrymen; the Mons had ten men killed, but 75 anti-tank regiment were also hard hit with eight men killed. All evening the ambulances shuttled back and forth with the wounded. At nightfall the German attack on Pavée came to a sudden end, as had happened at Le Grand Bonfait three days earlier. Running across the fields and down the slope were the enemy infantry. Tanks of 2nd Fife and Forfarshire advanced back up the ridge and fired smoke to screen themselves as they raced down to catch up with the retreating enemy. The Mons got their hot meal, the first for three days, hot tea brewed on the spot and much mail. Major How noticed the post corporal put an elastic band round the pile of mail for the many no longer there to receive it.

Enemy dead lay everywhere. Long spirals of black and grey smoke rose slowly in the evening air from half tracks, tanks, carriers, soft vehicles – but mainly British.

Sergeant Wheeler, 3rd Mons, wanted to start digging graves for those who had been killed: 'We decided it would be quicker to get the prisoners to do the digging. When we handed the shovels round one of them dropped his and spat at us.' Most of the prisoners were teenagers, exhausted, frightened. Some thought they would have to dig their own graves.

The General wrote:

The battle which followed raged on both sectors well into the night. Great valour was shown everywhere. It was certainly the toughest battle we had in the campaign: both sides received heavy casualties but the Germans had the heavier largely because they were advancing and not dug in. If it had not been for the Corps artillery, I doubt if we would have held the Germans.

The Aftermath: Days 9–14, 7–12 August

The storm had come and more or less gone; the killing grounds were a shambles – the little villages and hamlets of Chênedollé, Presles, Burcy, Pavée, Le Bas Perrier, Le Moulin and Le Grand Bonfaits. It was a good harvest that August of 1944. The corn stood high, there were cows to milk and livestock to feed. Many of the civilians had abandoned their homes and taken to the roads with their pathetic possessions. Wheelbarrows, prams, small carts, little groups trying to avoid the fighting, some on bicycles. Always the very old or the very young. The British soldiers had, unfortunately, brought battle, total destruction and often death. There was to be no easy liberation of the little hamlets, taken and retaken, bombarded and stonked by both sides.

Roden Orde, 2nd Household Cavalry, wrote on 7 August; 'The winding road out of Burcy towards Pavée was the biggest strain of all and the sight on reaching the Monmouth's position was appalling. A hurricane seemed to have hit the place. All their transport was gone, the farm burnt and the dead

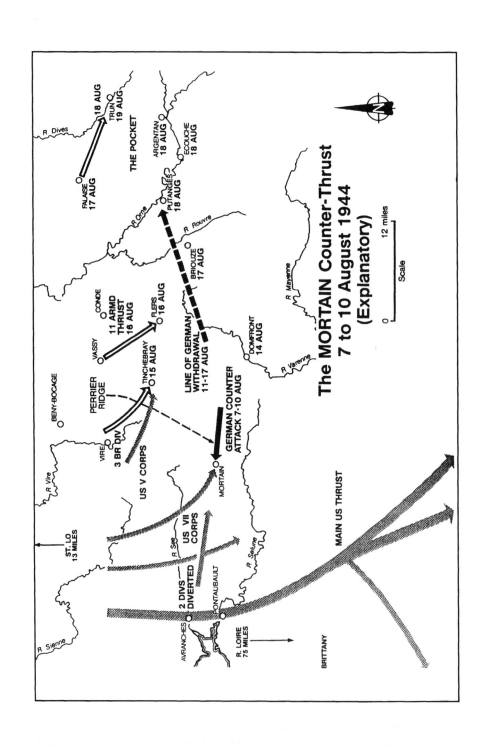

The MORTAIN Counter-Thrust
7 to 10 August 1944
(Explanatory)

were lying in rows awaiting burial.' And Major How, 3rd Mons, one of the survivors, noted: 'The two Shermans were still burning. There was not a living soul in the company HQ area. The Norfolks were all dead, lying half in and half out of our old slit trenches. Some had no visible wounds: they must have been killed by the blast. There was a strange silence. Around us was only death and destruction.' But it was not over yet.

8 RB stayed in Presles and sent out frequent patrols. They were based in the apple orchards on the slopes above the village. Most of the time was spent in or near their slit trenches, with steel helmets on, and despite intense shelling and mortaring on many occasions, their twelve casualties were, according to Noel Bell, 'not unduly high'. Three platoons were commanded by sergeants, as their officers were casualties. On 10 August 5 Battalion Coldstream Guards took over and 8 RB went back to Le Bény Bocage where reinforcements arrived from 8 KRRC.

2nd Fife and Forfarshire spent 7 and 8 August on the Bas-Perrier ridge being fired upon by Tigers from the high ground to the east around Chênedollé. Steel Brownlie fired at movements in Dump Wood and called on Typhoon shoots: 'How to deal with the Tigers? We could not see them, just received their 88–mm shots.' But on 7 August the 2nd Fife and Forfarshire knocked out almost as many tanks as they lost, despite being stonked on and off. On the 8th Brownlie crawled round their burnt-out tanks: 'I had a list of the wounded who had been evacuated, so knew what bodies to look for: crumpled heaps on this seat or that.' Relieved by the Scots Greys tanks, five out of nineteen tanks in his squadron moved back to La Quelle. 'I immediately had three large whiskies and soda and for four balmy days refitting, absorbing reinforcements, eating a roast goose, taking showerbaths, marking maps.'

Geoffrey Bishop wrote:

As the mist clears the ravages of the battle began to show. The cornfield beaten down, scarred with masses of tank tracks and literally pitted with bomb holes – the burnt out wrecks still smouldering with the blackened stubble all round them – the delightful vegetable field now just a mangled pulp, the stark black roof timbers of the once peaceful thatched farmhouse showing through the shattered trees – all the beauty gone. There are the charred remains of gallant men in these burned out vehicles – all is quiet. The village of Presles with its painted church spire seems deserted and beyond, the long road up the other side of the valley is empty.

Late that day as 23rd Hussars approached their harbour area, their Colonel and Adjutant walked across the field to greet the survivors:

The Colonel in his gay red and green side hat stands and salutes us – the tension breaks and I sob my heart out – we're back. Later Ted Harte lends me a mirror and a horrible apparition is reflected. Three days' growth of beard, dark lined eyes under filthy army glasses – grimy face, neck and matted hair. 'Even me Mum wouldn't recognize me', I thought.

Soon reinforcements from 24th Lancers arrived at La Barbière to replace Bluecoat casualties.

On 7 August 43rd Division took Mont Pinçon after a week's slow and extensive fighting, partly as a result of 10 SS Panzer moving away to counter-attack the Perrier Ridge salient. Hitler had ordered von Kluge to make a massed armoured counter-attack through Mortain to Avranches to cut off Patton's tanks sweeping into Brittany, towards the River Loire. 11th Armoured Division had fought 9 SS and 10 SS (2nd Panzer Corps) almost to a standstill, and as a result von Kluge could only muster 100 tanks for his counter-thrust against the Americans. Typhoon activity was intense. Ned Thornburn, 4 KSLI, remembered 'having a grandstand view of the Typhoons coming in and loosing off their rockets. We all got out of our trenches and cheered our heads off at the thought of the pasting the Germans were getting'.

The Irish Guards relieved half the battalion, while the rest concentrated near 8 RB at Presles with the Warwicks in their front. On 9 August the 4 KSLI moved to take over the Guards' positions at Bonfait and Le Busq to free them for an attack with 3 British Division to secure the Vire–Vassy road. A mobile bath-house was constructed by the Pioneer section and the men got their first decent wash for twelve days accompanied by a double issue of NAAFI rations. But mortar stonks happened most days, and on the 10th caused a dozen casualties. The weather was oppressively hot, day after day: 'We all felt extremely limp and battered and the dust made it worse.'

Meanwhile the long-suffering 2nd Warwicks were relieved on 9 August by the 1st Herefords and 3rd Mons were lent temporarily to 185 Infantry Brigade, who reverted back to 3rd British Division, now on the right flank. By the morning of the 10th the changeover was complete and 159 Brigade held the narrow front around Le Busq to give flank protection to the Guards. On 11 August the Guards reported – at long last – the village of Chênedollé clear of the enemy and occupied by 1st Herefords. 3rd Mons returned to 159 Infantry Brigade. A depleted 1st Norfolks reverted back to 185 Infantry Brigade and 2nd Household Cavalry were replaced by the Inns of Court scout car reconnaissance regiment.

13 RHA and the Ayrshire Yeomanry were in action every day with stonks on Dump Wood or Tiger Hill, a feature near Le Haut Perrier. Red smoke was fired to indicated targets for Typhoon attacks. On the 8th Basil target blanketed Tiger Hill with smoke screen, while the Scots Greys took over from the 2nd Fife and Forfarshire. Some concentrations were fired to support Guards Armoured Division, advancing slowly on the left.

Corporal Alastair Tait, 173 Troop Carrying Co. RASC, was attached to 3rd Mons during most of the campaign. One way or another he lost three motorbikes; one under a 3 RTR Sherman, one to a 'moaning minnie' and another to a shellburst. Around Burcy he saw that farm pigs had got loose and were beginning to eat some of the dead.

So Bluecoat was over and on 12 August the Black Bull came under XXX Corps, now taken over by Lieutenant-General Brian Horrocks (a personal friend of General Roberts), recovered from his severe wounds in North Africa. What had Bluecoat achieved? The General wrote: 'Our deep thrust had caused the Germans great concern. Our advance south from the Bény Bocage ridge had drawn and held the only German reserves to the great advantage of Patton's army.' During Bluecoat the division had killed in action: 3rd Mons 35, 4 KSLI 30, 1st Herefords 28, 23rd Hussars 22, 8 RB 21, 2nd Northants Yeomanry 21, 2 Fife and Forfarshire 13, 3 RTR 8, Inns of Court 6, and artillery regiments 16.

CHAPTER TWELVE

Breakout

Alan Moorehead's book *Eclipse* summarized the situation in early to mid-August:

> Somewhere to the south of Falaise in an ever-dwindling pocket of rolling countryside, there was a horde of broken and bewildered men, the survivors of some thirty or forty [German] divisions. And now they were being killed and captured and maimed at the rate of several thousand every day. It had been a dull and indifferent summer; since D-Day we had never been able to rely on the weather for two days at a time. But now the sun shone out day after day. The trampled corn turned brilliant yellow. The dust rose up with the smoke of the explosions. And through this hot August sun the Allied aircraft streamed down on the trapped German armies with such a blitz of bombing as western Europe had never seen. No German convoy could take the roads in safety before nightfall. But now in their extremity they were forced out into the open and the carnage along the roads was horrible.

On 7 August the Seventh Army reported: 'A break-down has occurred, the like of which we have never seen.' And on 10 August Hitler gave up Normandy with his order: 'Disengage'. On 13 August the retreat started and the remains of 1st, 2nd, 9th and 12th Panzer and Panzer Lehr started to force their way between the Argentan and Falaise gap. Monty ordered XXX Corps under Lieutenant-General Horrocks to advance south-east and make for Vassy and Flers with 11th Armoured leading, followed by 50th and 43rd Infantry Divisions. 15th Scottish had finally captured Estry on 13 August after a desperate defence. That night 4 KSLI had a rather uncomfortable roundabout march of 5 miles to enter Estry and at 0630 hrs on the 14th were ready to start the advance from the main crossroads towards Vassy, Flers and Briouze.

8 RB took over on 13 August from the Seaforths of 15th Scottish at Drury, west of Le Bény Bocage, and stayed there until the 15th when they linked up with 23rd Hussars.

The Division formed up on the line between Lassy and Estry south-east of Le Bény Bocage and south-west from Mont Pinçon. Initially there were to be three centre-lines of advance: 8 RB/23rd Hussars from La Caverie due south towards Vassy; on the far left 3rd Mons/2nd Fife and

Forfarshire from Lassy due south to La Rocque and St Germain-du-Crioult converging on Vassy; 1st Herefords/3 RTR from Estry on the right flank to Le Theil, La Herbalière and Hill 212, also heading for Vassy. Inns of Court would nip down the side roads and paths and act as the divisional 'eyes and ears'.

Infantry were riding on the backs of tanks, but after the Herefords advanced and took La Rocque and Le Theil, they found themselves under heavy fire from Hill 212 1,000 yards ahead, and lost twenty men, including eight killed. 13 RHA and Ayrshire Yeomanry fired 'Sleeper' target on Hill 212 to support them. The German habit was to fight like hell until dusk and then retreat during the night to their next defensive position. So when nightfall came 4 KSLI took over and Ned Thornburn noted: 'The Boche is definitely withdrawing leaving behind last ditch covering parties of odd MGs and Anti-Tank guns.'

On the 15th the advance went on slowly but surely. 8 RB/23rd Hussars took the lead on the right, taking Canteloupe by nightfall, which was, as Noel Bell reported, 'an unpleasant night of shelling and mortaring'.

The historian of the 23rd Hussars wrote: 'All this was dull, dangerous and unspectacular. Slow grinding work. 159 Brigade led by 3 RTR was on our right heading for Vassy and Fife and Forfarshire were working up on our left through Lassy and La Rocque.'

On the right flank 4 KSLI took over the lead at La Herbalière and pushed patrols into Vassy where the bridge was blown and the town empty of defenders and locals. Brigadier Churcher remarked: 'There wasn't a living person or animal to be seen, not even a cat.' The sappers cleared the bridge and the Inns of Court forded the river and nipped ahead to reconnoitre. 4 KSLI continued on, crossed the Condé–Vire main road towards Flers, and dug in for the night having advanced 2 miles in the day. Ayrshire Yeomanry had some fun firing propaganda leaflets into three selected areas, probably scaring the German defenders out of Vassy!

On the far left Steel Brownlie's troop was given the task of taking a platoon of 3rd Mons on the back of their tanks, plus a section of sappers, to inspect a bridge north-west of St Germain-du-Crioult: 'We covered ten miles of fields, hedges and woods without opposition and found the bridge intact. The road was cratered and mined and there was a wrecked Inns of Court scout car. The sappers cleared everything. The regiment came up and we bedded down in a potato field.' At La Rocque and Gacé 3rd Mons had a very difficult time with twenty-five casualties, including ten killed. But the main sadness of the day was that the battered and depleted 2nd Northants Yeomanry had fought their last battle as a regiment. Nearly 200 of the survivors would go as reinforcements to the armoured regiments of the 7th Armoured Division equipped with Cromwells. The remainder went to their sister regiment, 1st Northants Yeomanry. A new reconnaissance cavalry unit, the 15/19th Kings Royal Hussars, fresh from England, now arrived.

The gallant Northants had fought brave actions with outgunned Cromwells at Brettevillette, Cheux, around Caen, St Martin-des-Besaces and Vire and had had eighty-seven killed during sixty-four days' fighting.

On the morning of the 16th, 3rd Mons and 2nd Fife and Forfarshire were at La Faverie and La Poulladière, and 8 RB and 23rd Hussars at La Croarde; 1st Herefords at La Calbrasserie and La Tirlière; and 4 KSLI at La Poterie and south of Hamel. The Inns of Court had actually got into the remains of Condé, where the brothers Samuel and Joseph Tibbetts noted: 'There wasn't a sound, nothing but a terrifying silence, not one person, not a solitary living soul, not even a bird!' Their patrols discovered that the bridge at Pont de Vère near Aubusson was intact but well defended, and that Flers, a major objective, was not occupied – invaluable information.

But ahead lay well-defended positions with 363rd Infantry and 3rd Parachute Divisions intent on fanatical resistance. At 0745 hrs the divisional artillery from St Pierre-d'Entremont and Perlyer was in action supporting 4 KSLI and 3 RTR. 4 KSLI had started at 0715 hrs and soon found, Major Ellis reported: 'a Boche CQMS who had run over one of their own mines and gone for six. The food in his dumpers was still hot so B Company got a second breakfast which was a lot better than the first. The fellow also had 100,000 francs on him which was "carved up" as "blood money" among the leading platoons.' 4 KSLI crossed the River Noireau and then the Herefords came through, took Cerisi and with 3 RTR pushed on 1½ miles along towards Flers. Knowing Flers was not occupied Brigadier Churcher then ordered 4 KSLI to turn eastward and make for the Pont de Vère, 2½ miles north of Flers, a distance of 3 miles cross-country through narrow lanes. The descent down to the bridge by a narrow and steep road was heavily shelled by artillery, machine guns and mortars of the Germans 3rd Parachute Division. Aided by 3 RTR the bridge was eventually taken at 1900 hrs and the Flers–Condé road secured. Ayrshire Yeomanry fired 100 rounds per gun to break up a counter-attack but lost two experienced FOOs: Captains Garrett and Bennett were both killed. 123 Battery had lost its Battery Commander, Battery Captain and both Troop Commanders in the Normandy campaign. Major Ned Thornburn said later: 'In many ways the battle for Aubusson was the unhappiest of all my actions in France. It was an untidy battle in which we suffered grievous casualties'. The town was taken at 2300 hrs as the Germans skilfully withdrew to fight more rearguard actions.

In one of their last actions 2nd Northants Yeomanry, held in reserve with 159 Brigade, cleared an area north of Flers and assembled many prisoners at Mesleret. But German artillery shelled St Georges-des-Groseillers and Mesleret causing casualties.

Steel Brownlie, with 2nd Fife and Forfarshire, wrote on the 16th:

In many small, unspectacular actions we were delayed by mines or anti-tank guns, well sited by officers who beat it and left a handful of men to hold us up. We went through St Germain-du-Crioult [west of Condé] and the Fifes and 3rd Mons formed up in text book formation, then advanced south-east. We got on to the high ground overlooking the River Noireau. We sat all afternoon in the sun and had a wash and shave. A scissors bridge [a converted Sherman tank manned by REs, with a box-girder bridge that unfolded like a pair of scissors] was put over the river and we crossed at 6 p.m. near a lemonade factory.

They harboured the night at the next river crossing near Le Pont Montilly, south of Condé.

The line of advance planned for the 17th was for 159 Brigade group to go via Flers towards Briouze, 10 miles east-south-east; and parallel but north, 29 Brigade were to head from Aubusson north-east a little to Athis and then east-south-east towards Putanges. Divisional sappers were as usual indispensable, clearing mines and building scissor and Bailey bridges, since most of the bridges were blown by the retreating Germans. The Inns of Court patrols entered Ronfeugerai, where Vic Truss recalls: 'I can see myself driving through the village in pursuit of the German infantry, then getting down from my scout car and chasing them with my Bren gun.' Other patrols scurried through hamlets and later in the day met US patrols from V US Corps south-west of Briouze. On the other flank three officers were wounded on the edges of Putanges.

Early in the morning Steel Brownlie and David Voller raced their Shermans south-east to La Carneille, where the mayor – a butcher with apron and carving knife – and crowds of citizens welcomed the Fife and Forfarshire and Mons. The next race was to secure bridges over the river Rouvre. These were half blown so RE scissors bridges were required and a nasty battle developed, as the crossing was defended by MG and mortar fire. Major Todman of 3rd Mons recalls: '2nd Fife and Forfarshire tanks approached a hill overlooking the river at Pont-Huan, two of them were hit and the others stopped by very accurate enemy fire. As my company crossed the track to attack the high ground overlooking a very large rock-strewn field, a well-aimed barrage of mortars crashed down on them.' 3rd Mons suffered twenty-five casualties in a few minutes. Around Vassy prisoners, mainly Polish deserters, surrendered in groups as 23rd Hussars followed 2nd Fife and Forfarshire through Le Pont and Cerisy Belle Etoile.

In the cool breeze of a sunny afternoon they went through hamlets pillaged and vandalized by war. Stragglers picked up at Athis told of the German plan to withdraw nightly from river line to river line in 10–mile bounds. Roland Jefferson, 8 RB, noted that a long column of American tanks and vehicles passed through the British centre-line. Lost? 8 RB traversed St Germain and Athis to the banks of the River Roure, east of Vassy. 'Members of the Resistance (FFI), civilians wearing armbands, caused us some excitement when they reported there were German guns on our flank. Investigation showed that they were heavies but they had been abandoned with huge stocks of ammunition.' He was not keen on the FFI, who were shaving women of their hair at pistol point if they were suspected of collaborating. But at least they were useful for guarding German prisoners.

After several brisk actions 8 RB and 23rd Hussars reached the River Roye at Taillebois. The bridge spanning the deep gorge was blown. The enemy concealed and emplaced on the other side in Notre Dame du Rocher was mortaring and machine-gunning. Tanks and SPs were seen and heard. A ford over the river was found downstream and the regiment crossed over with H Co. 8 RB. Throughout the afternoon of the 17th they fought their way up the steep, high-banked road leading into Notre Dame in the face of heavy fire. By nightfall they had cleared most of the village but their close laager was under constant and accurate fire throughout the night. On the morning of the 18th sappers had completed the main bridge but the enemy had vanished in the early hours abandoning SPs, vehicles and fifty bedraggled, tired, despairing prisoners, amid the havoc caused by air bombardment and stonks. Noel Bell, 8 RB, reported: 'This was our first real Swan, some 15 miles south and east of Condé.'

159 Brigade heading for Briouze on the southern centre-line was led by 3 RTR and 1st Herefords. 'The crowd was delirious. Everyone wanted to thank the soldiers, to hug them or to shake their hands. This did rather slow down the advance,' wrote the Northants Yeomanry historian. The mayor proffered champagne toasts to liberty and to victory. The advance was delayed!

The Germans laid mines everywhere and civilians, animals, even the German troops retreating, suffered from them. Divisional sappers were kept very busy each day on mine clearance as well as their bridge-building activities. Many Germans troops were abandoning uniforms for civilian clothes, but the Resistance movement usually identified them. Resistance was strong, first at Durcet, then at Ste Opportune and Le Rocher, so 13 RHA and Ayrshire Yeomanry fired heavy stonks and the town was taken at 2300 hrs by 3 RTR and 4 KSLI. 900 SS troops had been rumoured to be in the area, but they rapidly withdrew late at night.

Back at Aubusson early that morning of the 17th, 4 KSLI woke up with low morale. No hot meal during the night and, in Tim Ellis's words: 'We were all feeling tired, hungry and rather fed-up.' But later that day in Flers:

We had a hell of a good party. The civilians had not been evacuated and were out in strength to meet us. We were covered in flowers and offered all sorts of venomous drinks (actually I got a bottle of excellent Sauterne). Everyone was Boche-hunting and it was priceless to see some of the 1914–18 French veterans suddenly appearing with a brace of miserable Boches in tow.

However, 4 KSLI company commanders were deeply worried by their CO's inexperience of joint armour/infantry attacks and, when difficult resistance was met, an inflexibility in his views and plans. 2nd Fife and Forfarshire squadron leaders were not happy with their temporary CO either and were delighted when their original CO, Colonel Scott, returned on the 19th. BBC radio reported that Canadian and Polish divisions had finally reached Falaise.

By midday on the 18th 23rd Hussars and 8 RB pushed around Ste Honorine and found themselves on the high spur overlooking Putanges from the west, where the main bridge over the River Orne predictably was blown. B squadron looked for a river crossing south and C squadron went north, but met a strong enemy rearguard in Launay. B squadron and F Company 8 RB encountered an American column of tanks using the same route but going in the opposite direction. Major Wigan, 23rd Hussars, smoked a pipe of peace that evening with the American CO. The 3rd Mons came up and that night, with only four officers left in the battalion, made a river crossing south of Putanges. Joe Logan recalls how C Company had had sixty casualties in the Normandy campaign including three successive company commanders. Twenty reinforcements had arrived but the company was forty men short, now led by a lieutenant, no CSM and only six NCOs. At midnight he collected his 18-set and sten gun: '[There was] no moon, warm, no noise apart from the burning of a house near the bridge. We moved silently, no talk, no orders. I sensed an atmosphere of apprehension. We had never done a night attack over a river before and we didn't like it.' Logan volunteered to swim across the River Orne and slid down the 3-ft. high bank into the water. He had never swum fully clothed before. He swam across, talked to the Mons sergeant on the hillside, swam back, collected a Bren gun and swam across again. Then he rescued another rifleman in distress who was about to drown.

This was a brave operation with swimmers, rafts and long ladders, which mercifully met with scant opposition. Noel Bell's company harboured in some pleasant parkland on the high ground overlooking Putanges – a town of the dead, most houses destroyed and looted – while the faithful sappers brought up bridge-making equipment.

During this breakout operation 11th Armoured Division occupied the extreme right flank position in the British 2nd Army, next and supposedly parallel to the American 3rd Infantry Division. When Briouze was about to be taken by 4 KSLI/3 RTR a short battle took place between the two allies in the early morning fog! Eventually Monty's HQ sent down their ruling that the vital road between Briouze (D924) east to Ecouché and Argentan, designated Club Route, was 11th Armoured Division property. Time was wasted before the Herefords and the newly-joined 15/19th Hussars set off in late afternoon of the 18th. Eventually 4 KSLI in their TCVs reached Ecouché, 12 miles on, and dug in at 0200 hrs. Guess who was there. The Germans? The Americans? No, it was General Leclerc's 2nd French Armoured Division.

Roland Jefferson noted:

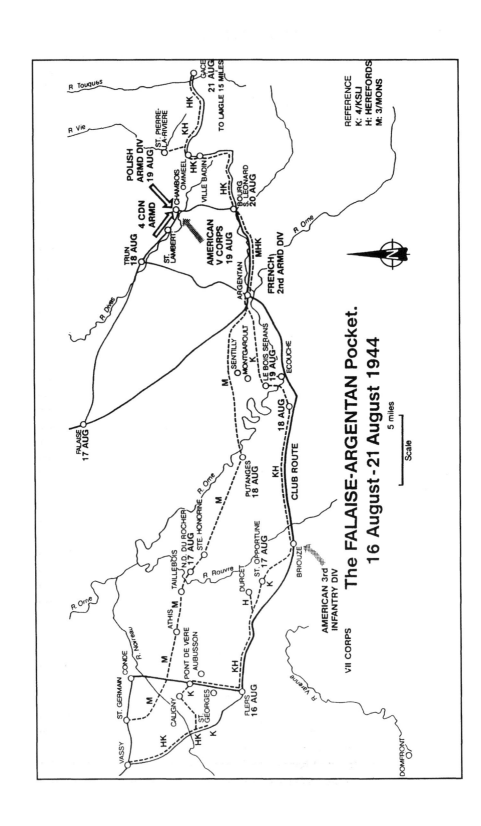

The FALAISE-ARGENTAN Pocket.
16 August - 21 August 1944

Even bulldozers were brought up to assist us. There was simply nowhere to push some of the German debris, it was piled so high. Literally thousands of German dead lay around and we did not envy the task of the French who would soon have the task of lifting all this litter of war from the roads and fields. The sun shone brightly as we passed through the ruins of Argentan.

The Americans were still fighting in the town and flushing out snipers.

Sergeant Frank Moppett, 1st Herefords, encountered the Americans at a crossroads near Briouze. He saw and heard a large GI shout out; 'Gee, Lootenant, we've knocked off a Kraut pay truck. Pay this in for me, it will pay for a Buick back home.' 'This' was a 6-inch wad of bank notes. Frank wondered whether he would ever get back home to buy his Buick.

2nd Fife and Forfarshire had motored unhindered almost to Putanges and the regiment harboured in a pleasant green meadow away from the stench of dead men and horses and flies buzzing in the hot sun. Steel Brownlie examined an undamaged Panther which was out of fuel, and it 'confirmed our opinion that German tanks were far better than ours'.

On the 19th 4 KSLI cleared the area 2 miles north of Ecouché, crossed the bridge over the River Orne and advanced towards Montgaroult and Sentilly. An air-OP in an Auster of 659 squadron provided divisional gunnery targets on the Montgaroult–Sentilly roads, supporting 3 RTR and the Herefords. In the village of Moulins-sur-Orne Trooper B. Cornwall, 15/19th Hussars, was killed when his Firefly tank gun went off accidentally. The villagers were so upset that they insisted on the funeral and burial taking place there and then. Christopher Mackonochie, Padre with 7 FDS recounts:

At 9 a.m. the cortège moved off led by the Mayor, with French tricolour and the majority of the civilian population carrying enormous wreaths. For ecumenical reasons the quiet simple service took place in the graveyard with the closing words 'Vive la France, Vive la Grande Bretagne'. The local village carpenter made a cross and after the service, a drink of calvados with our French friends with the hope that the fighting would soon be over.

At midday on the 19th the newly-joined 15/19th Hussars were in action for the first time as right flank protection. New Cromwell tanks had arrived two days before and they had a number of minor mechanical problems. They were on high ground overlooking Moulins-sur-Orne, 3 miles north-west of Argentan. C squadron engaged enemy transport at long range and at 1500 hrs B squadron moved to the hills in front of Argentan to shoot up enemy columns retreating eastwards from the 'pocket'. A concealed Panther knocked out Lieutenant Sharpe's tank and the crew were captured. But mortaring, minefields, appearance of enemy tanks, bad radio communications and mechanical breakdowns caused acute problems when B squadron and the recce troop were ordered to return to harbour. They would probably have been dead ducks if they had stayed the night where they had been in action, so eight tanks and three scout cars were left unguarded. Recovery parties went out early on the 20th and recovered all bar two Cromwells which had been knocked out. Simon Frazer, Troop Commander B squadron, wrote: 'Moving forward on to a forward slope through heavy corn stooks, I soon saw the Mark V at a range of no more than 400 yards below me silhouetted in front of a small dark copse. My gunner hit him seven times from seven alternative positions – six AP, one HE – all turret hits. Five other Cromwell 75s like mine also engaged, scoring at least four hits apiece. Our 'ricos' were flying upward with exasperating regularity. On my eighth appearance he had gone, presumed to ground in the copse.'

Liaison with 2nd French Armoured Division and 80th and 90th US Infantry Divisions took time and trouble and delayed the advance. 159 Brigade were clustered around Ecouché and 29th Brigade eventually crossed and forced the Putanges bridgehead at 1500 hrs with 3rd Mons and 2nd Fife and Forfarshire leading.

2nd Fife and Forfarshire pushed over the Orne at Naudière on roads cluttered with wrecked enemy vehicles which needed clearance by bulldozers. Steel Brownlie brewed up some horse-drawn ammo carts which exploded nicely.

Late that afternoon of the 19th, 23rd Hussars and 8 RB relieved 3rd Mons and 2nd Fife and Forfarshire and advanced east from Putanges to Courteilles taking many prisoners. At Cui Noel Bell found a large hospital in a chateau full of German wounded, with an over-large medical staff. There were a hundred seriously wounded Germans and a hundred staff, including saucy German nurses practising their charms on the walking wounded! It was a black and rain-swept night and the whole area was infested with Germans. The 23rd Hussars at Cui lost a tank but destroyed two rude SPs. Throughout the night the air was filled with planes, flares, long rumblings and vivid flashes of explosions. Ahead lay the Falaise–Argentan road, the neck of the pocket being battered by Polish, Canadian, American and British forces. It was hell to hear at night, even worse to see the carnage on the ground.

The 4 KSLI were dug in at Le Bois-Serans, west of Ecouché, 3rd Mons near Commeaux and 3 RTR at Sentilly. The whole division now occupied a large triangle just west of Argentan between the Argentan–Falaise, Argentan–Ecouché roads. Contact was made with 5th US Corps and until Argentan was finally cleared advance eastwards was difficult.

The next day, the 20th, was notable for a bag of nearly 1,000 prisoners. 8 RB and 23rd Hussars crossed the Argentan–Falaise highway at Occagnes, 3 miles north of the battered town, and ventured into the large woods of Forêt de Gouffern. There many abandoned AFVS were found and minefields, which the sappers duly cleared. Booby-trapped trees were pulled across the minor roads. The 23rd Hussars' historian wrote: 'Personal belongings of dead Germans who had fled were everywhere, an indescribable jumble of clothes, mess tins, helmets, etc. But worst of all was the stench, the acrid smell of a burning Sherman, nauseating stench of decomposing bodies and a smell peculiar to German troops.'

12 Platoon 8 RB captured General Kurt Badinsky commanding 276 Infantry Division and his entire staff on the 20th. The old general, according to Noel Bell: 'had no idea what was happening around him, had no division to command and was anxious to surrender to an officer. That night 8 RB fetched up on the edge of the famous Falaise pocket at Bailleul, on the east side of the Forêt de Gouffern.

2nd Fife and Forfarshire followed the same axis, as Steel Brownlie reported: 'It pelted with rain, we went through Occagnes to the Forêt de Gouffern, took hundreds of prisoners as well as a Volkswagen and Panther in running order and ended up near Ballieul (Argentan–Vimoutiers) watching fires and explosions for miles around – the closing of the Falaise gap. But a miserable night in pouring rain.' By 1800 hrs 4 KSLI were moving through Argentan, described by Ned Thornburn: 'The day was dull and wettish and the town looked awful – totally desolate.' The battalion then drove in TCVs to Le Bourg-St-Léonard, 6 miles east of Argentan. The Ayrshire Yeomanry met American troops who had been on the right flank from Caumont to Vire and a number of friendships were revived. 23rd Hussars had a brisk action on the edges of the Forêt de Gouffern, losing a tank but destroying two Panthers and finding many abandoned German tanks and SP guns. 3rd Mons and 2nd Fife and Forfarshire captured an entire German field hospital and released nearly 200 British and American wounded prisoners. The colonels of 23rd Hussars and 8 RB acquired respectively a Horch and a Lincoln Zephyr, magnificent staff cars, courtesy of General Badinsky.

The divisional objective was now to be L'Aigle, 35 miles to the east. Only two routes were possible from Le Bourg-St-Léonard at the south-east corner of the Forêt de Gouffern. 159 Brigade group were given the northern centre-line to Gacé via Avenelles and Omméel. 29 Brigade group had a more direct centre-line to the south of Exmes and Croisilles, south-east of Gacé. So on the 21st, the Inns of Court sent their scout cars ahead, followed by 3 RTR linked with 4 KSLI and the Herefords. 4 KSLI were held up by a blown bridge at Villebadin and the REs quickly put a scissors bridge across. They pushed on to take Omméel and St Pierre-la-Rivière and captured fifty-three prisoners, as Ned Thornburn pointed out 'from nine different divisions'. The Herefords took over for a bit but 4 KSLI reached the high ground west of Gacé at 1500 hrs, when they were greeted with well-directed shellfire. 15/19th Hussars were held up just to the east of Gacé and 2nd Fife and Forfarshire to the south. The divisional artillery now fired heavy stonks and a decisive bold move took place. Major Bill

Close, 3 RTR A squadron CO, sent a troop helterskelter down the main road through the town. One tank got through although hit by HE shells, and some time later the rest of the squadron joined Lieutenant Langdon's solitary tank high up on the north of the town. 4 KSLI professionally followed up and captured the railway station and the main town, taking over 100 prisoners in the process. Well might General Roberts send his personal congratulations.

The 20th Panzer Division plus Luftwaffe troops had defended tenaciously. Indeed Le Bourg-St Léonard had been taken and retaken four times in a few days. South of Gacé 2nd Fife and Forfarshire lost several tanks and took casualties near Coulmer and the bridge over the River Touques. So 8 RB and 23rd Hussars were diverted south from Croisilles, 4 miles south-east of Gacé, to take the villages of St André d'Echauffour and Les Authieux-du-Puits.

For a change the 22nd was a lovely day. With L'Aigle as the major objective 159 Brigade group pushed a few miles due east to La Trinité des Laitiers on the northern verges of the large Forêt de St Evroult, where the Herefords and 15/19th Hussars found few enemy. 4 KSLI came through without incident and moved south to Ste Gauburge on the main Argentan–L'Aigle road and dug in for the night. Meanwhile 3rd Mons and 2nd Fife and Forfarshire had cleared Echauffour. As usual most of the minor roads were mined and booby-trapped and the sappers were kept busy, particularly in the clearance of St André d'Echauffour. Scissors bridges were needed at Ste Gauburge, which was cleared by 23rd Hussars, although they were joined there by American troops and the FFI Resistance movement. South of the blown bridge at Ste Gauburge a very boggy ford over the River Rile was found and General 'Pip' arrived to spur the 23rd Hussars across. About four tanks including the Colonel's got ditched or bogged down on the approaches to the ford. A great deal of sweat and blasphemy followed. Very embarrassing! Moreover the sappers were trying to deal with the main blown bridge so the 'potato-pickers' of C squadron had to dispose of the many rows of mines now encountered. Once gingerly exposed, a rope lassoo was apprehensively attached to them and the usual procedure was to tow them away. When the REs arrived in time to take over the removal of the last row, it was noted with interest that the Hussar technique was correct but that the REs used a much longer rope!

Ste Gauburge was bypassed to the north and the 23rd Hussars bustled east, again on the main road, and by early evening were actually inside l'Aigle. There they were greeted by cheering, waving crowds throwing flowers and offering cups of cider. At 2000 hrs 3rd Mons arrived and took control of the east and south-east sectors of town. 8 RB arrived too, getting an enthusiastic welcome.

Steel Brownlie and 2nd Fife and Forfarshire in reserve 'motored' to Aube-sur-Rile, 3 miles south-east of L'Aigle and 'rest for at least three days. Baths in civvy houses, mess truck, sleep and more sleep. Glorious!'

Tim Ellis, 4 KSLI, wrote: 'Everyone woke up feeling soaked and tired. The news is damned good – a bridgehead over the Seine, 25,000 prisoners so far from the Falaise pocket. We moved out of Gacé with all our looted trailers from a German Q store with enough kit in it to stock an Army Group. They even had bunches of "cat o'nine tails" hanging up with the boots!'

On the 23rd the whole division was concentrated south and south-west of L'Aigle, and 3rd Mons were delighted to hand over the town to troops from 50 Division. 8 RB and 3rd Mons moved to Rai-Aube, where they spent the next few days, 23rd Hussars found some pleasant fields by the River Rile for their 'holiday', with ENSA parties and excellent bathing.

The Inns of Court moved on recce in front of the division from Briouze through Argentan, La Ferne Fresnel, L'Aigle and Rugles to Conches [wrote Peter Reeve]. Those who led this advance will remember all these towns with a mixture of joy and sorrow. Lieutenant Richards and Trooper Climie were killed near Courmeil, Troopers Brown and Price were killed near Tilly and Sergeant Clarke and Lance-Corporal Roberts wounded in the same incident. Corps HQ tribute was that no formation had ever had armoured car cover such as had been provided by the Inns of Court during those days.

One German gunner wrote home during the 'closing of the gap': 'We have no vehicles or guns left, and whoever is still alive will have to fight as infantrymen. But I won't stay with them very long. I really don't know what we are still fighting for. Very soon I shall run over to the Tommies if I am not killed before I get there.'

The pocket had been closed. The division had been in action continuously for twelve days, taking nearly 3,000 prisoners. They had 868 officers and men killed and another 3,000 casualties on the way from 'Epsom' to L'Aigle.

Aube-sur-Rile was the centre of the divisional concentration. Cafés and restaurants did a roaring trade and sentimental attachments were frequent. ENSA, cinema shows, dances, swimming and concerts given by regimental bands, enlivened this rest period. Reinforcements arrived, tanks were repaired and maintained, guns cleaned and General Roberts visited every regiment. Trooper Bob Walmsley, 23rd Hussars, had acute toothache and jeeped back to see the Corps dentist, whose operating drill worked from a foot treadle. This Heath Robinson machine broke the victim's crown and hit a nerve, so he flinched. 'Get back you big baby,' crowed the RAMC dentist. Which Bob, all of 6 foot 4 inches, did – rather reluctantly!

Ned Thornburn, 4 KSLI, said: 'It felt like the school holidays again!' 3 RTR harboured in a series of orchards west of L'Aigle and bivouacs were made between Sherman and hedgerow. Bill Close commented that a divisional dance held in the town was not much of a success. The local young ladies attended with their swains or their mothers or both!

CHAPTER THIRTEEN

The Great Swan

The result of the closing of the 'pocket' meant that 40,000 Germans had been made prisoner and a further 10,000 were dead. Nearly 350 tanks and SPs had been destroyed, 250 guns and about 2,500 lorries. The five SS Panzer divisions (1, 2, 9, 10 and 12) had been devastated. Their survivors numbered about three thousand men and forty-five tanks. In addition 2,21 and 116 Panzer Divisions had only six weakened infantry battalions and twenty tanks left between them. But about twenty thousand Germans, twenty-four tanks and sixty guns were eventually ferried east across the Seine, some 80 miles from L'Aigle.

When General Horrocks took over 30 Corps on 26 August, 43rd Division had skilfully forced a crossing of the Seine at Vernon, so at 0600 hrs on 28 August a rejuvenated 11th Armoured set off on a long journey, later described as the 'Great Swan'.

Mixed brigades were not needed so 29th Armoured led, followed by 2nd Household Cavalry, Divisional HQ and 159 Infantry Brigade. 8th Armoured Brigade were under command, operating on the right flank. An important role was given to the motor companies of 8 RB, who travelled with the armour from L'Aigle, Chambray and Evreux towards the Seine. 3 RTR led, followed by 2nd Fife and Forfarshire and 23rd Hussars.

Steel Brownlie remembers how he: 'motored in blinding dust, crossed the Seine at Vernon over a class 9 pontoon bridge [Goliath] in total darkness – a strange experience. Jimmy Samson and I conferred about where the hell to go next, passed two burning scout cars, then a burning Tiger, eventually found the regimental harbour. Orders [were] move north first light, all speed.' 3 RTR spent that night near Tilly, in the vicinity of blazing farms and haystacks. On the second day they set off at first light, 'swanned' an unheard-of 60 miles, charging through Etrépagny at 1330 hrs and Mainneville, where they met anti-tank, SP and infantry resistance.

On the left 2nd Fife and Forfarshire met strong resistance at Doudeauville, although Steel Brownlie was more fortunate: 'It was a wonderful sight, all the tanks deployed and belting over open country, Tournay, Guitry, Hacqueville and Longchamps.' Noel Bell, 8 RB, reported clearing several small villages, Etrépagny being reached without much difficulty. The civilian welcome was enthusiastic but the Germans came back: 'and all rejoicing had to subside at once.' The tanks had a small battle near Mainneville and 8 RB reached the outskirts of Amécourt and settled there for the night. Roland

Jefferson recorded the RB route as Guiviers, Guitry, Mouflaines and Valmesnile. 'After a skirmish at Etrépagny we took a lot more prisoners and pressed on to Longchamps, where the village priest stopped us. He was brandishing a pistol and beckoned us towards the church. There were about thirty more German soldiers there who had given up the fight and we made them all sit around in the graveyard of the church.'

Ned Thornburn with the 4 KSLI, following up with 159 Brigade, commented: 'The leading tanks were frequently checked by demolitions and by small pockets of infantry backed by anti-tank and SP guns, and 4 KSLI, after a frustrating day on 29 August, harboured near Cantiers with "only" 12 miles covered, mostly in their TCVs.' 8th Armoured Brigade on the far right had met more resistance, particularly at Bray and the River Epte crossing, but reached the line of Vesley-Dangu, south-west of Gisors, by the first night and by the second night were closing in on Beauvais. General Horrocks wrote: 'We had only advanced 21 miles on the 29th, which wasn't good enough if we were going to bounce the crossings over the Somme.'

Sergeant John Hooper, RASC, said:

Despite the very heavy traffic on the roads in the area 171 Company advanced 60 miles that day to rest briefly in the hours of darkness at Pacy-sur-Eure, 40 miles from Paris. Alas the fleshpots of Gay Paree were not for us. RASC lorries carrying precious petrol, food and ammo lurched across the swaying pontoon bridge over the Seine and made a supply Polpoint at Corbie.

On the third day of the Swan – 30 August – the well-tried partnership of 3 RTR and 8 RB had to deal with stiff resistance in Amécourt where the River Epte bridge was blown, taking 150 prisoners. House to house fighting took place. Noel Bell's command half track was knocked out by a 20-mm gun, so 13 RHA shelled the village, which was bypassed and left for 159 Brigade to clear up. 3 RTR and 4 KSLI moved on to Talmontiers, a couple of miles up the road towards Gournay, then 8 RB doubled back, crossed the river at Sérifontaine and went cross country to Neufmarché with over fifty prisoners on the bonnets of their half tracks. 23rd Hussars and H Company 8 RB took the lead and rushed north-east along the modern D930 round Gournay, through Marseille-en-Beauvais and east to Crèvecoeur-le-Grand. Here 3 RTR captured guns, half tracks and 150 prisoners, and the liberators had a splendid welcome. Noel Bell remembers the town's gendarmes giving away numerous cases of brandy, and saw many collaborators being summarily dealt with. As darkness fell 8 RB and 3 RTR entered Croissy-sur-Selle, 18 miles south of Amiens. 8 RB, as Roland Jefferson related, 'had drinks of all sorts pressed on to us. The French called us all Tommy and we realized that we were now into the battle zone of the First War which our fathers had known so well. A common joke was: "Come away from her, she's probably your sister."'

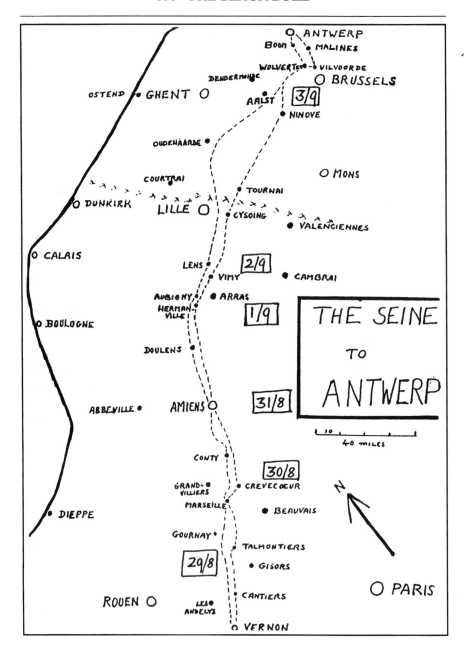

Earlier that day a right-flanking drive by 23rd Hussars started at Sancourt, went east to Sérifontaine, north to Cuigy-en-Bray and St Aubin-en-Bray and with nominal resistance crossed the main Gournay-Beauvais road, bypassed little Armentières, of the famous song, and reached Villembray by midday. By mid-afternoon 22 miles had been covered and both centre-lines converged at Marseille-en-Beauvais, that is 3 RTR/8 RB and 23rd Hussars/4 KSLI. 2nd Fife and Forfarshire were on the left flank starting from Longchamps, then to Neuf-Marché, St Germer-de-Fly, north to Villers-sur-Auchy, Songeons and Morvillers, and east to Prévillers and Hétomesnil. By now drenching rain had set in.

Near Gournay Ned Thornburn recalls:

Out of the blue our General's car drew up and 'Pip' Roberts got out to stretch his legs and see his troops at first hand. 'How would you like to be in Amiens?' 'That would be fine,' I said, 'but surely the Germans will defend the Somme?' 'They may, but they'll get an awful shock when we arrive there in the morning.' And that was my first intimation of the night drive to Amiens.

The next dramatic move is recounted by the General: 'It was quite simple: Ike said to Monty "Amiens tonight"; Monty said to Bimbo [Dempsey] "Amiens tonight"; Bimbo said to Jorrocks [Horrocks] "Amiens tonight" and Jorrocks said to 'Pip' Roberts "Amiens tonight"; and then the planning started.' Horrocks had used tanks at night on three occasions before and the bold plan to seize the Somme bridges in Amiens was typically daring.

Two key concerns were the availability of petrol and the fact that the taking of a large town like Amiens needed infantry easily available. The grouping of brigades now had to be altered, since armour alone might just be able to take a town, but not hold it. The General's plan was for two centre-lines. 29th Armoured Brigade (3 RTR, 8 RB, 13 RHA, 23rd Hussars, 4 KSLI) would follow the main road from Crèvecoeur to Amiens. 159 Brigade (2nd Fife and Forfarshire, 3rd Mons, Ayrshire Yeomanry, 15/19th Hussars, 1st Herefords) would take winding country roads through Conty and Taisnil to Amiens.

General Horrocks paid tribute to his two reconnaissance regiments – the Inns of Court and 2 Household Cavalry regiments:

The advance was a squadron affair, advancing by a separate route on a comparatively wide front. Suddenly hostile fire would open from a wood, an isolated farm, or from some hastily constructed trenches covering perhaps a crossroads. The leading troops would deploy and return this fire. Sometimes the Germans would surrender. If not the remaining troops, benefiting from the local knowledge of the Maquis, would outflank the opposition using by-roads or tracks, while one of the troops would turn back and engage the enemy post from the rear; the remainder of the squadron would continue the advance.

According to Trooper Ernie Hamilton, 15/19th Hussars: 'We really motored on after the Seine. We hoped the RAF Typhoons with rockets slung on each wing recognized the large white "Star of Liberation" painted on the tanks as belonging to "friendlies".' Roden Orde, 2 Household Cavalry Regiment, wrote:

> A night march through enemy territory is at the best of times a tense affair. The drivers peer out of visors intent on avoiding falling asleep or landing in the ditch. The armoured car commanders also stare ahead trying to penetrate the gloom for signs of the enemy and checkups on the right route. The operators live in a strange world of their own at the bottom of the turret tormented by crackles and demoniac wireless noises while map boards and chinagraph pencils drop on their heads. Gunners grip the trigger mechanism as much for support as anything else for they are almost blind at night. Over everyone the desire for sleep descends in recurrent and overpowering waves.

Normally armoured cars bear a role out of all proportion to their size, as they are the eyes and ears of the Corps Commanders. Advancing usually on a wide front, they constantly report back by wireless to their LO at TAC Corps HQ.

Much credit is due to the Resistance movement. They provided advice about German troops ahead, although it was a sensible rule of thumb to divide their figures by three! They also provided guides, guarded prisoners and bridges and, above all, offered a marvellous reception which was very good for morale. '*Vive les libérateurs. Vive les Anglais!*' Anyone who took part in the liberation from Normandy to Antwerp on the Great Swan will always remember the startling, intoxicating welcome.

The two artillery regiments, 13 RHA and Ayrshire Yeomanry, deployed into action several times a day. But by contrast with Normandy, the necessary fire support were usually quick troop or occasional battery targets, and then it was 'up sticks and on'.

The phrase 'it's moonlight tonight' had a fine ring to it. The General's memoirs state: 'I ordered that the advance [to Amiens] would continue at once and we would continue until last light when we would replenish and start again when the moon was well up, which would be about 2300 hrs. At that moment it was a lovely fine warm evening and the moon was nearing its fullness.' At last light the two brigade columns were almost level. 29th Brigade on the right about Catheux, 159 Brigade around La Houssaye on the left, both about 20 miles south of Amiens. The RASC petrol lorries had NOT caught up but there was reckoned to be just enough for the next vital stretch. At 2300 hrs the famous night march began in pitch darkness and pouring rain. Fighting sleep was the single biggest problem. Noel Bell got his RB sergeant major to ride up and down the column in a scout car to make sure drivers did not fall asleep. German vehicles joined the convoy and were usually dealt with, but some travelled in convoy tail-to-tail for several miles before detection and destruction. A German petrol lorry and several half tracks were dispatched. Major Bill Close, 3 RTR squadron, led the night march with orders that 'nothing was to stop us and to brush aside anything in the way'. Shermans followed blindly the dull red exhaust of the tank in front – the blind leading the blind. Everyone was soaking wet and bad tempered. When a German staff car met the 3 RTR column head on, the occupants were equally bad tempered until a Sherman Browning ended the conversation. At dawn – 0400 hrs – 3 RTR on the right centre-line were 3 miles south, and 2nd Fife and Forfarshire on the left, about 5 miles short of Amiens. The General ordered the well-tried partnership of 3 RTR/8 RB to seize the main bridge over the River Somme in the centre of Amiens, 23rd Hussars/4 KSLI were ordered to occupy the high ground south of the city astride the main road, and 2nd Fife and Forfarshire and 3rd Mons on the left, the main feature west of the River Celle.

Noel Bell tells the story:

Reports came in from civilians that there were approximately 5,000 Germans still in Amiens, and at that early hour and having had no sleep this information shook us a bit. It was now getting light and we could see enemy columns and single vehicles streaming into the city along the roads parallel to our own. After some discussion, negotiation and argument as to who should go first the leading section [of RB] carriers and the leading troop of tanks [3 RTR] advanced *abreast!*

A series of individual platoon battles then took place with Lieutenant Donald Sudlow and Co. destroying lorries, staff cars and sections of infantry with three Bren guns. The action was known as 'Sudlow's Shooting Gallery' 'with fifty POW and the same number killed or wounded. A bridge was blown in front of 11 Platoon's eyes but the main bridge was saved. Breakfast tasted wonderful that morning and despite our weariness we felt on top of the world'. Noel Bell's G Company totalled seventy riflemen, but Bill Close's 3 RTR squadron was at half strength with ten Shermans. Resistance men showed the way through the sleeping city. Fortunately later 2nd Fife and Forfarshire seized two bridges across the Somme.

As Steel Brownlie recounts:

Civilians were out in force and one hit me in the face with a bunch of flowers when I was doing 35 mph. *Merci bien!* I found the bridge at last undefended though a few small shells came down. [Later] we harboured in green fields near Coisy [4 miles north]. I was orderly officer which meant sitting all night beside the wireless tank with earphones round the neck. But there was a large rum ration which I supplemented. I was happy, still alive, doing my job, and winning. Lucky.

Noel Bell noticed signs of hardship and privations suffered by the townspeople, and much looting of food stores and dumps followed liberation. In the centre of Amiens early in the morning Trooper Bob

Walmesly, 23rd Hussars, filled up his Sherman from 50-litre cans at a civilian petrol station. A pretty young woman ceremoniously presented him and his crew with a ¼-pound of Lyons Tea, kept for five years to present to the eventual liberators.

After lunch 8 RB crossed the Seine and found a dump of brand new guns in a cemetery. 3 RTR occupied a German artillery HQ with a field kitchen where an excellent meal had just been cooked. Corporal Byrne of 2nd Fife and Forfarshire Recce Troop captured General Eberback, commander of the disintegrated German 7th Army. He was having breakfast at the time, and was unceremoniously dumped on the back of Byrne's Sherman and trundled off into captivity. His pockets revealed photographs of a comely young girl, whom the General swore was his wife!

South-west of the main town at 0600 hrs 4 KSLI suddenly encountered a Mark IV tank which knocked out four TCVs in quick succession. B Company broke all records for speed of de-bussing, so had only two men wounded. Ned Thornburn visited the 700-year-old cathedral, undamaged by air raids, and reflected on war and peace, battlefields and the house of God.

Early that morning B squadron 23rd Hussars went into Dury, south of Amiens, and did violent execution among a crowd of startled Germans. Major Blacker of A squadron, with unerring instinct, procured a large and powerful Horch staff car containing maps showing German dispositions over most of Europe. They were fascinating but obsolete. C squadron and H Company 8 RB entered Amiens by the Rue St Fuscien, Place du Maréchal Joffre, and were guided by excited FFI right into the tree-lined Boulevard d'Alsace-Lorraine where they made for the main bridge. A quick neat combined operation of tanks, riflemen and the Maquis led to a firm bridgehead being established by 1040 hrs despite interference by two Panther tanks. However, 23rd Hussars had not finished for the day. B squadron pushed over the captured main road towards the north-east and by mistake took a smaller minor road due east which brought them out into open country. To their astonishment they had come out *behind* a substantial AA Flak site. Joined by RHQ and a troop of C squadron they had a marvellous 'turkey' shoot, with Captain Blackman's troop causing mayhem in a matter of minutes: a hundred German casualties including a full colonel and four heavy AA and six light AA guns destroyed. Sergeant Roberts of A squadron knocked out a King Tiger tank and the squadron destroyed fifteen light AA guns. A very happy regiment harboured that night at Cardonnette (D919 north-east of Amiens).

The Ayrshire Yeomanry were not so happy. A survey party was ambushed near Vers-sur-Selle and during the day suffered eight casualties, including three officers.

The Corps Commander arrived at General Pip's HQ at 0800 hrs: 'I am glad to say he was quite astonished to find everything completely under control.' At 1800 hrs 151 Brigade from 50 Division came under command

and by 2300 hrs had taken over the city. At the same time the Guards Armoured on the right had reached Beauvais. In General Horrocks's memoirs he wrote of the capture of Amiens: 'This was a remarkable performance which could have been achieved only by a very highly trained division – but Pip Roberts was probably the most experienced British armoured commander and certainly one of the best.'

Geoffrey Dowman, 171 Company RASC, made the Amiens to beachhead run: '[to collect petrol and ammo] to keep the tanks moving. The trouble was the Division were leaving more enemy behind than what they were facing'. RASC drivers were farmed out to units 'for various jobs, i.e. bridging equipment (most unpleasant), collecting prisoners (some the Maquis used to shoot), shells and petrol galore'.

The cavalry 'gallop' continued. After sleep, replenishment of petrol, rations and mail, the objective for 1 September was to be Aubigny, 10 miles north-west of Arras, some 33 miles north-east of Amiens. The Guards were directed on Arras. Three centre-lines were available to Doullens due north, Thièvres due north-north-east, and Varennes due north-east. Steel Brownlie recalls:

Off we went again, via Villers-Bocage (where there were 88s but the crews surrendered), then Talmas, Beauquesne, Halloy, Grande-Rullecourt, Savy and Estrée. It was a hectic dash mostly cross country, map reading not easy. Voller and I competed (as so often) as to who could go faster. We brewed up a German convoy coming from our left. We began to run out of petrol. Corporal Vallance fell out. I just got to a firing position on high ground near Estrée when the engine conked. [As Echelon arrived to fill up] a squadron of Spitfires attacked the Fifes and brewed up one petrol truck and destroyed our barbers' tools. The order to 'get your hair cut' was now meaningless.

8 RB had a peaceful day. Noel Bell noticed the 'great number of flying bomb sites abandoned'. The many Londoners realized that the liberation was now 'close to home'. The Maquis in northern France 'were in great form and had performed many brave deeds'. They took over prisoner guard duty and in return 8 RB helped in as many local battles as possible. 8 RB harboured at Gouy and Servins, north of Arras.

23rd Hussars' route to Thièvres took them over the River Authie, where the French were beside themselves with joy. They screamed and waved, rushing forward with bottles of wine and fruit. It was an intoxicating occasion but there were hazards of course. Admiring *jeunes filles* threw loving missiles which rendered commanders and drivers *hors de combat*. Steel helmets were vital during *la libération*. Also the Maquis would rush out of side streets firing their antique musketry into the air quite indiscriminately. The 23rd Hussars' historian commented: 'They would advance in the most friendly manner to shake hands, while in the left hand a full loaded rifle pointed straight at one's stomach. In their enthusiasm they were far the most dangerous individuals we met.'

The 1-in. maps issued by Division were now useless and Brigade couriers produced ¼-in. maps and little pieces of paper with route continuations! Luckily the road signs were good and there was little opposition in front. Signs to Dunquerque, Arras, Vimy and Lens raised painful, nostalgic feelings. By 1600 hrs 50 miles had been covered and the Hussars were on objective 10 miles north-west of Arras. The general told the brigadiers who told the colonels, that Brussels was the divisional target for the following day, which proved to be inaccurate!

Sergeant John Hooper's 171 Company RASC operated a long-distance shuttle service from the Normandy beachhead with petrol, Derv, and some food to catch up with the Division – just – and return with some of the thousands of prisoners of war. He described: 'Many of the POW looked in poor shape – hungry, tired, dirty and dispirited, especially those conscripted from the occupied countries, but in sharp contrast to those from SS formations who were smartly dressed, disciplined and arrogant.' Many officers including Generals were shunted rapidly towards the Channel ports.

The Ayrshire Yeomanry's FOO, Captain Spence, took his OP Sherman into action in a wood and emerged with eighty-eight prisoners, and 13 RHA harboured astride the Arras–St Pol road near Aubigny, having had a peaceful 35-mile 'Swan'. The Inns of Court had scampered briskly through Pentencourt, Acheux and Arquèves, shooting up enemy infantry and transport. They then moved ahead to Lieven, reported clear, and Houdain, where they met minor resistance. 15/19th Hussars put a squadron into Doullens, where they met up with 8th Armoured Brigade from the right flank.

It was surprising that when vehicles ran out of petrol it was generally just outside a *bistro* or *estaminet*, where the friendly natives proffered military advice and liquid refreshment.

The fifth day of the Great Swan, 2 September, was unusual. The Airborne divisions back in the UK, having recovered from their epic landings on D-Day, were champing at the bit for fresh action. So the High Command decided on a large-scale airdrop in the vicinity of Tournai, east of Lille, beyond the River Escaut. Since Horrocks's two armoured divisions were both going like bats out of hell with nominal opposition, this proposed landing was pointless. The Division's objectives were therefore limited to the area of Lens, north of Arras, 14 miles north-east. By mid-afternoon 29 Brigade was concentrated north-east of Lens. 4 KSLI set off in high spirits and by 1100 hrs had covered 10 miles. Almost by mistake Ned Thornburn captured and cleared the ill-omened Vimy Ridge, marked on the map as 'MEM'orial: 'It was a strange feeling advancing unopposed over so many thousands of graves. The wood opened out into a wide glade opposite the Canadian War Memorial.' Suddenly a jeep-load of Canadian war correspondents appeared and wired the news back to Montreal.

For the Inns of Court, Peter Reeve wrote:

Each day was a mad rush from harbour to start line; each day the fierce competition to keep ahead of the tanks. 'Our heavy friends are at X – what is your position now?' Bets were laid whether the petrol lorry or water cart would ever be seen again; the Sergeant-Major's 'party' last heard of 30 miles back heavily engaged by well-concealed A/Tk guns; a startled 2 i/c C squadron [Peter Reeve] missing a target by a mile at 200 yards (only fired in the air of course – just to frighten the buggers); another Paymaster in the bag, and at Lille eggs, tomatoes, cheers and kisses, champagne and flowers.

Brigadier Churcher, 159 Brigade commander, announced to Division: 'he was holding Vimy Ridge, a place well known to him, and was this as it should be?' It was! 8 RB's route lay through the factory towns near Lens to Pont-à-Vendin. The reception from the obviously poverty-stricken districts was moving, but the riflemen were in peril of flying tomatoes and splintering glass from beer bottles. 8 RB were ordered to hold the two bridges across the canal between Bauvin and Anneullin. At midnight a mortar bombardment began with a strong German attack on the bridge held by 12 Platoon. Casualties were taken and three carriers lost, but by dawn a troop of 3 RTR arrived and the attack was beaten off. 2nd Fife and Forfarshire started early in pouring rain with orders for maximum speed. Steel Brownlie's troop led as his squadron commander 'had more confidence in my map-reading than I had. Vimy, Acheville, Billy-Montigny, Courrières, Oignies. In Billy-Montigny the tank crews were drinking from bottles and smoking cigars. Colonel Alec, his voice rather thick, came upon the air and said that nobody should partake too freely.' Steel Brownlie made a speech to a FFI guard of honour in his best Greenock Academy French, explaining that the liberation was effected not by '*les Anglais*' but by '*les Ecossais*'. His troop took up defensive positions in Oignies where the Scotsmen were fed steak and chips and allowed hot baths in private homes. They guarded the bridges in torrents of rain.

Sergeant John Hooper, with 171 Company RASC, stopped for a drink with gendarmes in Arras and met a lady with a broad Lancastrian accent who had lived in Lens for twenty-five years and produced cups of tea in her best Crown Derby teacups. But outside Lens an 88-mm gun picked off several RASC trucks before rescue arrived.

Ginger Wilson was a young lieutenant in the RAMC. Small medical units of about twenty men including the MO, a padre, plus the RAMC crews of four vehicles, formed 7 FDs. They followed behind the two main divisional attack brigades mopping up casualties – British, German, and frequently civilian. A quiet Sunday afternoon on the Great Swan found them near Lens, based on a farmstead:

Suddenly a very excitable French farmer, who might have come out of the cast of 'Clochmerle' burst into our midst gesticulating like a windmill and shouting: '*Les Boches, ils se sont cachés en les meules* [ricks].' In my atrocious French I did my best to explain that we were 'Croix Rouge' and therefore non-combatant, but this had little effect. General mobilization was taking place among those of the Section in possession of arms. The farmer's rather pretty daughter may have had some influence!

In pouring rain the young 'Dad's Army' set off across the fields and with bayonets discovered eight Boche hiding in the haystacks, who seemed relieved to be taken prisoner. A cynical name for the RAMC is 'rob all my comrades'. On this occasion the enemy were relieved of a pair of jackboots, a camera, a compass and a pair of scissors. The parson still has the compass but he 'lost' the jackboots and camera!

3 RTR were in overnight laager 7 miles from Seclin. Earlier Bill Close's tank crews had a bathe in a large water tank and had their backs scrubbed by three jolly Polish girls. As Roland Jefferson remarked: 'We were constantly reminded of the sacrifice of 1914–18 when we passed numerous huge war cemeteries. They all looked so neat and tidy even though they had been under German occupation for over four years. There was an air of stillness and reverence as we passed them.' The 23rd Hussars travelled past the ugly black slagheaps and went through Lens at 1000 hrs:

This black and dreary town was packed and jammed with cheering, shouting, waving people. They hurled fruit and biscuits wildly at us, they dashed forward with cups of coffee, bottles of wine and beer, they scrawled their names on the sides of tanks. Crowds of girls flung their arms around the necks of carrier crews, the most convenient target. People scrambled on to the tanks, feeding the crews with fruit, cakes, making them drink out of bottles – the people were in a kind of delirium.

The 23rd Hussars laagered at Carvin and like the rest of the division were told that the new objective was Antwerp, not Brussels, and that predictably the airborne drop had been cancelled. On a map it was clear that the fleshpots of Brussels were a logical target for Guards Armoured on the right flank, who had taken Arras the night before. Still it was considered at the time 'a bitter disappointment. Antwerp, a greater prize strategically, was with its ring of forts likely to be more strongly defended'. 7th Armoured were given Ghent as their objective.

General 'Pip' asked the Corps Commander: 'what my main task was at Antwerp, and he told me to go for the docks and prevent their destruction'. The Germans in the Channel ports would be looked after by the Canadians, Poles and 12 Corps on the immediate left flank. So, early in the morning of 3 September, 23rd Hussars with H Company 8 RB led with 4 KSLI behind on the right centre line, and on the left were the ubiquitous 8 RB including

Noel Bell's G Company with John Dunlop's squadron of 3 RTR. F Company with 2nd Fife and Forfarshire were to sweep up behind.

Opposition was met at Seclin, but the Maquis helped with the clearance. A squadron 3 RTR had a rude shock when 88s destroyed two recce Honey tanks. Colonel Silvertop was cross and all three squadrons of 3 RTR joined in to shoot hell out of the sheltering wood. The result was one battery of horse-drawn 88 mms demolished and four more 88s knocked out in the wood, plus a large Wehrmacht treasure house of wine and spirits. Bill Close told how 'the advance continued with crates of brandy or champagne stowed behind their turrets'. Skirting south of Lille, the advance parties reached the border town of Willems. Noel Bell remembered their last location back in UK, Willems Barracks, Aldershot.

By midday Seclin was cleared and Steel Brownlie and F Company 8 RB secured the town against counter-attack by eating lavish helpings of steak and chips, till 15/19th Hussars came up and took over. F Company had no maps. If 2nd Fife and Forfarshire went too fast, the RBs might get lost; too slow and they might not catch up with the regiment now ahead. The colour of the welcoming flags changed at Pecq, 'and we were in Belgium'. Lille was still enemy-held so 15/19th Hussars' task was to watch the southern approaches of the city until 50 Division turned up. The 2nd Fife and Forfarshire route was from Carvin north-east to Seclin, past the east side of Lille to Willems, north-east to Estaimbourg, east to Ronse (Renaix), east to Sottegem and north-east to Aalst. At Sottegem burning wreckage blocked the main road, so Steel Brownlie's whole column was quite lost. A bright Belgian guided him '*pour suivre vos amis*' through a maze of streets and lanes back to the centre-line and was rewarded with the last (looted) bottle of Calvados. At 3 a.m., having covered 87 miles, 2nd Fife and Forfarshire, avoiding flying plums, jet-propelled apples and rocket-projected pears, reached Aalst 20 miles north-west of Brussels. All the cafés were open and Corporal Vallance's Sherman had run out of petrol in the town square: 'He was getting on very well with the natives.'

Roland Jefferson noted that the flags that flew from every vantage point were now the red, yellow and black of Belgium. At Fretin his RB Company with 23rd Hussars encountered a full German infantry company. Bren gun fire over their heads had no effect but the Sherman 17-pounder lined up on them persuaded them otherwise. The officer in charge fired one shot from his pistol as token resistance, then they formed up and marched away in style to captivity. In Tournai astride the tramlines the RB brewed up and had a hot dinner of stewed steak direct from the tins with the aid of their petrol-fired 'tommy cookers'. The mood was jolly and Roland's carrier resembled a fruit and flower stall. They finally harboured at Brosseghen, 4 miles west of Brussels, where the German cooking fires were still burning. When 8 RB reached Renaix, to his great surprise and amusement, Noel Bell met their A1 Echelon who had taken the wrong turning further back and had raced on, acting as a 'soft' vanguard to the armoured columns. In

Audenarde a sharp counter-attack destroyed a tank and half track of the Divisional sappers – 'a feeling of over-confidence had crept in' after relatively little opposition. In Termonde H Company got lost as pyjama-clad men, women and children thronged and blocked the streets.

It was a fairly peaceful 88-mile run for the 23rd Hussars apart from some opposition in Ninove and then, after reaching Assche, there was a noisy fracas in Wolverthem where B squadron had a battle involving bazookas, hand grenades and sten fire with a German column. Some sixteen German vehicles, some carrying speedboats, were destroyed. The night was uncomfortable surrounded by disorganized but belligerent enemy.

3 RTR had a similar run through late in the day over the Escaut canal, over a wooden bridge at Warcoing, to Ronse/Renaix, where Bill Close, now an expert on 'liberation' reckoned: 'the population went mad with joy – much more so than anywhere in France', past the Duke of Marlborough's victory-site of Oudenarde, a bazooka party at Sotteghem and by 0300 hrs reached Aalst, 10 miles west of Brussels. Brigade HQ had heard of the liquor booty they had 'found' at Seclin, and demanded it should be handed over, possibly for wider distribution. 15/19th Hussars harboured west of Sotteghem for left flank protection while Inns of Court sent patrols into Ghent and Termonde.

For the Division it had been an exhilarating day as Ned Thornburn described: 'Crowds lined the streets in every town and village cheering, waving flags singing and dancing, pressing wine and flowers on every vehicle. It was like a Cup Final homecoming. It was a day of retribution however for 'les collaborateurs'', with women's heads shaved and certain houses deliberately burned.' The KSLI halted for the night 5 miles beyond Ninove, having advanced over 60 miles in the day.

By the time they reached Antwerp the Division had made a fighting advance of 230 miles in the six days since crossing the Seine at Vernon. The General wrote:

> I did not want to try getting into Antwerp in the dark – the possibility of absolute chaos was much too great – but we had to start on first light the next day. As a result of Inns of Court reports, 23rd Hussars on the right-hand route would enter Antwerp via Malines and 3 RTR on the left route would enter via Boom. 2nd Fife and Forfarshire were in reserve and 159 Bd with 15/19th Hussars were looking after the rear, and the Inns of Court guarded both flanks.

The divisional supply lines were now immensely long and infiltration and temporary blocking happened on several occasions.

Starting from Wolverton, 5 miles north of Brussels, 23rd Hussars headed at first light for Malines. They crossed the rivers Dyle and Nethe but then found canals blocking the way and bridges blown. C squadron destroyed the 'Last Train to Berlin', allegedly full of U-boat commanders and beautiful spies. So they doubled back, crossed a bridge at Vilvoorde, and went north towards Malines, where the main bridge was intact. Across the centre was an enormous bomb. As usual a resourceful sapper engineer cut the wires, a tram blocking the road was towed away and the town quickly secured. By early afternoon via Kontich the Hussars were in the outskirts of Antwerp, to be greeted by 88-mm guns which delayed them. This dug-in flak site was heavily shelled by 13 RHA.

2nd Fife and Forfarshire followed up and Steel Brownlie wrote: 'We passed Breendonk, said to be a concentration camp, and went through Boom.' Patrick Delaforce, with I battery 13 RHA, also went through Breendonk, 7 miles east of Malines. Rather desperate FFI begged him to have a look in the large sinister grey fortress on the right near the main crossroads. Alan Moorehead's account in *Eclipse* describes the scene encountered:

Fifty of the Belgian White Army [Resistance movement] were handed over to the Gestapo. They were taken to the camp at Breendonk and tortured. Ten days was the usual length of the torture. That is to say the special torture used to get members of the Resistance to give away the names of their comrades. It was very severe. When the Gestapo constructed the [concentration camp at Breendonk] they made special runnels in the cement floors for the blood.

The bodies, the blood and the smell of horrible death was still there on the morning of 4 September.

G Company 8 RB with Noel Bell and Major John Dunlop's squadron of 3 RTR raced along the broad highway east to Willebroeck from Termonde, then turned north to Boom, where the main bridge was blown. A Belgian former lieutenant of engineers named Robert Vekemans, had reconnoitred a largely hidden route. It was half a mile to the east along a cinder track and over an old toll bridge which crossed the River Rupel, prepared for blowing up at one point only, thence over the canal just beyond the river. Vekemans stopped the second 3 RTR Sherman commanded by Lieutenant Gibson Stubbs and asked to speak to the squadron commander. Dunlop at once realized the importance of a local right hook and passed on his recommendation to his CO. Colonel David Silvertop immediately agreed to this change in plan. Vekemans bravely cut the demolition charge firing leads. Dunlop sent two Shermans and a scout car across and 8 RB protected both ends of the vital bridge, Pont Van Enschodt. Better still, Dunlop's squadron raced through back streets to come up behind the Germans and prevent them from blowing the main bridge. Vekemans was later awarded the Military Cross.

13 RHA FOOs were with 3 RTR and 23rd Hussars as they battered or sneaked their way into Antwerp. Tony Bicket of H Battery with 3 RTR brought down a heavy concentration on the 88-mm guns in one of the five

forts covering the city's approaches. Lieutenant A.P.G. Bluett, GPO A Troop, was killed going forward to receive a sniper's surrender and Buck Taylor, Bt Capt of I battery was hit in both legs by an 88-mm shell and had bullet wounds in his back. He was evacuated and the ambulance in which he was travelling ran into the canal at Boom. Buck, despite all his wounds, swam to the bank and survived.

To replace the main bridges blown up at Boom, 13 Field Squadron RE cleared the charges at one site and built a fine 110-foot Bailey nearby, and 612 Field Squadron RE built a 120-foot Bailey, both completed on the night of 4–5 September. The two main roads into Antwerp were thus quickly made usable again.

CHAPTER FOURTEEN

The Taking of Antwerp

Day One

General von Zangen, who commanded the German 15th Army which was swept aside to the west by 11th Armoured's dash to Amiens and Antwerp wrote:

When we retired from the Somme about 1 September, I planned slowly to fight my way to Brussels and Antwerp and then take up a line in Holland. I had no fear that Antwerp would be taken since it was far behind the front line and there was a special staff organized to defend it. When I heard on 4 September that it had been captured it came as a stunning surprise. The reason for the fall of Antwerp was the failure of the High Command to appreciate how badly beaten 5th Panzer Army really was. Instead of an army on my left flank there was an empty gap. It was not yet realized how weak our forces had become. My own forces were neither strong enough nor fast enough to get back to Antwerp in time to defend it. We had no motorized equipment and we were constantly being attacked by armoured columns [i.e. 11th Armoured Division].

The defence of Antwerp district was in the hands of Major General Graf Stolberg-zu-Stolberg, who had 15,000 troops under command, widely scattered, modestly equipped and of poor quality. The hurriedly manned defences were road blocks at the important cross roads covered by mines, anti-tank and machine guns, bazookas and mortars. Although General Horrocks had ordered 11th Armoured to seize the Antwerp docks before the Germans could carry out any large-scale demolitions, he did not realize that the River Scheldt would be mined and thus render the port unusable. Nor did he realize that the Germans would be able to evacuate large numbers of troops trapped in the coastal areas across the mouth of the Scheldt from Breskens to Flushing. Subsequently General Schwabe, commanding the German 5th Army, was able to evacuate more than 65,000 men from eight battered divisions. They escaped to defend the Siegfried Line. Horrocks admitted afterwards that if 11th Armoured had been told to *bypass* Antwerp on the east, cross the Albert Canal and advance only 15 miles north-west to Woensdrecht, the Beveland isthmus

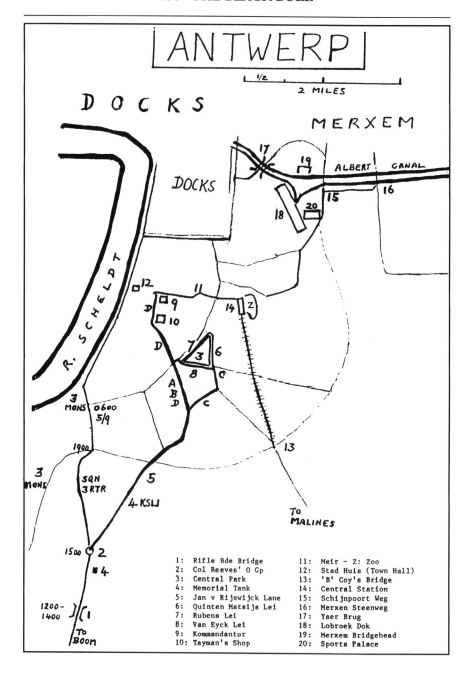

1: Rifle Bde Bridge
2: Col Reeves' O Gp
3: Central Park
4: Memorial Tank
5: Jan v Rijswijck Lane
6: Quinten Matsijs Lei
7: Rubens Lei
8: Van Eyck Lei
9: Kommandantur
10: Tayman's Shop
11: Meir – Z: Zoo
12: Stad Huis (Town Hall)
13: 'B' Coy's Bridge
14: Central Station
15: Schijnpoort Weg
16: Merxen Steenweg
17: Yser Brug
18: Lobroek Dok
19: Merxem Bridgehead
20: Sports Palace

would have been blocked and the German 5th Army trapped: 'My eyes were fixed entirely on the Rhine.' Nor did Eisenhower, Monty or Dempsey see this opportunity. All their eyes were turned towards the east and the occupation of the Ruhr. Antwerp is a large sprawling city with a population of 2½ million and if it had been defended professionally (like Caen) it would have been impossible for one armoured division to take. As it was the 159 Infantry Brigade was going to be under immense pressure quite shortly.

The Resistance leaders estimated that 5,000 enemy infantry were in the city with General von Stolberg's HQ in a network of bunkers in the Central Park. The General ordered 4 KSLI plus C squadron 2nd Fife and Forfarshire to take on the Central Park garrison at 1600 hrs, and 3rd Mons to move to and occupy the dock area. Maps were very poor and neither the General nor his two brigadiers realized that the vital Albert Canal did not go through the *centre* of the city but was in fact in the northern suburbs, separated from the suburb of Merxem. Horrocks admitted that the division simply did not have sufficient troops to clear the town, seize the docks, force *and* occupy a strong bridgehead over the canal. Nevertheless that is what the division now proceeded to try to do.

Under cover of the artillery smokescreen 3 RTR plus G Company 8 RB attacked and cleared the defences and by 1400 hrs had reached the dock area. It was a huge deep-sea complex of 1,000 acres with warehouses, cranes, bridges, 6 miles of wharves, quays, locks, electrically controlled sluice gates and railway rolling stock.

> As we arrived at the city itself [Noel Bell reported] shots rang out, Germans began throwing grenades on to us from a window of a high building near us, 20-mm guns opened up and we knew we should have to fight for it. The main streets were densely packed with crowds awaiting us. Our vehicles were unable to move and were smothered with people; we were overwhelmed by flowers, bottles and kisses. Everyone had gone mad. We had to get to the docks at all costs to save them from being destroyed by the Germans who might now be getting organized.

But the riflemen in their carriers were separated from the tanks by the immense crowds: 'We then came under fire from the far bank of the Scheldt at the same time as we were engaged in two different street battles on the near side. I began to wonder whether we should ever see the tanks again. It was difficult to describe over the wireless exactly where we were.' Eventually 3 RTR arrived, running a gauntlet of German bazooka fire. There were snipers everywhere, as Bill Close, 3 RTR, wrote: 'I found myself crouching in the turret looking for the source of the bullets pinging about, while pretty girls waved madly from blocks of flats pointing out the enemy positions.' John Dunlop's C squadron went for the docks with 8 RB and Bill Close took his squadron to Antwerp-South railway station. The White Brigade

Noel Bell's half track enters Antwerp

resistance fighters conducted their own private wars, often vendettas, settling old scores with the Germans or collaborators. The Shermans were pelted with fruit and flowers and every head exposed was offered a glass of cognac or champagne, plus cigars. John Dunlop led 3 RTR to the docks. He had stayed in Antwerp before and spoke French and enough Flemish to get by:

> We never closed the lids of our turrets, because we then became so blind and so deaf that we felt too vulnerable. We felt a lot safer with them open. But that afternoon I remember seriously considering closing down. Sporadic firing from above (from Germans at the upper windows of houses) was confined to the outskirts of the town and later rather more intensively to some parts of the centre. Civilians climbed on our tanks. We kept on meeting bursts of small arms fire and an occasional grenade and there were civilian casualties.

Lieutenant Gibson Stubbs's troop sank a small steamer full of Germans in the Scheldt river. He fired AP at 1,000 yards and the boat went aground enveloped in steam.

Bill Close sensibly refrained from brewing up the steam locomotives, which offered tempting targets. Most of the division were unaware of a strange order that no artillery or mortars were to be used in the centre of town without reference to the Corps Commander, in order to save civilian lives.

3rd Mons in their TCVs had driven through the night of 3–4 September and Major Joe How noted: 'The men were dirty and hungry and the cooks' trucks were welcome as they arrived in the company areas to prepare food.' They heard on the radio that Guards Armoured had entered Brussels. After a small action at Londerzeel, a few miles south of Breendonk, 3rd Mons crossed the River Rupel at Boom, entered Antwerp by the main road, turned off left and west for the Scheldt and the docks after passing the inner line of forts. They were ordered to secure the sluice gates vital to the port and these they captured intact. Near the river A Company came under fire at a narrow bridge. After several attempts and casualties they established a firm bridgehead in the darkness. On the east side of town the 23rd Hussars had a more difficult time. On their advance line the roads were mined and covered by a Flak unit and there were anti-tank guns in some of the forts and on the roofs of houses. C squadron brewed up a number of staff cars leaving the town. Their guide was a young Belgian boy scout, who outlined in accurate detail the defences ahead. A White Army man insisted one corner was safe to go round; the boy scout said: 'No it wasn't.' Geoffrey Bishop put it to the test, walked round the corner and was machine-gunned. He darted back, unhurt but wiser. A squadron faced the same problems: '"Hello Able-Two, they are firing 'black' (i.e. HE) at me. What are you going to do about it?" Answer: "What do you think they are firing at *me* – confetti?"' Despite Captain Budgen, 13 RHA, firing stonks, the impasse continued. H Company 8 RB did not have enough manpower to clear the area dominated by anti-tank guns and mined roads. Eventually 23rd Hussars withdrew and spent a very comfortable night at Contich.

Colonel Ivor Rees, CO 4 KSLI, described part of his O group given out at 1500 hrs on the outskirts of Antwerp on the Boom road:

The difficulties of collecting one's 'Order Group', thinking and giving out orders, making oneself heard, linking various sub-units together among this mass of the populace crowding round, still kissing you, asking you to post a letter to America, to give them some petrol, some more arms for the White Brigade, holding a baby under your nose to be kissed, trying to give you a drink, inviting you to their house, trying to carry you away, offering information about the enemy, had to be seen to be understood, and were the same, but about three times as great, as in Amiens. In addition Brigadier [Churcher] would say at intervals: 'I want you to be as quick as possible.'

4 KSLI next marched two miles in a straight line from the Boomse–Steenweg roundabout towards the Central Park, cheered on by hordes of well-wishers thronging the tightly packed pavements. The large triangular park, each side about ¼-mile long, was covered with bushes and tall trees and was overlooked by high buildings. Three substantial bunkers, screened by thick shrubs, sheltered the main German HQ, with a subway under the

road to the Kommandantur building. A large lake was another obstacle and snipers on the rooftops a distinct menace. A Company attacked from the west and C Company from the east and by 2200 hrs the park HQ was taken. C squadron 2nd Fife and Forfarshire did a good deal of intimidation by milling about in the park, and certainly helped in compelling the complete surrender. Captain Fruin took his tank and another off to deal with the SS HQ and shelled the building briskly. Each time an empty shell case was pushed out of the tank's open port, a Belgian civilian put a hand in with a large glass of wine!

The Ayrshire Yeomanry FOO, Captain Robin Burton, used his Sherman machine guns now to good effect, since he was not allowed to call down pinpoint fire on the bunkers!

Corporal Ted Jones with A Company 4 KSLI noted that his platoon sergeant, Paddy Cahill, was offered a precious bottle of White Horse whisky, which had been kept safe for the day of liberation. 'When we finally reached the park we found a high bank covered in shrubs and trees. The only access was over a narrow footbridge covered from the far side by two enemy machine-gun posts.' Sergeant Cahill, Major Tom Maddocks and the determined A Company fought their way through the park, and captured 280 prisoners in the bunkers, including General Stolberg and a resplendent chap who turned out to be the bandmaster.

Ned Thornburn with D Company 4 KSLI was given the task to capture the Kommandantur in the Banque Hypothecaire, half a mile north-west of Central Park. Supported by a troop of 3 RTR, the three platoons attacked the building from various angles with sten guns and grenades. Bill Close ordered a Firefly to fire its 'beeg cannon' at the main doors. The KSLI platoon commander, Jimmy Bratland, was a Norwegian and with his fluent German helped Ned Thornburn negotiate the surrender. Eventually seven officers including the smartly-dressed Commandant and eighty-four ORs came out and were marched off to Antwerp Zoo, which had been organized by the Resistance as a collecting centre for prisoners and collaborators. (Sverre Bratland was an officer in the Norwegian army at the outbreak of war. After Resistance work he was posted to 4 KSLI, was wounded twice, won the MC in Holland, and rose to the rank of General in the post-war Norwegian army.) After that very successful little battle Ned imbibed Pils with the Resistance leaders in a nearby café until 0200 hrs and slept on a doormat at Taymans toy shop in the Huidvetter-Straat.

The third KSLI battle on 4 September involved B Company under Dick Mullock. They were ordered to seize a bridge on the south-east perimeter and block one of the main east–west roads in the southern suburbs. Admiring crowds impeded their march and the KSLI burst into song with 'Tipperary' and 'Pack up your troubles', many arm in arm with the (prettier) Belgians. Just as well Colonel Reeves did not see them. CQMS Bob Howells arrived with a proper hot meal: 'The locals were amazed to see such delicious food being ladled out to us.' Two brisk skirmishes took place.

The FOO, Captain Burton, mowed down a column of German troops and horse-drawn vehicles, and the dead horses were hung, skinned and quartered by a local *boucher*. Later Sergeant Hughes almost single-handedly destroyed a retreating column of fifteen vehicles, causing forty-five casualties. Altogether 4 KSLI had a marvellous day. The city of Antwerp was in their hands, 2,000 prisoners taken and the German GOC and Town Commandant captured.

'It was unrestrained joy – mad and crazy,' according to Captain CKO Spence, Ayrshire Yeomanry, 'and all the time sporadic firing against stubborn remnants of resisting Germans. No war can have been more crazy.' Spence tried to capture a beautiful Mercedes staff car, but the Belgians got there first, so he had to settle for a moth-eaten Volkswagen, which did at least 60 miles to the gallon!

That night was chaotic. Café parties went on until dawn. Snipers fired and were hunted down by the Resistance. There was dancing in the streets. A Company commander of the Herefords told Bill Close that he hadn't a clue where half his men were!

Day Two – 5 September

Captain Moody, 2 i/c C Company 3rd Mons, had a strange visitation during the night of the 4th–5th: 'The sound of approaching tracks brought the company to "stand to". It was a Bren carrier painted white with gun etc., in perfect order, manned by the Resistance, furious that 3rd Mons had arrived in their patch "so early". The Belgian crew had hidden and serviced the vehicle and weapons since it had been abandoned by the BEF in *1940!*'

At first light the Herefords started to clear the eastern and south-eastern part of the city. Slowly but surely they succeeded, taking many prisoners. Major Joe How, 3rd Mons, noted:

Even at this early hour (0600 hrs) the people of Antwerp thronged into the roadway to greet the advancing troops as they made their way in long files on either side of the road. Fair ladies of Antwerp showing signs of having been hurriedly disturbed from their slumbers, pressed bunches of flowers on the soldiers who, not wishing to appear ungrateful by throwing them into the gutter, continued on their way with bouquets in one hand and their firearms in the other.

At 0900 hrs on 5 September General 'Pip' received an unpleasant shock. The main bridge over the Albert Canal had been blown up: 'This was a blow to me and I realized that I had made a great error in not going into the city the evening before. I had thought that the canal went through the centre of the city . . . had I braved the crowds and gone into the city myself I would have realized the situation.' In the absence of adequate maps, patrols of

4 KSLI were sent out to locate the Albert Canal and to discover whether it could be crossed. The Schijnpoort-Weg carried the main road to Breda and Bergen-op-Zoom. Half a mile east was the Merxem Steenweg bridge and to the west in the dock areas was the Yserbrug bridge. Major Andy Hardy, CO C Company 4 KSLI, said:

> My task on the 5th was to seize a main road bridge over the [60-yard wide] Albert Canal somewhere west of Merxem. The scene was as usual: dense accompanying crowds making control difficult, all mysteriously vanishing as we approached the bridge and shortly before we came under fire from MGs from across the canal. I must say that I regarded the task of rushing the bridge as doomed to bloody failure.

As one platoon got across there was a loud explosion and the middle span dropped into the canal. Major Hardy's men remained in their positions until dusk.

At 2000 hrs Colonel Reeves, CO 4 KSLI, was ordered to put the whole battalion across the Schijnpoort-Weg bridge. The maps were unreliable. There was no time for a detailed reconnaissance. The Belgian guides disappeared. The assault boats carried from Normandy on the sides of TCVs all had holes in the canvas and leaked badly. Colonel Reeves's Ayrshire Yeomanry FOO's key wireless set failed to work. Nevertheless the indomitable Sergeant Ted Jones, A Company, found some local boats and, despite a strong current, rowed across a 150-yard stretch of canal. During the night three companies got across and, backed by their own mortar sections, formed a bridgehead near the Sports Palace south of the canal. The Sextons of I Battery 13 RHA were ready for action in the Central park. They could not fire on targets *within* the city but they were soon to be in action. Patrick Delaforce noticed that his troop commander's Sherman OP tank had eighteen civilians clustered on it. Norman Young was a good-looking chap and he had lost his beret, his steel helmet, his RHA insignia and much of his dignity, but not his nerve! Delaforce visited the lion house in the zoo, a broad high building with barred cages on both sides. Two pretty Belgian girls checked in the new arrivals. Each cage had a different category of prisoner: male collaborators, female collaborators, important Belgian traitors, German NCOs, German ORs and finally German officers. When Alan Moorehead visited the zoo he compared it to the Colosseum in Rome in the time of Emperor Caligula. A large crowd was permanently baying at the entrance to the zoo; they wanted to get inside and carry out a lynching party. 'These,' explained the Belgian officer in charge, indicating the Germans, 'we will turn over to the British authorities. These,' indicating the collaborators, 'will be shot this evening *after a fair trial.*' A couple of photographers had gone into the cages and were arranging the condemned men in convenient and artistic groups to have their photographs taken. The models stayed rigid like wax figures. Another man was going among them taking their money and watches. By midday on the 5th Brigadier Churcher ordered the 6,000 German prisoners in the zoo to be marched out of the city and escorted and protected from retribution by the carrier platoons of the three infantry battalions. Three months later Brigadier Churcher, then on the Maas, received a letter from Switzerland accusing him of contravening the Geneva Convention by humiliating German prisoners placed in a zoo! Appropriately most of the German POWs were marched to the infamous Breendonk concentration camp.

8 RB enjoyed themselves. They continued mopping up in the morning and their mortar detachment had their 'best ever' shoot, as Noel Bell reported:

Large parties of Germans had been reported on the far bank and the prospects of targets appeared good. We entered a tall bank building on the waterfront and an obliging life attendant took us up to the sixth floor. Here we got the most wonderful view of the country on the far side of the river including a collection of stationary German transport. We wirelessed back to the mortars to engage this target. A salvo of bombs fell among the transport, whereupon some sixty Germans who must have been taking it easy within the vehicles, leapt out and began milling around in the open. The new target was worked out and within a few seconds down came bomb after bomb right into the middle of them, scoring the most direct hits I have ever seen. Hardly a German escaped this murderous hail of bombs.

FOOs from 13 RHA and Ayrshire Yeomanry found OPs on top of high blocks of flats, on the roof of the Town Hall and on a factory building, and many useful shoots were carried out. One gunner major with 13 RHA was sitting with John Dunlop, 3 RTR, in a comfortable office on the top floor of a skyscraper bringing down fire across the Scheldt: 'Meanwhile a trim little Antwerpoise office secretary was bringing in relays of *café*, cognac and playing us pre-war American blues on the office record player. Now that was the right way to fight a war.' Fortunately the well-constructed eighteenth-century forts were not strongly defended, but large stocks of weapons were found which were handed over to the Belgian White Brigade. By midday the Herefords were concentrated in the Berchem area.

The opposition was the 7/9 Division (elderly gentlemen according to the Corps Commander), a battalion of Dutch SS troops, and a few Luftwaffe detachments. But the 85th Division under General Chill quickly arrived from Turnhout, so on the 5th there was a lot of German reinforcement activity on the west and north of Antwerp along the line of the Albert Canal.

It was difficult to assess how effective the local resistance groups had been. Certainly they were in guarding prisoners, hunting down single snipers and providing somewhat unreliable guides (except for the boy scout), and also resistance groups under M. Edouard Pilaet and M. Eugene Colson sent fighting patrols around the docks and co-operated particularly with 3 RTR. The Resistance suffered 200 casualties during the week of the capture of Antwerp.

The armoured regiments had little action on the 5th but much maintenance was needed after the 300 miles or more which they had travelled since L'Aigle. As Steel Brownlie wrote:

[they] worked on the tanks, [which had] many faults after the long drive. We then did a sweep with the Herefords in carriers through the western part of the city. A Belgian black-shirt fired a spandau from a window but was killed by the infantry. We signed autograph books, posed for photographs, halted for refreshments. In the evening David Voller and I went into town in our liberated Volkswagen with a bottle of champagne and had a party. Met Irma. Voller drove into a minefield on the way back, but what the hell?

23rd Hussars harboured round the Pulhof, a large villa on the southern outskirts, where they, the RTR and the 15/19th Hussars, rested, relaxed and repaired.

Day Three – 6 September

Colonel Ivor Reeves, CO 4 KSLI, described his bridgehead at dawn on the 6th:

We found ourselves in the most ghastly factory area, one mass of small streets, lanes, passages, walls, walls within walls, piles of iron and waste of every description. We soon discovered some machine-gun posts and started to clear them. That started two days and a night's street fighting, the most tiring and trying type of fighting even under the best conditions. The Boche found us and soon [1100 hrs] had five tanks among us. We knocked out two and then ran out of all Piat anti-tank arms. They shot us up with machine guns, AP shot and HE, knowing we couldn't touch them, stalking round and round day and night, blasting us out of houses as they discovered us.

The three companies were trapped without food in a factory area, 150 yards square.

A section of C Company was forced out of a burning building into the gardens and thirteen of the KSLI were taken prisoner. Colonel Reeves noted: 'We were surrounded by snipers and counter attacks by up to two battalions of SS infantry. The Boche put down mortars, 88s and 155s his heaviest field gun.' However, the KSLI mortars, 13 RHA, Ayrshire Yeomanry put down accurate stonks which helped prevent the bridgehead being overrun.

Captain Bowden, Ayrshire Yeomanry, was FOO in the KSLI factory bridgehead in the Schijnpoort area, and with an 18 set brought down many DF plans including 'Navy' to help the Belgian harbourmaster rescue three motor launches. Other stonks were to cover rations being ferried across on the 6th.

Stretcher-bearer Sergeant Ron Cookson persuaded a courageous barge skipper to swing his barge across the 100-yard canal and punt it to the Antwerp bank with sixteen of the KSLI casualties in it. A German tank spotted the barge, set it on fire, wounded the barge skipper and killed a lance-corporal.

The General wrote:

With the object of entering Merxem from the flank and taking pressure off the 4 KSLI, the 3rd Mons (less one company who were down at the main lock gates) and two squadrons of 23rd Hussars organized an attack on Merxem from the flank. At the second of two bridges on their route, this force was held up by a road block protected by mines and covered by heavy fire.

A squadron 23rd Hussars made good progress towards the railway bridge at Merxem but Lieutenant Drake's troop was held up by infantry supported by A/Tank guns and Lieutenant Unwin's troop, trying a flanking movement, had two Shermans bogged down near the canal in view of the enemy. So 3rd Mons and 23rd Hussars spent a most unpleasant night. Captain Moody, 3rd Mons, recalls how: 'In answer to a call for medics, two young, very attractive Belgian girls in white uniforms walked down the dock, tended our wounded and walked back. The enemy made no effort to interfere. A wonderful act, very brave, never to be forgotten.' Alastair Tait, RASC with 3rd Mons, remembers a bakery with enemy dug in around. Corporal Gordon Harris, his friend from Yorkshire swimming days, was killed by a bullet that entered through his web belt, and 'along the street a Belgian doctor hanging out a flag from an upper window was shot by a retreating member of the Wehrmacht'.

Colonel Reeves, 4 KSLI, asked Brigadier Churcher for permission to withdraw his battered, defenceless three companies on the night of the 6th. Churcher sought permission from the General. His intention was still for the division to move north with 29th Brigade leading and 159 Brigade clearing up Merxem. The sappers were ordered to construct one or more bridges in the night. So that evening 4 KSLI clung on to their small factory area bridgehead, 3 Mons beat off a counter-attack on the vital sluice gates, while 23rd Hussars/3rd Mons were also in trouble.

Day Four – 7 September

The Divisional historian, Edgar Palamountain, wrote: 'Nor were we ourselves to find Antwerp a rose without a thorn, for besides the intermittent shelling which continued for some weeks, we were to fight a battle there and an unsuccessful battle at that!' The General wrote: 'The 4 KSLI situation was becoming worrying: they were suffering steady casualties and it was decided, reluctantly, to withdraw them. This was successfully done under cover of intense artillery fire in the late afternoon.' It was tempting to think that Corps HQ were having such a jolly time in Brussels – which they were – that 11th Armoured Division were left out on a limb. Eventually on the morning of the 7th, Lieutenant-General Horrocks came, saw the problem for himself and said: 'You must get them back.' At 0300 hrs in pitch darkness and pouring rain 3rd Mons were ordered to attack eastward starting from No. 7 dry docks and crossing the Yserbrug bridge towards Merxem. But they met tough opposition in their efforts to relieve pressure on the KSLI bridgehead. In confused hand to hand fighting 3rd Mons took the Groenendaallaan bridge under the railway. Two supporting 23rd Hussars tanks were knocked out by two 88-mm guns. Once Colonel Orr heard of the 4 KSLI rescue plans, there was no further point in risking lives. It was not until midnight that 5th Dorsets (of 50 Division) took over the docks and relieved them. But for another four weeks the Germans continued to hold Merxem until the great Canadian offensive finally drove them out.

Major Andy Hardy, 4 KSLI, describes the final rescue:

At last orders came that the sappers would take us off in boats at 1500 hrs under a heavy artillery programme. A delay was caused by a sudden squall but at 1530 hrs our guns opened up with a very tight box barrage of HE and smoke around the minute bridgehead. It was a shattering barrage, it came down with pinpoint accuracy, some shells landing dangerously close but I'm sure it was that closeness which made the evacuation such a success. In came the assault boats with their sapper crews paddling like maniacs. The whole party was back within fifteen minutes without a single casualty. C Company was down to forty all ranks, A similar and B substantially less.

4 KSLI took 150 casualties including thirty-one killed and Colonel Ivor Reeves was seriously wounded. The Merxem bridgehead at Antwerp is a famous battle honour.

Patrick Delaforce, 13 RHA, remembers the extra special care needed for the rectangular barrage to protect the KSLI evacuation. For thirty minutes at four rounds a minute, the divisional artillery plus borrowed Corps mediums, pounded the far bank of the Scheldt.

The battle for Antwerp was over. In a sense it was also starting. The first flying V-2 landed on 12 October, the first V-1 on 23 October, and altogether 1,214 rockets landed in greater Antwerp, another 302 in the dock area. 15,000 civilians were killed or wounded in these attacks. On 12 December the Rex Cinema was hit, killing 242 soldiers on leave and 250 civilians. But even worse. Between 1 October and 8 November the 1st Canadian Army suffered 12,873 casualties (50 per cent Canadian, 50 per cent British and Polish) in the brutal clearance of the River Scheldt.

CHAPTER FIFTEEN

Prelude and Right Flank to Market Garden

We were well and truly ready for a bit of a rest. For days and nights ever since coming away from the carnage in the Falaise area we had been active, getting little or no sleep [Roland Jefferson remembers]. We had not changed our underclothes or socks for well over two weeks. Indeed I do not remember even taking off my boots in all that time and we began to be smelly. Anyone who has never experienced being an infantry soldier in the front line might tend to overlook the fact that the natural bodily functions still have to be attended to. A visit to the toilet normally meant digging a small hole with a spade and crouching down under fire. This required a certain amount of expertise and speed was vital.

With admiring Belgian crowds around it was even more difficult than usual. The 8 RBs stayed for four days in the grounds of the Château de Baron de Coeur. The riflemen presented the grey army blankets, ideal for tailoring into smart (warm) coats, to the young ladies of Antwerp. Cafés and *estaminets* did a roaring business, although business was not quite an accurate term, as all the drinks were free! The Antwerp newspaper *Het Handelblad van Antwerpen* of 14 September 1944 carried a leading editorial article about the Division's advance. Many long-lasting friendships were made. Divisional clubs formed and eventually many leave parties went 'back' to Antwerp. Noel Bell's G Company spent thirty-six hours in the pleasant suburb of Hemixem. The battalion had had twenty-eight casualties on the Great Swan. B squadron 23rd Hussars' historian noted: 'We had four days of luxury relaxation swamped by the hospitality of grateful citizens, while fighting still raged in the suburbs.' There was even an officers' dance run by 29 Armoured Brigade HQ which Steel Brownlie found 'deadly dull'. There was a temporary feeling of frustration even though 75th Anti/Tank brewed up a barge in the Albert Canal. As Steel Brownlie put it succinctly: 'At dusk we returned to our old harbour, feeling that we were being buggered about by a higher command that had no clear idea of what it was doing.'

7 September was a day of coming and going, and 29 Brigade tanks and 8 RB were sent on a false alarm to move through the Merxem bridgehead, but of course the operation had to be abandoned. 347 German Division had

Sergeant O.R. Wilson, Deurne

now joined the 719th to block the advance. One bright spot however was the divisional occupation of the Antwerp Customs House. Each regiment received 800 bottles of wine and 8,000 cigars, roughly one bottle and ten cigars per man. Patrick Delaforce's 13 RHA half track crew all stood 5 inches taller when they left Antwerp than when they went in as they were standing on cases of Cointreau – a delicious liqueur, but taken in abundance it produces heartburn.

At Holsbeek, 3 miles east of Louvain, 171 Company RASC 'found' the contents of a German NAAFI depot. The ersatz food included tubes of cheese like shaving soap and blocks of solid jam, probably 95 per cent turnip. John Hooper was more enthusiastic about '15,000 bottles of all kinds of wines and spirits, which worked out at 3 per man in the Brigade plus a small extra allowance for each officers' and sergeants' mess. Bottles marked Cassis, Pastis or Geneva meant nothing to us. The cigarettes were awful but the cigars were the best Dutch.'

'The REME were most extended after the Seine crossing at Vernon', Jimmy Carson wrote later. 'After Amiens fell and right through to Antwerp we had [vehicle] casualties scattered over what seemed hundreds of miles with our own workshops far behind the main body of the Division.'

Bob Wilson, Sergeant CMP Provost Company, was in charge of POWs after the taking of Antwerp. They were to be housed in Breendonk concentration

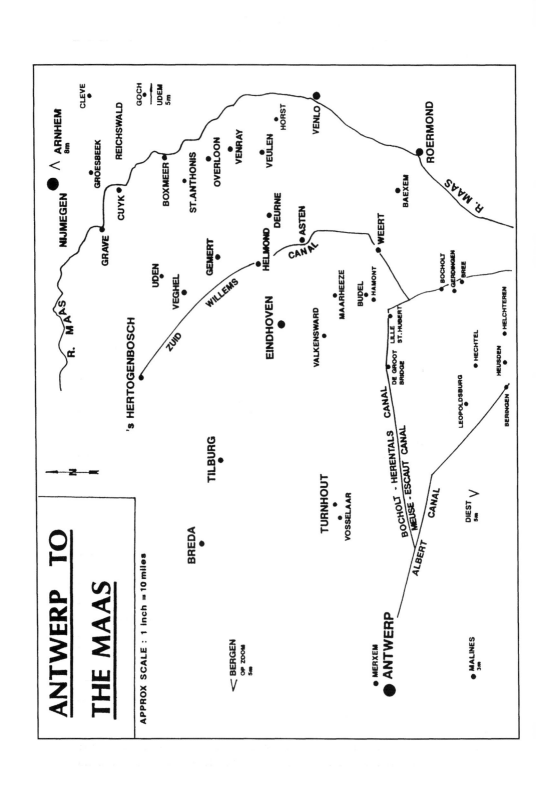

3rd Mons and 3 RTR having lunch

camp near Boom: 'I was allocated two tanks from Div. HQ which were positioned in the perimeter of the compound. There must have been a thousand prisoners – they came in lorry loads, NOT having been searched – this was a mammoth task as many were still carrying weapons and even hand grenades.'

So the advance resumed against hardening opposition. On 8 September 29th Armoured Brigade moved off eastwards. 3 RTR and 15/19th Hussars came under 159 Brigade and 1st Herefords under 29th Armoured.

8 RB and 3 RTR went off on a 'peacetime' march through liberated territory – Malines, Aarschot to Diest – where they harboured alongside the Americans who had more or less run out of petrol. Roland Jefferson's route followed the Guards Armoured centre line to Diest, where his RB company met the Princess Irene's Netherlands Regiment. The Inns of Court patrolled the Albert Canal as far east as Herenthals; the 15/19th Hussars silenced some enemy guns at Burght on the west bank of the River Scheldt; and the 23rd Hussars were diverted to Beringen where the Guards had already bridged the Albert Canal. Everyone was sad to leave the fleshpots of Antwerp behind, except the 4 KSLI who had survived forty hours of continuous close-quarter fighting across the Albert Canal. Their fighting strength was now 211 below the war establishment of 809. Ned Thornburn used to ask the new reinforcements: "How many A/Tk guns were you used to in your old company?" "Oh, we sometimes had one," came the reply, to which I said: "Well, I never have less than three or four and usually three tanks as well. Whoever attacks me will get a very bloody nose," after which they cheered up considerably.'

On the 9th the Division crossed the Albert Canal on a Bailey bridge immediately next to the Guards bridge. By 0600 hrs Steel Brownlie and the Fifes were 'having a café breakfast party with the owner and his daughters who played the piano, eating fried eggs, drinking coffee and cognac. Never miss a chance.' Then Noel Bell observed 'one of the biggest "brews" we had ever set eyes on'. Unfortunately this was a long column of supply vehicles of 8th Armoured Brigade blown up by infiltrating panzergrenadiers. The woods around gave them shelter and the huge slag heaps dominating the area gave cover to the snipers. 8 RB and 3 RTR occupied Beringen and combed immense woodlands around, a slow and tiring operation helped by Princess Irene's Dutch infantry. Noel Bell noted sadly that the working relationship 8 RB/3 RTR now ended – a 'historic partnership'. South of the village of Helchteren that evening 1st Herefords met their new partners, 2nd Fife and Forfarshire Yeomanry. The other new partners were 23rd Hussars and 8 RB, 15/19th Hussars and 4 KSLI and 3 RTR with 3rd Mons.

On the following day the 10th, 8 RB and 23rd Hussars led on the right, and immediately ran into tough opposition a mile north-east at Kunsel. Noel Bell's G Company and A squadron 23rd Hussars looped round to the north and caught the enemy looking the wrong way, but as they moved on 8 RB ran into a considerable number of German paratroopers. They were part of General Kurt Student's hastily assembled First Paratroop Army: 'very lightly armed, very badly organized but who fought fanatically, preferring to shoot themselves rather than be taken prisoner. They suffered enormous casualties and the carnage over the whole area was the greatest we had yet witnessed. Darkness fell and we spent the night in a field with the tanks expecting to be attacked.'

Captain Budgen, G Battery, 13 RHA FOO with the leading troop, used tank HE and Browning fire on enemy pockets. When the Browning jammed, he used his rifle: 'The forward tanks were in bazooka range. The one in front was hit, set on fire.' Budgen then with his trusty musket shot a bazooka team of three and another close by – there were fifteen in an area no bigger than Battersea Park – fired two shots at his tank. This too he dealt with. Two bazooka crews surrendered to him and two others left their weapons and ran. He did not leave his task until every bazooka had been eliminated. He earned the MC.

The grounded Luftwaffe crews, young men of high morale, fanatical and desperate, suffered 500 casualties. Each paratrooper was armed with a bazooka but few tanks or carriers were hit. 8 RB had eleven killed and 23rd Hussars three – a real classic victory by a determined, well-planned attack.

Meanwhile the Herefords and 2nd Fife and Forfarshire pushed north towards Hechtel early on the 10th and reached Wychmael against equally determined resistance, and took 400 prisoners. Lieutenant Ken Crockford was commanding 14 platoon C company and wrote:

We were in reserve and under fire by 81–mm mortars. It was a great relief to move forward. 13 platoon was making slow progress through the woods. 15 platoon had lost their commander (Lieutenant Kotchapan, a CANLOAN officer), their platoon sergeant Lobb and three section leaders and was now commanded by Lance-Corporal Everall who was later awarded the DCM.

The Herefords took fifteen casualties that day from German mortar fire, which plastered the whole area despite the large number of their own troops that was still there. Only three prisoners were taken in the fierce hand-to-hand fighting. Most of the enemy were killed by bayonet at close quarters. Steel Brownlie was, as usual, in the thick of the fighting. Here C squadron and C company Herefords fought an action that has been described as a model of its kind:

I took my troop across the railway line and gave chase. Why not round up a few prisoners? That was not exactly what happened. It was sandy heath with heathery dunes. Soon we were in the middle of a large area of dug-in Germans who were firing at us from all sides with small arms and panzerfausts. I gave the order that we should keep moving among the enemy positions, never halt, run over trenches, fire at all possible targets. Soon there were forty Germans out of their holes with their hands up. Easy! David Voller and I were herding the prisoners when he was hit in the neck. I hurriedly remounted and resumed the previous tactics. There were far more enemy than we had supposed in a honeycomb of dugouts. They kept appearing and disappearing as we drove round and round, flat out. We shot them, crushed them, blew them out of their holes, but as soon as we passed others popped up and let fly at us. They seemed to be everywhere. Voller was taken away in his tank. Corporal Vallance was hit in the track by a Panzerfaust and had to limp away. Corporal Corney was shot and wounded, his tank withdrew. A grenade was lobbed into Corporal Barlow's turret, he and all his crew badly wounded.

Steel Brownlie's tank was hit but without penetration. The heather was burning, and smoke obscured the view. The Herefords then arrived and cleared the enemy with their bayonets. 400 Germans paratroopers (so-called) were disarmed and herded up by the railway line: 'They had been dug in, in a piece of ground not much larger than a rugby pitch, over which I had been charging for about half an hour.' A marvellous effort. The battle group then headed for Peer, bypassing Hechtel, where practically every Fife tank was bogged down in low-lying marshland. 'We sat there till night fell.' The Herefords had men killed in the fighting around Hectel and Helchteren. 4 KSLI and the 15/19th Hussars moved south-east and 4 miles north of Hasselt.

It was close country with lots of marsh and short fields of view; treacherous going for tanks and the fighting was severe and confused [wrote Ted Deeming, 15/19th Hussars]. The opposition was A/Tk guns of all calibres, at least 2 SP guns and probably a Panther tank, all located east of the road [3½ miles north of the Albert Canal]. The regiment inflicted many casualties on the enemy, destroyed two SP guns, four A/Tk guns and three tanks but lost twenty-one casualties themselves. Squadron Leader Lord Rathdonnell found himself 60 yards away from a Jagd-Panzer IV. His gun jammed, the SP fired and missed and a bazookaman hit the Cromwell, but no real damage!

The Ayrshire Yeomanry FOO, Captain Burton, was killed along with several 15/19th Hussar tank commanders. The 3 RTR/3rd Mons group moved south from Helchteren towards Laak, where Captain Spence, Ayrshire Yeomanry FOO, engaged several enemy strongpoints. 75th A/Tank were in action around Helchteren and also at Wichmael. Altogether it was a very good day for the Division.

The following day, the 11th, 8 RB and 23rd Hussars advanced to Peer and met some resistance. It was a beautiful, clear autumn morning and strangely peaceful after the battles the day before. The enemy had vanished as in a dream, leaving many dead behind. But bazookas soon claimed several Hussar tanks, and Lieutenant Evans was captured, but fortunately recaptured a few hours later. Captain Norman Young, I Battery 13 RHA, had a narrow squeak. Fired at by an 88-mm gun he replied with his 75-mm and hit it with his first shot, even though his sights were 400 yards out of true! The battle group advanced to Petit Brogel, Linove and Grand Brogel, where the villagers gave 8 RB a warm welcome.

B squadron 23rd Hussars with F company 8 RB was sent that afternoon through Caulille for a crossing of the Meuse–Escaut canal. The bridge had already been destroyed but a nasty skirmish took place when 88 mms, heavy mortars and infantry brewed up two tanks and a carrier. At nightfall the whole party was recalled to Petit Brogel. Hussar Lieutenants Drake and Garai, in an acquired Mercedes, swanned off and liberated a hamlet on their own before 3 RTR reached it.

In the afternoon 1st Herefords and 2nd Fife and Forfarshire approached Peer from the west, and then sent patrols eastwards towards Bree. Steel Brownlie and his 'little friends' met up in Peer high street and then harboured in a potato field: 'Glory be, we were put on twenty-four hours notice to move, told to make ourselves comfortable and "maintain" the tanks. A mess was set up in a house and the officers slept in a barn – the first time under a roof for quite a time.'

During the day the Inns of Court had investigated all possible canal crossings between Peer and Neerpelt – all bridges were blown and covered by enemy fire from the far bank, as 23rd Hussars had discovered.

159 Infantry Brigade had a relatively peaceful day. 3rd Mons/3 RTR cleared up Laak and concentrated round Helchteren, and 4 KSLI and 15/19th Hussars took over, approached Bree from the south-west, had some skirmishes, and found the bridge, not surprisingly, was blown up in their faces. Divisional contact was made with the Guards on the left and 2nd US Armoured Division on the south flank.

On the 12th the Inns of Court kept up their canal patrols and found the town of Bree on the west bank to be free of the enemy. 13 RHA and Ayrshire Yeomanry fired heavy stonks on the defenders between 0815 hrs and 0845 hrs in support of the 1st and 2nd Welsh Guards, who finally turfed the spirited German resistance out of Hechtel. Many Guards tanks were knocked out in the morning attack amid savage fighting. 3rd Mons/3 RTR then moved in to occupy Hechtel or what was left of it:

We arrived at a small bridgehead [on 13 September] over the Meuse–Escaut Canal to protect the road on the left of the regiment [wrote Trooper Ernie Hamilton, 15/19th Hussars], some 200 yards from the Dutch border. Next morning brought 2nd troop C squadron's first tank battle; to our front appeared four Mark IV tanks. It was here the troop made regimental history; this battle brought us an MC, two MMs and a mention-in-dispatches. We had knocked out the German tanks but not without our own casualties, two tanks hit. My own hit twice, my guns were damaged unable to fire and our 19 set filled with shrapnel like myself. My operator Percie Downing was killed, his first moments in action, he was eighteen years old.

Ernie spent the next five months convalescing from his wounds in England.

The Division spent another five days, until the 16th, resting and reorganizing, the first real break since L'Aigle. 8 RB and the infantry sent out patrols to the line of the Escaut Canal. Roland Jefferson recorded: 'German patrols were active and there was many a skirmish. On night patrols it was an uncomfortable feeling to go out in the dead of night, face blackened.' He carried a 38 radio set, of short range but with a throat microphone. Words were whispered, translated into pulses through the throat mikes and thus transmitted back. Steel Brownlie and Geoff Hales 'explored Peer's cafés, scrounged for eggs in a liberated Volkswagen, drank much Cointreau (ex-Wehrmacht), had a hot shower in a pit-head baths, had a letter from Maria in Antwerp, were shelled occasionally, played piano in cafés, put clocks back one hour. What next?' During their stay at Petit and Grand Brogel, 23rd Hussars, 8 RB and the rest of the Division enjoyed the vast collection of wines, liqueurs and cigars, 'liquid booty', acquired in Antwerp. On the 13th a deception force consisting of a company of Herefords and a squadron of Fifes engaged the enemy around Bree to persuade him that a big attack was coming. FOOs of 13 RHA and Ayrshire Yeomanry occupied OPs in Bree church tower and every other high building on the west bank of the canal to harass the enemy with minor fire targets.

On the same day a Feldwebel with 712 Infantry Division, west of Antwerp, wrote in his diary: 'We have to leave the dead lying in the street for with fighter bombers overhead any unnecessary movement may be fatal. One of our mates commits suicide by hanging during the night. British aircraft drop flares and attack with fighter bombers.'

8 RB sent 'liberty' parties to Brussels and quite a few veterans, wounded in Normandy, returned to fight again. As usual both gunner regiments stayed in action within 5 miles of the Dutch border for that week. The dashing 23rd Hussars had several squadron dances and parties. Captain Taylor played a mean clarinet and Lieutenant Drake was visited by two beautiful Belgian girls. 2nd Fife and Forfarshire showed off by firing five shots from a 17-pounder Firefly at maximum elevation, hoping they would land in Germany, but had to settle for Holland instead.

On 16 September at 1200 hrs 11th Armoured Division came under command of General O'Connor's 8 Corps together with 3rd and 50th Divisions. General Horrocks, GOC 30 Corps with Guards Armoured, 43 Division and 8th Armoured Brigade would make a bold dash to link up with 1st British Airborne, 82nd US Airborne and 101 US Airborne in the audacious dash of 70 miles into the heart of Holland to seize the Grave–Nijmegen–Arnhem area. This was the famous, eventually doomed Market Garden operation. 12 Corps would be left-flanking and 8 Corps right-flanking protection and also responsible for clearing the area to the River Maas and down to Venlo.

The General described the new German opposition: 'The Germans now consisted of a number of "battle groups" bearing the name of their commanders [Hermann, Haregg, Hubner and Grassmehl]: their divisions had broken up but the groups still had a very high morale, particularly those of SS or Paratroops: they would often fight on without any officers.' The killing-grounds were going to be different too: 'The country was heavily "canalized" and with natural obstacles little work is required to convert them into a strong line of defence very quickly.' To deal with this situation the Division was once again organized into mixed brigade groups with the Inns of Court armoured cars – like busy little fox terriers – aggressively reconnoitring ahead and on the flanks. General Roberts also wrote:

In Normandy there was always real anxiety: if one made wrong decisions, if the front were penetrated by the Germans, if our line of communication was cut, the result could be catastrophic. Now mistakes or failures could only delay the end. Unless morale was high we would not achieve our objectives; heavy casualties in a fruitless battle will not help morale. We must try to win our battles without heavy casualties; not very easy.

Between 16 and 18 September 107 German Panzer Brigade, hauled all the way back from Poland, unloaded their 36 Panther tanks at Venlo station and went into action straight away.

On the 17th the two gunner regiments moved north to Neerpelt to support the start of Operation Market Garden. Two targets were engaged just after midday and between H-hour at 1435 hrs and 1450 hrs there were three more heavy concentrations. Rocket-firing Typhoons were also in action. On the 18th vigorous enemy patrols crossed the canal in the factory area of Neerpelt and bombarded Ayrshire Yeomanry rather intensely. But there were no casualties and the enemy were pushed back. 'Taurus Pursuant' mentions that two small mercenary forces now appeared to protect the canal towns of Bree and Bocholt. They were a mixed bag of Russians and French dressed in various uniforms with German arms and equipment. The Germans were amazed, the Belgians perplexed, the Division amused and the FFI miffed. On the 18th 4 KSLI replaced Breeforce and Tineforce and also occupied Bochotz. 3rd Mons were holding the line at Wychmael.

For six days, 17–22 September, 15/19th Hussars were lent to 30 Corps to link up with 101 US Airborne Division at Zon and Eindhoven and protect the long lines of communication. On the 17th they admired the great armada of gliders, Dakotas and bombers protected by a fighter screen as Operation Market Garden was launched. B and C squadrons fought in support of the Dorsets and Devons, but three tanks including the COs went up on mines. On the 18th B squadron reached Valkensward and the regiment was bombed around the Escaut bridge. On the 19th they passed through Eindhoven in brilliant sunshine with Dutch Orange-Nassau flags flying everywhere. Then A squadron went under command of 506 US Parachute Regiment at Eindhoven and the rest of the regiment at Zon under 101 US Airborne Division. They protected a supply-dropping zone on a large heath north of the canal. In the afternoon joint operations around Best produced fifty prisoners and much captured equipment. C squadron lost a 17-pounder Challenger, which turned up in Best five months later. German REME must have enjoyed looking at this 'new' British tank. Trooper Crump of A squadron destroyed two Panthers with seven hits out of eight shots. In support of the Americans and then the Guards Armoured, 15/19th Hussars were in action until the 22nd, giving a good account of themselves but suffering fifteen casualties. Their CO, Colonel Taylor, received the DSO for the successful six-day campaign.

CHAPTER SIXTEEN

Holland and the Peel Country

The Germans now worked miracles. Robert Kershaw's book *It never snows in September* is a masterpiece of detail derived from many German field-troop diarists. The beaten, weary, desperate survivors from Normandy straggled into Belgium and Holland in dribs and drabs. Hardly a fighting formation existed and the amazing collection of disparate services was hauled into battlegroups. There were few tanks or armoured cars or half tracks that survived the long journey, but new equipment was still being made in the German armaments factories. There were five groups of enemy troops – a small minority of tough old ex-Russian front sweats, some steady Wehrmacht, some dedicated SS cadets and the invalids (earless, limbless, deaf) – formed into regiments. The deaf soldiers could not of course hear incoming fire and took heavy casualties. The final group was the Hiwis or Hilfswillige, pressed men, mainly Poles, Czechs or Alsace Germans, who were unreliable and often deserted at the first opportunity. The Battle of Arnhem sucked in many of these freebooting battlegroups, but the two or three weeks of grace after the capture of Antwerp gave time for other battlegroups to dig in opposite Guards Armoured and 11th Armoured and thus defend every canal and river crossing.

The division did not of course realize that their visit to this, the third country of liberation, was going to be extended for another five months. The Peel country is a large tract of reclaimed marshland extending along the west bank of the River Maas for about 20 miles on either side of Venlo. Each field is surrounded by a deep dyke to drain off water, but in the autumn and rainy season these fill up and the whole becomes a quagmire. Poor quality roads from Venlo through Meijel and Deurne to Helmond were not capable of standing up to heavy traffic, certainly not to tanks and AFVs. The minor roads and tracks disappeared under water at the first shower of rain. The Engineers and Pioneers were always kept very busy, using utmost ingenuity to keep supplies going. No tank dared leave the roads, and minefields caused enormous delays. The digging of slit trenches, waterlogged before they were dug, became a grim shivering joke. A leading tank was virtually certain to meet a mine or an 88-mm A/Tk gun sooner or later.

Tank recovery in Holland was most difficult [recalls Jimmy Carson], not only due to the poor terrain and dreadful weather but also to the nasty habits of the Boche. At Veulen we had two tanks to get out, both being up to their turrets in soft ground and in full view of the enemy. The REME crews worked until dusk and started again at first light to find the tanks had been boobytrapped. This took hours to sort out and eventually we took three days to get the tanks out and on to transporters.

85 miles north the airborne warriors of Arnhem, after thirteen days of hopeless gallantry, surrendered or were evacuated on 26 September. First Airborne had been sacrificed and slaughtered with nearly 8,000 casualties. Guards Armoured had fought their way on the high dangerous road from Nijmegen towards Arnhem. They had done their best but it was not quite good enough. General 'Pip' Roberts wrote: 'After the operation there were many in 11th Armoured Division who said: "We should have been given this task – we would have got there" [i.e. from Nijmegen to Arnhem]. I doubted it myself but I did not disagree with them as I thought it was a sign of high morale and a fine divisional spirit.' So on 19 September the Black Bull moved across the Escaut canal at Lille-St-Hubert through 3 British Division's bridgehead. 2nd Fife and Forfarshire, 1st Hereford and a squadron of Inns of Court led, but were held up by a blown bridge at Schaft, then headed north towards Volkenswaard.

Steel Brownlie remembered: 'Around the Escaut Canal there was much wreckage; at last we reached the outskirts of Volkenswaard, clean, tidy, very Dutch and undamaged. Just outside there were nine Guards tanks nose to tail, all burned out and graves by the roadside. We harboured a mile beyond the town and saw and heard an air raid on Eindhoven.' The following day the advance continued east-north-east with two centre-lines. On the left 8 RB and 23rd Hussars reached Heeze, which they cleared without difficulty. The 2nd Fife and Forfarshire and Herefords passed through Heeze via Leende. Steel Brownlie's route was 'via a maze of sandy tracks among fir trees, inadequate maps but help from Dutch patriots. Small bridges kept collapsing. We finally harboured, shell and mortar fire all night, near the blown bridge between Zomeren and Asten. No sleep, refuelling risky.' On the right flank 3rd Mons and 3 RTR had cleared Budel and Soerendonig and were nearing Maarheeze. 13 RHA passed into Holland via Heeze, Someren and then Geldrop – awkward country for guns, the open ground marshy, with coppices giving good cover for snipers. The Ayrshire Yeomanry supported 3rd Mons with crash action targets fired on Toom, north-east of Hamont, and on Budel reached by 4 KSLI. The night of the 20th the advance battlegroups were altered. 3 RTR/3rd Mons with 23rd Hussars/8 RB were under command of 29 Brigade, and 2nd Fife and Forfarshire 1st Herefords with 4 KSLI/15/19th Hussars (on their return to the fold) were under command of 159 Brigade. 29 Brigade were directed north and 159 Brigade to Zomeren on the Willems canal, via Asten to

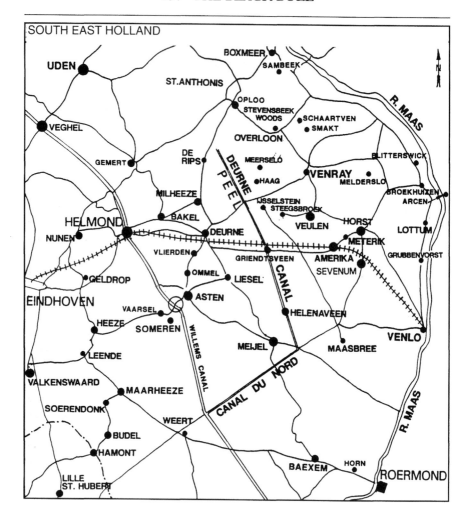

SOUTH EAST HOLLAND

Deurne with a view eventually of taking Helmond from the rear. On the 21st 8 RB found Geldrop a 'very friendly place'. Noel Bell's riflemen had time to dive into a local barber's and have a haircut and shampoo, but ran into determined resistance at Gerwen, where 23rd Hussar tanks and a carrier were brewed up.

At the hamlet of Stiphout, radio codename STRIPTEASE (for Jane of the *Daily Mirror*), C squadron ambushed a force of five Panthers on their way to reinforce Gerwen. Three were destroyed about 1630 hrs, and two Shermans were brewed up. Despite artillery and mortar stonks on Gernan, 107 Panzer Brigade defended stoutly – but evaporated during the night. A single 88 mm destroyed three RB carriers in the darkness. Roland Jefferson remembers: 'Some of our wounded pals who had caught their packet in the early days of Normandy rejoined 8 RB.' He did not mention what they thought of the Peel country.

Maarheeze had been cleared in the morning of the 21st by 3rd Mons and 3 RTR who then followed 23rd Hussars and 8 RB north via Nunen towards Geldrop. Later 3 RTR pushed on to Hout, south of Helmond. Meanwhile in the Zomeren area due east of Eindhoven, 1st Herefords, 2nd Fife and Forfarshire and 4 KSLI found the town bridges over the Bois le Duc Canal blown and covered by fire. Steel Brownlie's squadron spread along the Willems canal looking for a crossing: 'We worked south in thick country with a high bank on our side of the canal, making it difficult to see the far bank. We harboured near the Zomeren/Asten bridge with rain, shells and mortars coming down. We were shocked.' A daring plan had been hatched for the morrow: 'A and D Companies of the Herefords in assault boats had got across to make a bridgehead while the Sappers were starting to build a Bailey bridge. This was the cause of all the noise as dusk fell, for the enemy were obviously sensitive and were bombarding the area. The opposing force of Assault Engineers were reputed to be good fighters.'

An attack with two Herefords companies took place about 2100 hrs [explained Sergeant Frank Moppet, i/c carrier platoon 1st Herefords], against little opposition and the sappers started to erect a Bailey bridge. About 0200 hrs the Germans made a determined attack on our bridgehead with artillery and mortar fire. I was ordered to take my section on foot across the lock gates to support 'C' Company and cover the road about 500 yards towards Asten. The night was pitch black and machine-gun fire from the right flank was very worrying. About 0330 hrs a burst of fire brought down the overhead electric cables arcing and sparking along the road. From the screams we heard we were sure some of our lads were electrocuted. The Germans were coming closer, leading horses and calling 'Tommy surrender'. I threw six or seven grenades at them. All movement on the road stopped.

Defending their precarious bridgehead Reg Worton of the Herefords recalls how Joe Barnham's carrier was knocked off the bridge deep down to the bottom of the canal with its lights still visible under the water. And a shell sent shrapnel through his carrier engine, also hitting Battalion HQ wireless truck and wounding his mate Harry Hackett.

The General related:

By 2100 hrs two companies of Herefords had crossed. Our engineers began to construct a bridge and a searchlight battery had been brought up to give them a better light. At 0200 hrs the enemy pressed home a fierce attack on the bridgehead; work had to be stopped. The Herefords rallied, restored the situation. By morning the bridge was ready.

Major Mitchell, FOO Ayrshire Yeomanry, was in the tiny, beleaguered bridgehead and brought down 'ORANGE' defensive fire plan. Throughout the night the divisional artillery thundered down DF stonks while the poor Herefords suffered and had twelve killed. The dawn chorus fire plan was predictably called 'LEMON'.

At dawn on the 22nd Don Bulley with his three Fife and Forfarshire Shermans led the charge, followed by Steel Brownlie's 4 Troop and three KSLI carriers:

> Don Bulley was a fair-haired cheerful young man of about my age [21] who had a habit of singing to himself popular tunes like 'I'm just biding my time, that's the kind of guy I am . . .'. We motored over the bridge, through the little cluster of houses. Don had got about 50 yards beyond the last one when his tank disappeared in a cloud of smoke and flame. His second tank swerved to the right in an attempt to bypass over a field but it stuck fast in the ditch. His third tank tried to do the same to the left but also stuck. Me next. All I could see dead ahead was smoke and dust but this was no place to hang about, so we just drove on. There was a tremendous crash but the tank kept moving and emerged with a rush, still on the road. There were enemy infantry all over the place so I kept the guns firing and threw grenades out of the turret at random.

Captain Alec Wardman, 1st Herefords, was in the lock-keeper's house and saw Don Bulley's troop pass over the Bailey bridge: 'A few Germans had hidden in a culvert under the road. When the first [Fife] tank arrived the Jerrys drew a cable with mines on it over the road. Although we could see what was happening we fired on the Germans but it was too late.' Sergeant Frank Moppett recalls: 'the Germans attacked the tanks with bazookas and guns. Two tanks crewmen who tried to escape were killed.' Don Bulley was killed, as were five others.

John Prott was the OP tank driver to Captain Miller, Ayrshire Yeomanry, who took part in this daring charge:

> We married up with A squadron of the Fifes, tucked in behind Major Hutchinson. Bump on to bridge, lots of smoke, bump off bridge, houses on both sides of us, MG bullets rattling on the hull, first corner three tanks and one scout car knocked out, a Fife crewman lying injured on right of road. I kept my foot down, just missed him and the smoking tank on my left. Captain Miller ordered: 'Drive like hell, Prott.'

Halfway up the road to Asten, Steel Brownlie looked around: 'I was horrified to see that nobody was coming along behind. What the hell had happened?' So he charged flat out *tout seul* into Asten, hard left at the church to the objective on the north side of the village. Shortly he was joined by Corporal Vallance and they both opened fire with every weapon they had on a company of enemy infantry. When two KSLI carriers went forward they collected thirty-seven prisoners and found sixty dead. Altogether the Fifes lost four tanks and a scoutcar, and the KSLI two carriers. But it was a magnificent action.

Ned Thornburn, 4 KSLI recalls: 'The bridgehead had been 250 yards deep but the German counter-attack pushed it in to 30 yards when we were due to cross. Jimmy Bratland with the leading platoon, crossed over and with tank support and hand grenade actions extended the bridgehead to allow my other two platoons across.' And later, after Asten was captured: 'That day we took hundreds of prisoners with great help from the tanks.' The KSLI dug in north-east and south of the village to guard the roads and fended off counter-attacks with their 3-inch mortars. The Asten church was used as a first aid station and was full of wounded from both sides. Lance-Corporal George Perks, DR with the KSLI, recalled: 'The air was full of the smell of death and destruction. The streets were full of the dead.' Ned Thornburn and Jimmy Bratland both won MCs at the Zomeren/Asten battle.

The General wrote: 'Despite a lot of small arms fire, the foremost tanks were moving on towards Ommel by 0900 hrs. I was near the bridgehead at the time and was delighted to see this very dashing action.'

8 RB and 23rd Hussars took over from the Fifes at Ommel. Noel Bell reported: 'The Germans had been using cavalry in Ommel, so many dead horses littered the area. Hell was then let loose and the village came in for shelling and mortaring, the like of which we had not seen since Normandy. The Germans were using huge rocket mortars.' Among the RB casualties was their padre, Jeff Taylor, who was killed trying to locate some wounded and helpless Dutch children – as well as a French driver, M. Clermont, who had joined 8 RB earlier in the war and hoped to return to his liberated home in Northern France. A squadron 23rd Hussars were shelled and minnied in Ommel all day. At night there was some noisy 'relief'. Our tame 'Dr Goebbels wagon', consisting of loudspeakers mounted on a vehicle, appealed to the Panzer Grenadiers to surrender, promising in return food, rest and all the other attractions of a prisoner-of-war camp. Renderings of 'Lili Marlene' were more melodious but there appeared to be no wild rush of deserters.

On the same day 29 Brigade continued to clear the area between the Canal d'Embranchement and the Zuid Willems-Waal Canal. 3 RTR and G & H Batteries 13 RHA were in the outskirts of Helmond clearing the western approaches. 3rd Mons/3 RTR remained in the region of Gerwen and 23rd Hussars and 8 RB moved to a position on the Heeze–Zomeren road and collected thirty POWs, 'raw and lousy recruits, convalescents and ex-Marines fighting with obstinacy born of despair'.

23 September was a cold wet morning but Major Belmain and Captain Prestwich, 15/19th Hussars, tended their 'RHQ farm', milking the cows and feeding the pigs and chickens. Hussars like their creature comforts.

29 Armoured Brigade found considerable resistance across the Wilhemina Canal at Zomeren but 23rd Hussars and 8 RB led off at dawn towards Deurne via Liesel. At 1000 hrs 3rd Mons/3 RTR, who had moved south from Helmond, crossed the Zomeren bridge and advanced towards Liesel. South of Ommel on the Deurne road Major Mitchell, FOO Ayrshire Yeomanry, was astonished to see a group of mounted men approaching from the village. They were not farmers. They were 1944 'Uhlans', who charged the Fife's Shermans and were destroyed. A small revenge perhaps for the Polish lancers who charged the Nazi panzers in 1939–40.

Vlierden was cleared at midday by 23rd Hussars and 3 RTR converging on the town, having knocked out four A/Tk guns. On the Liesel road one Panther and two 88s were disposed of and by 1900 Liesel itself was reached by 3rd Mons/3 RTR. After his Asten bridge exploits Steel Brownlie rested in a nunnery, where he was offered fresh bread, basins and hot water for a wash.

The Jewish New Year, on 23 September, meant that Trooper Tony Matza, 2 Troop A squadron 23rd Hussars, was given dispensation to be LOB that day on account of his Jewish faith. However, he decided not to take advantage of the offer. He remembers that it rained most of the day, he was stonked outside his tank, fell over into a dungheap and was wounded in the back by airburst. He was sent back to hospital in the UK and his sister said that it was God's judgement on him for working at the Jewish New Year!

Sunday 24 September was another grey drenching day when 15/19th Hussars took over the defence of Liesel. They had some encounters with, and destroyed three 88-mm guns in close wooded country to the south-east, giving and taking casualties. Corporal E. Nicholls was told by his troop leader, Lieutenant Egerton, A squadron 15/19th Hussars: 'You lead today.' On the Deurne–Liesel road an 88-mm hit the Cromwell, bounced down, hit the road and ricocheted up into the engine. The next shot hit the turret. 'I thought, we have had it, shouted "Bale out", climbed on to the engine cowling and helped the wounded crew out.' Under fire Nicholls pulled troopers Angel, Brown and Burrows to safety. When Lieutenant Ireland, the commander of the follow-up troop, was hit and killed, Nicholls took charge and went back into battle.

A schoolteacher in the village of Zeulberg near Deurne gave Corporal Alastair Tait, RASC with 3rd Mons, a brooch from her dress and pinned it to his battledress – the first English soldier she had met. His section had collected twenty POWs and as the village was being mortared they all took shelter in a windmill owned by the Veltman family. Later the village was re-taken by the Germans. 8 RB were in Deurne and Roland Jefferson remembers: 'The great traffic jam, tanks, carriers, AFVs blocked the street and air-burst shells made life a bit dodgy.' By 1100 hrs 3 RTR had cut the Venlo–Helmond railway, entered Zeilberg and threatened the north-east sector of Deurne. In Vlierden the 'Goebbels wagon' sounded off and POWs came in. Four regiments had a hand in the capture of Deurne; 23rd Hussars and 3 RTR, with 8 RB and 3rd Mons clearing up by 1500 hrs. The Fifes took the lead and were passing through Deurne towards Bakel when Panthers brewed up several C squadron tanks and that of 'Brigham' Young, Ayrshire Yeomanry FOO. Steel Brownlie's troop harboured in a downpour of rain, were soaked to the skin, but comforted by mail from home and the rum ration. By coincidence Captain Norman Young, FOO 13 RHA, had his tank brewed by an AP shot on the Helmond road.

It was 25 September. The Guards Armoured had failed to relieve Arnhem. That was the first bad news of the day. The second horror on that day occurred at St Anthonis crossroads. Brigadier Roscoe Harvey, his Brigade major, Colonel David Silvertop (CO 3 RTR), and Colonel H.G. Orr (CO 3rd Mons) were meeting for an O Group. Two 'rogue' German half tracks were flushed out of hiding by 15/19th Hussars, made a bolt for safety and in the ensuing melée Silvertop and Orr were killed, and Harvey and the BM wounded. Both were well-respected veteran leaders. Noel Bell wrote of Colonel Silvertop: 'We had lost in him, as well as a very great commander, a personal friend who was admired and greatly liked by all ranks of G Company 8 RB.'

4 KSLI and 2nd Fife and Forfarshire pushed ahead on the Bakel road and reached Gemert, where they discovered four abandoned Panther tanks – one apparently set alight by its crew, another in a ditch, another with its engine damaged by a shell.

On the night of the 25th 15/19th Hussars reached St Anthonis after an impressive sunset which seemed to stain a brilliant backcloth of colour to the windmills, church spires and flat-dyked country, which for the first time seemed like the imaginary picture postcard Holland. It was to prove a delusion. The next day 15/19th Hussars found Boxmeer clear and some enemy infantry in Sambeek to the south. The recce troop captured a rare species – a German officer who proved of considerable intelligence value. From the 26th to the 28th 15/19th Hussars pushed and probed towards Overloon and Vortum, often heavily shelled and mortared, losing tanks, taking casualties, but giving as good as they got, including a Tiger tank.

At 1827 hrs on 25 September H Battery 13 RHA, in action along the Milheeze–Oploo road, fired a salvo into Germany, the first RHA regiment in the British Army and first regiment in 8 Corps to do this. It probably did very little damage!

1st Hereford with 159 Infantry Brigade cleared the woods round Helmond and entered the main town, and the Inns of Court put a patrol into Boxmeer on the River Maas. The General noted: 'At Cuijk south-east of Nijmegen, we joined up with 30 Corps. The Arnhem operation was over.'

For the time being the division halted in its tracks. The 23rd Hussars in De Rips, the Fifes at Rijkvoort and Handel, 8 RB at Judiths Hoeve and the rest of the Division round St Anthonis, Lamperstraat, Mortel and Gemert. For a week or so, rest, cleaning and maintenance took place. 'Liberty' trucks were sent into Helmond to cinemas and baths. Local concert parties were held, as were evening church services in converted barns. Steel Brownlie recced the Maas bank, observed the dark shape of the Reichswald, his first view of Germany, and was promoted, aged twenty, to captain. Football and basketball matches were played and a brisk barter trade with American troops produced fine sheepskin coats. There was even opportunity for countryside walks, and some twenty-four or forty-eight hour passes were granted for leave in Brussels. 13 RHA and Ayrshire Yeomanry stayed in action, with FOOs nesting in church towers. Targets were engaged on the strong German pockets of resistance around Overloon and Venray. In turn the enemy shelled Oploo, and Boxmeer was a no man's land occupied by the British during the day, the Germans at night. The 'Pocket' in the bend of the Maas opposite Venlo – a miserable peatbog known as Peel Land – would keep the Division engaged, one way or another, for the next few months.

On the 'other side of the hill', a sergeant in the German 712 Infantry Division kept this diary on the 'Der Englander' front in Holland:

13 Sep. '44. Near Bath a convoy has been shot up by fighter-bombers. We bandage the wounded and send them back. Some of the dead are so mutilated as to be unrecognizable. We are in a hell of a fine place . . .

25 Sep. '44. We march about 45 kms. Everybody is dead tired.

27 Sep. '44. The men are done. They are all old chaps.
Unnecessary marching and counter-marching is making them discontented. We have now been two days without food. Three companies attacked Hees. Only a few stragglers came back . . . Poor Germany.

28 Sep. '44. We are again fighting tanks with rifles. A fresh attack is to be mounted. Murder! I go back to my foxhole.

29 Sep. '44. About 5 p.m. we hear the noise of tanks coming towards us. One of the monsters comes up behind us. I take up my panzerfaust but the distance is too great. There is nothing left now but to surrender. The Britishers however are not taking any prisoners, but open fire on us. Four men are mown down at once. Now another tank rolls up on our left. We run along a ditch. Both tanks are firing all their guns. There will not be much left of our battalion.

CHAPTER SEVENTEEN

In the Bleak Midwinter: October

There was no doubt that the various German paratroop groups were going to defend their Fatherland with skill, tenacity and low cunning. Their first line of defence was the Peel country west of the River Maas, then the wide-flowing Maas river itself, and then finally a defensive fall back on the Rhine. They defended the dozen little villages with utmost bravery. Overloon, Venray, Oploo and others will long be remembered, not alas happily! They had excellent defensive positions and they made the attacking forces pay for every yard gained. The low cunning showed itself with the Teller and Schu mines. They were laid everywhere, frequently at night.

> German patrols had been laying mines in our area at Judiths Hoeve [wrote Noel Bell], and our first notification of this activity was when James Ramsden, Donald Sudlow and a troopleader of A squadron [Lieutenant Unwin] proceeded out on a reconnaissance in a carrier and went up on a mine, the troopleader being killed and Donald and James badly concussed. More mines were found nearby and were speedily neutralized.

> John Thorpe, 2nd Fife and Forfarshire noted: 'We were held up by a minefield and 3rd Mons, our infantry, were engaged poking out German wooden box mines with their bayonets before we could advance.'

Probing attacks by 23rd Hussars and 15/19th Hussars against Venray and Overloon in wooded, marshy countryside against 107 Panzer Brigade had been firmly resisted. General Roberts described the situation:

> 7th US Armoured were given the specific task of occupying Overloon and Venray. Major-General Sylvester came to see me soon after his arrival. He quite clearly thought his task was easy in spite of my warnings that the country was difficult and the enemy very determined. 'Oh!' he said, 'we'll turn on the heat and be down in Overloon in no time.' By turning on the heat he meant that he would call up their escorting Thunderbolts on anything that held them up and they would be in Venray in no time. I wished them luck but was not very hopeful. One of the troubles was that they had not experienced any positional fighting so far, but had arrived in time to assist in the 'gallop' across France.

So on 30 September the divisional artillery went into action south of Oploo, engaging many targets beyond Vortum and Lactaria. The US commander sent back a letter of appreciation, and then asked for more! A huge target, indicating red smoke shoot to guide the US Thunderbolts and RAF Typhoons, was fired across the Maas on enemy positions and the thick woods near Overloon. For five days the Americans put in a full divisional attack driving towards Venlo. The flat open land and woods were littered with the charred hulks of American Shermans and US artillery pieces. 'The KSLI', Ned Thornburn recalls, 'later found thirteen of their tanks knocked out *nose to tail* by a single 88-mm gun a couple of miles south of St Anthonis. The Americans' total progress was less than 3 miles in a week.'

They suffered considerable losses and on 4 October were heavily counter-attacked, needing three substantial DF targets fired by 13 RHA, Ayrshire Yeomanry and their own guns. On the 6th the Americans admitted defeat and moved to a sector between Deurne and Meijel. They referred to the divisional sign as a 'swell bison', were generous with their good humour, tinned chicken and bartered everything in sight – Lugers and SS daggers being in demand. 'You English are fighting for freedom, the Russians are fighting for Russia and we Americans are fighting for souvenirs,' said one American officer. 3rd Mons reported that the price for German Lugers sold to the Americans had settled down to a steady level of £5 each.

During the same week Noel Bell commanded Meijelforce, a mixed force of G Company and part of E Company 8 RB, a troop of 23rd Hussars and E troop Ayrshire Yeomanry. Their task from 3 October was to clear and hold the 'no man's land' village of Meijel, 8 miles south-east of Asten, and guard the Deurne canal to the east. The first three days were quite peaceful, but at 0515 hrs on 6 October a strong raiding party made a three-sided attack on the 25-pounder guns' positions, and Ayrshire Yeomanry took eight casualties including two officers killed. BSM Wilson eventually drove the attackers off with bren-gun fire. In the same week David Swiney's 119 Troop, 75 A/Tk, was placed in direct support of 1st Welsh Guards in a small hamlet enclosed by orchards near Veulen, 8 miles east of Deurne: 'The weather was foul, mud everywhere, we were shelled or mortared heavily several times a day. My SPs supported a company attack and fired newly arrived low velocity HE shells. The guns did not recoil property, so unloading had to be done by hand!' On the 9th the Herefords took prisoners for interrogation in a forested area near Overloon and raided German positions in Boot Wood.

German patrols were always active at night, laying mines across tracks, ambushing 'soft' vehicles including one RA truck with NAAFI stores. Troops going to Helmond on 'recreation' were possible targets at night. Morale sank a little with the arrival and issue of captured German rations, some fresh, some tinned, and all equally unpopular. Every BQMS, CQMS and SQMS was very low in the popularity stakes but eventually AFV and Compo packs came back. John Hooper's RASC unit was initially based in

H Troop 75 A/Tk Regiment RA firing at enemy pillboxes, Holland

Heeze, but on 3 October moved to Helmond, where it stayed for another eleven weeks. Bitter Army chocolate was popular with the children of Mijnheer and Mevrouw Eerenbeek. The Dutch family on whom Hooper and Co. were billeted had an evening meal of one small boiled potato, half an apple and a cup of hot water each!

On the 12th there was a colossal fireplan to support a new attack on Overloon and 13 RHA fired a barrage of 300 rounds per gun in a period of 170 minutes with no rests. Patrick Delaforce, I Battery, recalls: 'It was as ferocious a fireplan as anything we did in Normandy. It must have shattered the opposition in front of 3rd British.' And a few days later he was setting up an OP in front of the 15/19th Hussars near Oploo. Snow covered the tracks and a Teller mine brewed up his carrier:

Despite standing on thick sandbags, the force of the explosion directly under my driver – John Smith of Liverpool – tore him to pieces and threw me almost casually 20 yards away into the hedgerows. When I came to, perhaps twenty minutes later, the carrier was overturned and burning furiously. I looked for my driver among the carnage and found only fragments, limbs and khaki rags. Concussed, with broken rib, forearm and a paralysed leg, I crawled back some 300 yards along the snowy verges to the Hussars warming themselves by a brazier. By nightfall I was in Eindhoven hospital.

On 13 October General 'Pip' met King George VI at 8 Corps HQ and at this 'tea party' the top generals gossiped.

Clearing the Pocket was not getting very far, so a further operation, Constellation, was planned by 8 Corps. On 12 October 3 British Division and 6th Guards Tank Brigade (with Churchill tanks) were to try to take Overloon and advance south to Venray. To put the operation in perspective these were small Dutch towns held grimly by now highly experienced paratroopers, attacked by highly experienced infantry and armour, backed by immense artillery and air force fire power.

The follow-up second stage was to be by the 7th US Armoured, 15th Scottish and 1st Belgian Brigade. Initially 3 Division was to operate towards Overloon and Venray, as the Americans had tried and failed to do. 11th Armoured would pass through them and advance on Amerika to the right and Horst on the left in the direction of Venlo on the Maas. On 15 October 23rd Hussars/8 RB leading, were to cross the Deurne canal, push towards Venray from the east, bypass the town to the south and take the road to Venlo on the Maas. In desperate battles 3 Division plus the Guards' Churchills took Overloon on the 16th, Venray on the 17th, despite well-sited tanks, anti-tank guns, bazooka-men and schu-mines. Casualties were heavy.

The battlegroup of Herefords and 15/19th Hussars had started on the 14th at St Anthonis, then moved south to the outskirts of Overloon. There they stayed till the 15th when 159 Infantry Brigade, which included Herefords/15/19th Hussars and 2nd Fife and Forfarshire/4 KSLI, were switched to the west flank near Deurne to launch an attack to link up with 3 British Division. It was a wooded area with sandy ground and occasional sand dunes, and during the KSLI/Fife attack from Schaartven, 1 mile east of Overloon, in confused fighting the KSLI had thirty-five casualties. Sergeant George Eardley, A Company, carried out three brave actions against paratrooper MG posts under heavy fire and deservedly won the Victoria Cross. And Ned Thornburn's company first encountered the dreaded schu-mines, usually laid along road verges.

Noel Bell's G Company and B squadron 23rd Hussars crossed the canal south of De Rips on the 16th and minefields were cleared on the way to the hamlet of Haag. The next day, going to Weverslo, 'we ran into demolitions and the going was appalling, shelling added to the discomfort of mud and pouring rain'. The sappers put a scissors bridge over a canal but three tanks and a flail were well and truly bogged down. Everyone was drenched to the skin. On the 18th the RB/23rd Hussars group reached Heide, took a lot of prisoners and finally on the 19th entered the large village of Leunen without opposition.

In the same three days H Company 8 RB/C squadron 23rd Hussars, G Company 8 RB/A squadron 23rd Hussars fought their way to Merselo, south to Weversloo, east to Heijde and finally, on the 18th, into Leunen. Comic coded place-names were bandied over the radio, which certainly defeated Teuton listeners, and most of the British recipients too. Examples

Sergeant G.H. Eardley,
4 KSLI, who was awarded
the VC

were: Haag (Old Woman place), Heide (Colonel Gates, as in *ITMA*, the well-known radio programme), and Walle (Mrs Simpson). Colonel Perry Harding was the most inventive 'coder'.

The Herefords and 15/19th Hussars tried to pass through the US 7th Armoured bridgehead over the canal on the Deurne–Venray road, but were impeded by mines and nebelwerfers.

The Fife and Forfarshire/4 KSLI battlegroup was on the right flank. Steel Brownlie, who had just celebrated his twenty-first birthday, ate a boiled hen and played 'The lady is a tramp' in a squadron mess west of Boxmeer. At his lecture to his troop about 'non-fraternization' in Germany, a rude trooper uttered the immortal words: 'Fraternization? Blaw their bluddy heids aff.' Brownlie was LOB for Constellation and set up his HQ 'in a shrapnel-riddled metal shed beside which lay a tall, long-dead German. We put signal wire round his ankles, towed him into a slit-trench for burial. His helmet fell off, filled with maggots. I slept in a filthy hen house.' All the divisional tank crews were issued with the new tank suits which had zips, were warm and waterproof – ideal for the filthy winter conditions in the Peel

Country. From Deurne the Fifes and KSLI fought their way to Veulen by the 18th, where they lost seven tanks but brewed up several Panthers and SP guns and found another ditched and took 450 prisoners. B and C squadrons lost two troop leaders killed on the way, but A squadron were so heavily camouflaged with branches and foliage that they looked like Christmas trees, as in *Macbeth*: 'Till Burnham wood doth come to Dunsinane.' The Fifes took twenty-one casualties during Constellation.

Trooper John Thorpe's Sherman was hit south of Overloon by mortar bombs: 'They're getting very close, time to close the turret hatch or we'll be goners. At that moment they exploded on the tank. One on Robby's hatch alongside me, blowing in the periscope and its housing into his lap and pieces of shrapnel hitting me in the face, like being struck by a cricket ball.' That night he was evacuated to the Field Dressing station, then to Helmond Hospital and finally to No. 8 Military Hospital in Brussels. The Queen Alexandra nurses were in full dress uniform and Lady Mountbatten offered him a cake of soap!

Finally 3 RTR and 3rd Mons cleared the woods and main area around Ijsselstein, taking 250 prisoners. Since 15th Scottish Division were now required to move west for an attack on Tilburg, Operation Constellation started to grind to a halt. 29th Brigade held Leunen and 159 Brigade Veulen, but the Boche was determined to keep the Maas pocket for as long as possible. The unsung heroes of the Peel were, besides the FOOs, the sappers, who performed miracles with bulldozers, constructing a mile road of logs, clearing minefields and bridging and rebridging canals, usually under fire. The Germans were always aggressive and had mortars, bazooka-men, A/Tk guns, Panthers and minefields everywhere, which made every advance in teeming rain over swamps, an absolute nightmare. Four cooks with 159 Brigade HQ had been killed in their beds by a bloody-minded Paratroop patrol. Jack Lockyer wrote:

> 612 Field squadron built a 1½ mile log road to Veulen, under constant observation and stonking on the working parties. No wonder it took a week to build. We erected a large notice: 'Veulen – One-Mile (Hope you get there quicker than we did)' with the Black Bull 41 signs. One of our bigger problems was getting in-fill for roads, so our bulldozers knocked down damaged farmhouses for material. We even hired and paid for a vintage Dutch steamroller operated by Sergeant Robbins for work on the main centre-line from Deurne to Venray. We also converted the railway line from Deurne to Amerika into a 'new' road. We had problems, however, when our very heavy armoured dozers and AVREs got bogged down, usually the rescuer got bogged down too!

A Canadian forestry squadron cut down 10,000 trees and the new log road was finished by 25 October. The railway line had been heavily mined with Tellers and Schumines, so a special mine-sniffing dog troop was

The notice that 612 Field Squadron built under fire

employed, with great success. The dogs got bored quickly, so dummy mines were laid to enliven their ennui!

3rd Mons spent five weeks from 18 October to 23 November in the front line, sharing duties where possible with 3 RTR. During the first two weeks at Leunen/Heide/Scher they were often only 200 yards from the enemy line. The battalion snipers were kept busy and patrolling took place every day, as well as mine laying, mine lifting and booby-trapping. The next two weeks were spent at Veulen, and the last week at Ijsselstein, opposing the battlegroups Hubner, Grassmehl and Hardegg. They found the Germans far superior in all mining techniques with the brutal schu-mines, trip-wired traps and fuses. A minor comfort was the Dutch farmhouses, well stocked with bottled preserves and cherries. The Herefords spent three weeks in Ijsselstein defending the Grientsveen bridgehead with occasional short rest spells in Deurne. Reg Worton was asked by a farmer to end the suffering of four cows and a horse wounded by shrapnel: 'I shall never forget the way they looked at me as I shot them. Then the farmer cut their throats.' Near Gruberost on the Maas, Reg's platoon lived off chicken, turkey, eggs and pork, all cooked on a Jerry petrol blowlamp; 'and we had bottled pears and plums for afters'.

On the 19th 15/19th Hussars had one of their toughest actions of the war, operating south across marshy orchard country towards Amerika. Ted Deeming recalls meeting groups of static 88-mm A/A guns covering roads bordered by flat marshland and large dykes, so tanks could not manoeuvre off the roads. Eleven Cromwells were put out of action either by 88s, bazookas or the Peel mud, but five were recovered. In the process a tank and four 88s were destroyed and St Petrus Hoeve captured. During Constellation 15/19th Hussars suffered thirty-three casualties.

For a few more weeks 3 RTR and KSLI resided in Veulen, 23rd Hussars in Leunen, Fife and Forfars and 15/19th Hussars around Ijsselstein.

Two 13 RHA FOOs, Captains Garry Davidge and Bill Budgen, remained in Leunen church tower for a month picking out targets, while their German opposite number in the church spire in Amerika did the same thing. Life in Leunen and Veulen, according to the 23rd Hussar historian, resembled a scene from the First World War's *Journey's End*. Everyone, apart from the FOOs, went underground or into a room on the safe side of a very thick house with a tank drawn up to the window. Troopers stayed in muddy holes under tanks and infantry converted pigsties and built log cabins. Frequently German patrols would get right into Leunen and Veulen at night. Noel Bell, OC G Company 8 RB, was responsible for the defence of Leunen. One platoon consisted of cooks, fitters, storemen and clerks: 'This gallant band of warriors did great work in their most unpleasant position and, at times, enjoyed it all.' Dutch spies with radios sent back information that produced pin-point enemy stonking. Roland Jefferson was hit by a mortar bomb fragment and his mate, Corporal Norris, was killed instantly. Roland went to the military hospital in Brussels, then Dieppe and Rouen, but eventually rejoined the battalion five weeks later.

Major Leith, Fife and Forfarshire, noted: 'Never-ending rain and mud, the Boche night patrols, stonks on Dead Horse Corner, squadron shoots on Amerika. As to Veulen itself as the weeks went by it became more and more battle-weary, ultimately becoming wholly repulsive. Livestock set off tripwires in the night. The place was littered with dead horses, cattle – an awful stench.'

On the morning of the 27th, battlegroups from 9th Panzer and 15th Panzer divisions launched a severe counter attack on the hapless 7th US Armoured Division 10 miles south. They quickly recaptured Meijel, 8 miles south-east of Asten, and were pushing strongly towards Helmond and Deurne. So 15/19th Hussars and 1st Herefords, plus borrowed 2nd East Yorks from 3 Division, were sent to help. Reg Horton recalls how the Herefords' front around Amerika was taken over by 'the Yanks who came with a full battalion, stacks of artillery, ice-cream cart and cinema, and Jerry took it off them in two days'. Even 15th Scottish were hauled back from the capture of Tilburg to help block this counter-attack, which had retaken Liesel on the 29th. 2nd Army HQ at Helmond, only 7 miles from Asten, were quite startled, as were Corps, Division and Brigade HQs! 13 RHA and Ayrshire Yeomanry fired several DF fire plans to help relieve the Americans – codenames DAINTY and DRAKE – and by the 30th the counter-attack had been repelled, and Liesel and Meijel rather painfully recovered.

CHAPTER EIGHTEEN

In the Bleak Midwinter: November

Peter Reeve, Inns of Court, remembered the Maas winter. Like the rest of the division the 'Devil's Own' were to spend the winter in alternating periods of luxury and discomfort: 'like hounds on a leash the opposing forces growled menacingly at each other across the River Maas'. C squadron commuted between Helmond, Beck, Gun, Legert, Asten and Maaseyck. The Blitz troop had two encounters, one of which they lost, and the other – beating off a night attack – they won. Dismounted winter guard over isolated farmhouses in the mud, rain and freezing cold was not for the fainthearted. Most front line tasks were rotated on a weekly basis.

The KSLI spent twenty-one days in Veulen. Ned Thornburn wrote:

More shells fell in the battalion area than we had faced at any time since the Odon bridgehead; we lost seventeen men killed without a yard of ground gained. There was not much romance about Veulen. Each time the heavy mortars of the Northumberland Fusiliers were fired, the Germans replied. The weather had deteriorated, there was mud everywhere and it was very cold. We looked forward to the rum ration every morning.

On 4 November 8 RB were relieved by 5 Coldstream Guards, 4 KSLI by 1 Welsh Guards and 4 Grenadier Guards, and vice versa on the 11th. On the 19th 8 RB were relieved by a battalion of 9 Brigade, 3 British Division. The 15/19th Hussars spent the first nineteen days on the 'Veulen' roster. Reinforcements arrived, and there was some reorganization and training in increasingly wet, cold, stormy days. When 8 RB were out of the line they moved north to Hathert, south of Nijmegen. They became temporary members of Guards Armoured: 'No sign of war, no damaged houses, no shell holes, no noise,' wrote Noel Bell, 'a most welcome change. Cinemas, ENSA shows, football, balls and clubs were all laid on.' Back in the line 'Weasels', small nippy tracked vehicles, brought up supplies across the Peel marshland. Gumboots and leather jerkins arrived. Tankies wore their new pixie suits. Patrick Delaforce, FOO 13 RHA, with some friendly Canadian airborne troops acquired a naval duffle coat for stonks rendered. Dutch pigs, turkeys and chickens had a high mortality rate. Their legal owners had been pushed out, either for their own protection, or because of suspected espionage. A pot roast was ideal for the Peel winter. The 23rd Hussars chased one pig down the road to Horst, straight into the arms of the Germans. One third of the 23rd Hussars went to Helmond for five days' leave, as well as to Antwerp and Brussels. Ned Thornburn wrote: 'The KSLI were in Griendtsveen [previously held by 7th US Armoured]. We were there for fourteen days. It was even more depressing than Veulen because it was even more water-logged. We were shelled and mortared quite heavily at regular intervals throughout the day, as if the Bosches were anxious to demonstrate that they were still there. But the mud deadened the bangs!'

The divisional artillery west of Ijsselstein were in action most days with small shoots and support of 1st Herefords or 4 KSLI at Griendtsveen, Welsh Guards south-east of Veulen, Inns of Court, or any other front line unit; occasionally AOB (airburst), counter-battery, targets on nebelwerfer areas, smoke screens for patrols and propaganda leaflets fired at dusk.

Nutcracker was the name of the 8 and 12 Corps operation which started on 19 November, to close out the remaining pockets west of the Maas. 3 Division would take over the Veulen–Leunen front, 29 Armoured Brigade would concentrate around Deurne and 159 Infantry Brigade, with 15/19th Hussars and 2nd Fife and Forfarshire under command, would attack Griendtsveen. D-Day was put back to 22 November, but conditions were so bad that the leading A squadron of 15/19th Hussars was bogged down head to tail in the veritable swamp of mud along the double road to Amerika. The only movement was along the famous log track made by the Sappers. 4 KSLI started at 0700 hrs, 1st Herefords at 0740 hrs, and Amerika was occupied at 1230 hrs. Still unchallenged they moved on a further 2 miles north-east to Meterik and Schadijk. The main deterrents were schu-mines, booby traps and mud. Mike Sayer, commanding Ned Thornburn's D company 4 KSLI (Ned had diptheria at the time and had been evacuated) had an appalling march through a minefield:

A series of explosions and within two minutes about eight men were lying on the ground with their feet blown off by schu-mines, small wooden mines looking like cigar boxes, impossible to see in the rough heathy ground. How do you extricate fifty men including the dead and wounded from an extensive minefield without incurring even more casualties? It was a nightmare. We did an 'about turn' and retraced our steps. It was a terrifying experience knowing that every step might prove fatal. The casualties were evacuated by Weasel.

Churchill and Sherman tanks slipped sideways into ditches and the recovery tank would then also get bogged down. The mobile Bailey bridges over craters fell out of kilter so permanent Baileys were needed. The Sappers brought up more and more equipment to try and keep traffic moving down the appalling roads. All rations had to be brought up 6 miles to the lead troops on foot. Never had an army crossed the Heide before, and the Dutch said it was an impossible feat. B squadron 23rd Hussars and a Churchill flail troop advanced in single file. Mines, an enemy SP and spandaus caused losses of men and tanks on the way to Erika Hoeve. Captain Blackman spent two days recovering the derelict tanks in the middle of a thick minefield. Shades again of the First World War, he found the German defences had a comprehensive network of underground tunnels, with alternative positions for spandau and mortars, surrounded by more than seventy mines. Outflanked by 15th Scottish, the Germans had skilfully withdrawn. As the 23rd Hussar historian wrote: 'a miniature classic of a delaying action in the face of superior strength'. The divisional artillery now supported 15th Scottish, who were attacking Horst until the 27th. On the road to Amerika Reg Worton, with the Herefords, raced his carriers round and round the fields to set off the deadly schu-mines:

Later I saw Jerry helmets in the window of a house. I yelled out at the top of my voice, jumped out, ran round the side of the house, bumped into two of them. They turned round, one with a Schmeisser. I pulled it out of his hand and sent them both to my crew. The German sergeant was running to a zig-zag trench. I shouted, he never turned, so I shot him. I was armed with a Yankee repeating rifle I had had since St Lô. I must have been on a high, that's the honest truth. My lads had their watches.

On the 23rd 4 KSLI were joined at Schadijk by the Herefords, but two days later returned to Deurne for three days' rest before relieving 7 Seaforths on the 28th at Houthuizen and Grubbenvorst, 2 miles north of the Venlo pocket.

On the 28th Patrick Delaforce had his twenty-first birthday 'party' in his Sherman OP tank sited in the courtyard of a large tannery OP on the banks of the Maas. His Canadian airborne 'friends' had caused so much havoc on their night raids that retaliation with airburst and mortars was inevitable. His whisky supply held out – just!

General 'Pip' wrote:

We took over a sector of the Maas from Blitterswijk and Grubbenvorst just north of Venlo. There were still a few German outpost positions on the west bank. One of these was Broekhuizen and its fortress or 'Kasteel'. Clearly we had to tidy this up and to do this 3rd Mons supported by 15/19th Hussars, plus two troops of flail tanks launched an attack [on the 30th] supported by our divisional artillery.

On the 19th 3rd Mons had moved from Ijsselstein north to Mook near Nijmegen in reserve to the Guards. They noted that the Dutch beer was rather weak compared to their usual Welsh brews. Four days later they had a few days' rest at Asten before moving into position between the hamlets of Lottum and Homberg. Unfortunately the Cameronians whom they were relieving, although they had had their attack repulsed the day before, seemed sure that the 'Kasteel' and the village of Broekhuizen were lightly held. Major L. Moody, then 2 i/c 3rd Mons, took part in the ill-fated attack. He recalls:

The enemy garrison of fanatical SS parachute cadets were in the 'Kasteel', a fortified, moated farmhouse with battlements and drawbridge [which] was protected by heavy minefields, a thick circular crescent of pinewoods on the west side and by artillery and mortars from the east side of the river. Flail tanks from the Westminster Dragoons led to clear a gap in the minefields from the south. A company led with the objective of taking the 'Kasteel', with C company to follow through and take Broekhuizen village. B company under command of Major Joe How would attack from the north-west towards the village. C squadron 15/19th Hussars would support 3rd Mons from the south and B squadron from the north-west. The artillery barrage started on plan at dawn to support the combined attack. The Ayrshire Yeomanry FOOs, Major Mitchell and Captain Caffyn, in their Shermans were in the thick of the battle. The flail tanks were destroyed and B company was pinned down by heavy fire from the 'Kasteel' and unexpectedly heavy 150-mm fire from across the river. B company lost all its officers, took many casualties and did not move again. C company followed through and was caught at a house just east of the 'Kasteel'. It too was pinned down by heavy fire and also suffered heavy losses, and lost prisoners. This awful stalemate lasted for many hours until the combined C squadron 15/19th Hussars and Major How's company burst into action. HE was fired point-blank into the Kasteel, but Colonel R.C. Stockley was killed near the drawbridge leading an attack.

Colonel Taylor of the 15/19th Hussars now took charge of the battle and after ferocious fighting in face of minefields, shelling, AP fire and intense small arms fire, finally by last light took the village. Although the Germans lost 112 prisoners and had the same number killed, many escaped across the river. The Mons A and C companies had 140 casualties, including 27 killed. It was a terrible day for the Mons. On the following day Ted Deeming, signals rear link 15/19th Hussars viewed the field of battle at close range:

The dead still lay where they died in the orchard near the Kasteel, a few German but many 3rd Mons. The weapons of the British dead had been retrieved. Some of the dead lay stiff in the prone position with their arms forward as if clutching their rifles. Some expressions were of pain and shock and some of sheer surprise. There's not much dignity to violent death.

It was a shattering blow to the regiment and brigade. The Mons had lost two COs in a matter of weeks (Lieutenant-Colonel Orr had been killed at St Anthonis) as well as many experienced officers and men. A and C companies virtually no longer existed. The stricken battalion was withdrawn to Horst until 17 December to absorb reinforcements.

CHAPTER NINETEEN

In the Bleak Midwinter: Leave

Patrick Delaforce liked Brussels. He had three rather unfair advantages. Both times he was wounded he arranged to be received at the Red Cross and St John Hospital (No. 1 Officers Convalescent Home) near Waterloo. For walking wounded this was a marvellous base. Secondly, his father was on the SHAEF HQ in Avenue Louise, with a staff car, attractive FANY, etc. Thirdly, his command of French was more than adequate. Although Guards Armoured reckoned they 'owned' Brussels, the various Black Bull clubs there had a non-stop welcome, often provided by the pretty young Belgian ladies. The photograph of the author with Belgian FANY Marie Deschamps was taken in the Boulevard Adolf Max. Her family owned the largest factory manufacturing mattresses in Belgium. 13 RHA thought that was quite funny. In the nightclubs he would ask the band leader to play 'Lili Marlene', the famous desert tune beloved by both opposing armies. The band leader would usually plead ignorance of a *German* song, which of course he had been playing every night for the last four years. In any case how could the British actually like a Teutonic tune. Forceful logic always produced a spirited rendering – 'Underneath the lamp post . . .' .

David Swiney, 75 A/Tk, had twenty-four hours' leave at the end of October. He met three old schoolmates in uniform, visited the bistro Le Cerf in the Grand Place, drank champagne and crooned songs into the microphone, unappreciated by band or vocalists. Steel Brownlie's leave started on 26 October:

> I saw A squadron off into action – with a grin on my face, for I was bound for leave in Brussels. Eric Lamont and I took turns driving the 3-ton leave truck, sometimes getting up to 60 mph on the flat and getting there in four and a half hours. With pee-halts and the roads as they were, this was pretty good. We found ourselves in Heaven. Hotel Plaza, hot bath, afternoon tea, waiters lighting matches when you produced a cigarette. Eric needed a soft seat as he had six or seven bits of shrapnel in his bottom, but we went everywhere, bought souvenirs, ate pounds of fruit, gloried in the comforts of the city.

> Rifleman Kingsmill, 8 RB, wrote: 'What is it that makes the girls of Paris and Brussels so attractive and exciting? Not mere beauty but an indefinable

Patrick Delaforce and Marie
Deschamps, Brussels,
November 1944

something that is not to be found among the women of any other city in the
world. And the Black Market! Luxuries of all types can be had in plenty.
Champagne and silk stockings of course.'

On his second visit to Brussels in late November, Steel Brownlie, back
from a Comet tank indoctrination course, entered the town in a small van
crammed full with three large Guards sergeants and stayed at the
Metropole, said to be the largest hotel in Europe with 600 beds. He and Bill
Peterkin then drank 14 pints of beer each at the Villevorde Rhu: 'a great
evening out'. Reg Worton and his Hereford mates visited the capital from
Hacht and went to a sex exhibition.

General 'Pip' took forty-eight hours leave and went to Brussels for a
couple of nights. He stayed with Bobbie Erskine, who having lost command
of 7th Armoured Division, was in command of the rear area based in
Brussels: 'I also visited our officers' club which had been set up by the A/Q
(Geoffrey Thwaites), and was most excellently run. Mary Churchill, serving
with an AA regiment, came to dine with us in the Club, later in our Officers'
Mess, a delightful and charming person.'

CHAPTER TWENTY

In the Bleak Midwinter: December

The good news was that the three armoured regiments were withdrawn from the front line to start going back to the rear area to change their Sherman tanks for new British Comets which had thicker armour and mounted a new high velocity 77-mm gun. Indeed 2nd Fife and Forfarshire had moved back to Deurne to become familiar with Cromwells, which were first cousins to the new Comets. The bad news was that 159 Infantry Brigade, plus 8 RB, 15/19th Hussars, Inns of Court and the three artillery regiments, were to continue the winter vigil along the Maas. With the last pockets painfully squeezed out, the river barrier would act as a temporary boundary line. The river was very swollen from heavy rains and even a crossing by rowing boat would have been hazardous. On 2 December the Germans cut the dykes in Holland, Metz was taken on the 13th and Antwerp started to suffer from V-bombs.

G Company 8 RB produced a spectacular fire at their Melderslo HQ (petrol apparently looks like water on some occasions) and the neighbouring 159 Brigade HQ was unamused when Boche shelling directed at the conflagration landed unexpectedly close. Roland Jefferson, back with 8 RB after his 'Blighty', found his mates again stationed at Broechuizervorst, a hamlet on the river. Intermittent shelling, spandau fire and night patrols across the river in collapsible boats were part of the routine. Coming back one night, Roland's platoon commander declared the password to the look-out: 'Mother Goose'. To which the look-out replied: 'Lucky I know your voice, Sir, "Mother Goose" was yesterday.' 8 RB swapped weekly with 1st Herefords, who were guarding Houthuizen, and their mortar sections had almost daily stonks on the village of Lomm on the German side of the river.

The 7th Field Dressing Station was settled in a convent in Helmond. Padre Christopher Mackonochie suggested to his CO, Major Desmond Murphy, that the unit organize a Christmas party for the local children. The traditional occasion is St Nicholas Day on 6 December. Funds were raised and loads of toys and gifts were purchased in Brussels. A co-operative Quartermaster, a supportive Captain John Wilson, RAMC, and an enthusiastic Staff-Sergeant Eustace, conjured up some wonderful food, an issue of medical comforts from reserves (for whom, the nuns or the party sponsors?), even an iced Christmas cake. A decorated stretcher loaded with

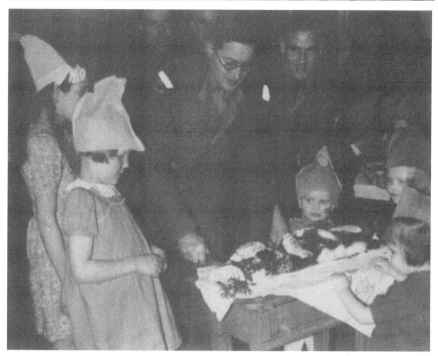

Children's Christmas party, given by 7 FDS (RAMC), Helmond, 1944

gifts served as a sleigh for the arrival of St Nicholas, accompanied by the traditional Black Peter. It is probable that the men of 7 FDS enjoyed themselves as much as the sixty or seventy joyful and happy children of Helmond.

Meanwhile Lieutenant-General O'Connor left for India and Lieutenant-General E.H. Barker, formerly GOC 49 Division, became GOC 8 Corps. And 11th Armoured Division had three GSO 1s in the space of a month! The General and CRA visited regiments in the first two weeks and presented medals. Steel Brownlie was told about his MC gained in August at Vire. Afterwards he wrote: 'I've always been suspicious of citations, preferring personal versions of how one got a gong. Mine is that I stayed out all night. Houston Shaw Stewart's is that he got lost. David Veitch's was "We were all running away at the time, but I fell."' Patrick Delaforce was given a Dutch medal: 'I brought a regimental target down on top of myself as well as on some unlucky Inns of Court.' Four Ayrshire Yeomanry FOOs were awarded MCs for the Perrier ridge actions in Bluecoat, and MMs were presented to Sergeant 'Curly' Brettle and Sergeant Wright of 75 A/Tk Regiment.

On 9 December Steel Brownlie led 2nd Fife and Forfarshire advance party back into Belgium: 'Diest, Louvain, Brussels where Jimmy Samson and I had a good lunch in a civvy restaurant with steak and chips about 18*s* 6*d* each, Oudenaarde, then it should have been Courtrai, only I map-read us to Roubaix instead – France instead of Belgium. Maybe it was the lunch. We got to Ypres in the evening.' 23rd Hussars moved to Geldrop on the 10th and were billeted in a vast bulb factory among over two million electric light bulbs. On the 14th the three armoured regiments motored to Brussels, left their Shermans there and moved back to Ypres. A change of mind now sent 8 RB on the night of the 16th off on the long trek back to Poperinghe, having handed over their front to the Warwicks – friends from Perrier Ridge battles. 'We were going to have a slap-up Christmas and really enjoy ourselves' enthused Noel Bell. The 23rd Hussars historian wrote: 'The Regiment arrived in extremely comfortable quarters in the historic town of Ypres where the hospitality of the citizens boded well for our immediate future. It was certainly a great change from De Rips, Leunen and Isselsteijn.' RHQ lived in a chateau and the old Cloth Hall was used as a Mess room. The Fifes tried to match up the billeting 'partners' in Ypres: Steel Brownlie over a café, the logically minded squadron leader, Pinkie Hutchinson, with a lawyer, Desmond Chute with a wine merchant. 'Years later my gunner, Buck Buchanan, stated that we billeted him and the rest of my crew in a brothel, but if so it was certainly not deliberate!' Roland Jefferson's unit was billeted in a school at Poperinghe. 'We settled into these warm surroundings where we were going to enjoy the best Christmas we had ever known.' While 29 Armoured Brigade were on the brink of Paradise in Ypres, the rest of the division moved again. On the 17th 3 British Division took over and 11th replaced 53 Welsh Division on the Maas 'frontier' opposite Roermond, and south to Maesyck, some 25 miles to the south-east. 8 Corps, which still included 159 Brigade, plus borrowed 4 Armoured Brigade, were to hold the entire 2nd Army front on the Maas from Cuyk in the north to Maesyck in the south. The Inns of Court were again much in demand, holding isolated farmsteads around Maesyck.

Signalman Roy Gillespie mended broken telephone cables damaged by mortar bombs and maintained no fewer than thirty 19 sets in the field. Laying lines through woods, frozen dykes and minefields was an unpleasant necessity in the winter river 'watches'.

15/19th Hussars had their RHQ at Kelpen, A squadron at Leveroi, and B and C squadrons at Baexem. It was during this week of cold, foggy weather that von Runstedt's dramatic offensive started in the Ardennes (Chapter 21) 15/19th Hussars celebrated their traditional Sahagun day on 21 December, with sports in the morning and considerable quantities of food and drink consumed in the afternoon and evening.

13 RHA's guns were at Neeritter on the north-east tip of Belgium, fending off German patrols, in and out of action in support of all and sundry including 3 British Division, losing a man here and there. Modified festivities – much pork but little liquor – marked the regiment's first and only Christmas overseas.

German positions and mortar batteries across the river were constantly engaged. The LAA brought down a stray Messerschmidt, and 75 A/Tk RA laid aside their guns and acted as infantrymen from the 25th. 338 Battery took over from D Company 1st Herefords at Haelensch Broek. David Swiney's troop defended a farm at Geystingen in thick fog and snow, and laid more wire and trip flares: 'From an OP in a barn we could see the Germans on the far side of the river. Our part of the front was pretty quiet with occasional shelling, with patrols being carried out at night by the Inns of Court and by the enemy.'

The first noisy German jet planes were now heard and seen and disliked – the 'moaning minnies' of the air.

4 KSLI occupied Lottum and Broekhuizen for the first half of December. The 'Kasteel' proved to be a comfortable company HQ for D company with A company nearby in Lottum. On the 16th 2 KSLI from 3 Division relieved them and 4 KSLI moved to 159 Brigade rest area at Baexem. 'Rain fell almost continuously,' wrote Kemp, their historian, 'and the battalion's Weasels churned all tracks into a sea of mud.'

D company 4 KSLI had a short spell out of the line in a small inhabited village. 'This was a tonic for the troops who in the evenings, except for those on guard duty, spent time in people's cottages. I could hear animated conversation,' noted Captain Mike Sayers, 'the language barrier not apparently causing much difficulty.' Many lifelong Dutch friends were made by the Division during the winter of 1944. 'On Christmas Day the talented musicians in No. 7 platoon played, with local civilians joining in. We had a good time,' recalls Corporal Bob Bignell.

3rd Mons relieved their sister regiment, 2nd Mons of 53 Welsh Division, on the 17th and took over a front line near the river with the three hamlets, Beegden, Heel and Panheel, south of Roermond. It was a 4,000-yard stretch and included an artificial island which needed a permanent guard in three lock-houses. At its narrowest the Maas, in full spate, was 100 yards across. The Germans naturally had commandeered all the available boats, making their night patrols more effective. The Mons Christmas lunch was, however, up to scratch – tinned turkey, roast potatoes, green peas, brussels sprouts, Christmas pudding and beer. They stayed there, still licking their wounds from Broeckhuizen, until 8 January, and then moved 3 miles west to Baexem, and out of the line.

The Herefords spent ten days from the 17th in the Horn sector, north-west of Roermond, where enemy cross-river patrols were particularly aggressive. In between training and integrating reinforcements from the RASC, CMP and the RAF, Ken Crockford, 1st Herefords, led a patrol to Hatenboer on 26–27th. During the fighting their ammo ran out and their CO said on the phone: 'If you are taken prisoners I know you will all uphold the best traditions of the British Army.' Fortunately the 4 KSLI arrived in time! They celebrated their Christmas belatedly on the 27th in the reserve area at Baexen, where they stayed peacefully until 21 January.

In the last week of December Recce Troop and HQ squadron 15/19th Hussars relieved the Herefords opposite Roermond. The weather became cold, crisp and sunny and ice on various ponds and meres was used for skating and ice hockey. Those with (shot)guns frightened the local birds, and visits to Weert and Eindhoven for cinemas and concerts were the main entertainment.

The Ayrshire Yeomanry fired a rather bloody-minded fire-plan, SANTA, on the 23rd to disrupt enemy arrangements for Christmas, and in heavy frost had their festive dinner on Christmas Eve. Tinned beer prompted toasts and speeches – and the strains of 'Loch Lomond' and 'Annie Laurie' rang out. But SOS tasks were fired on enemy patrols infiltrating the Herefords' lines intent on disrupting their Noel. FOOs reported on Christmas Day that similar celebrations were evidently in progress on the enemy side of the river.

CHAPTER TWENTY-ONE

The Ardennes

'Then the incredible happened,' wrote Lieutenant-General Horrocks, 'The telephone rang and the voice of a senior staff officer at General Dempsey's 2nd Army HQ said: "The Germans have smashed through the American front in the Ardennes and the situation is extremely confused."' So too were the armoured regiments. Comet tanks had been collected from Menin and firing ranges and shoots had been organized at Gravelines with 'overs' falling in German-held Dunkirk. A team of instructors were doing the dirty work supervising gunnery lessons with the Comets. The bombshell fell on the 20th. 21st Army Group in Brussels ordered 29 Armoured Brigade to get back in action with their battered old Shermans and act as 'long-stop' to fend off 6th SS Panzer Army now thrusting for Liège and 5th Panzer on its left flank heading via Namur and Dinant for the seizure of Antwerp. On 21 December Steel Brownlie wrote:

> We were to move to the Ardennes soonest. Forget the Comets, leave all heavy kit behind, pick up old Shermans in Brussels, get to the Meuse and help stop von Runstedt. Advance party to leave at 1330 hrs, self for A squadron, Jimmy for B squadron – all in scout cars. Cup of coffee in Aalst, Brussels in turmoil, population very scared. It was cold and pouring with rain, V-1s were passing overhead, very depressing.

Ted Harte, commanding A squadron 23rd Hussars, had his HQ in Ypres in a small comfortable hotel only yards from the famous Menin gate: 'To my surprise the Last Post was still sounded every evening.' 23rd Hussars completed the fastest move they had ever been asked to make. 'That night we harboured in the streets of Brussels near the Second Armoured Reinforcement Group, where we were to collect once more the tanks we had handed in only a week before,' noted the regimental historian. 8 RB had almost burned Poperinghe down when a petrol tanker containing 600 gallons caused the greatest conflagration Noel Bell, Roland Jefferson and the local burghers had ever seen. Nevertheless: 'We had only been in the place for three nights and yet scores of firm friendships had been made, many of which live to this day.'

The Brigade had been allocated a 40-km north–south stretch of the River Meuse to defend. 23rd Hussars were to guard the bridge at Givet (France), 2nd Fife and Forfarshire that at Namur and 3 RTR at Dinant. 8 RB were to lead the advance and establish the three vital bridgeheads, H with 23rd Hussars, G with 3 RTR, F with 2nd Fife and Forfarshire. The first night was spent harboured near Waterloo south of Brussels, despite a rather strange CMP routing. Noel Bell noticed: 'Signs of the alarm and despondency caused by the German offensive were already evident. Reinforcement holding units were all standing-to manning road blocks. In the city itself the "Whitehall Warriors" were packing their bags and preparing to evacuate themselves and probably their girlfriends too, to safer climes.'

Steel Brownlie harboured in Belgrade, a suburb of Namur, and parked his tanks in a street of brick-built houses. A delightful damsel served the Fifes with a four-course meal, but unfortunately she had a large policeman husband who arrived from late shift, and a baby daughter in the back room. 'You can't win them all!'

8 RB found a hastily assembled scratch force defending the bridges, which were wired for demolition: American Air Service Corps (non-combatant), American police, a platoon of American infantry. Noel Bell became OC forces at Dinant. His most appalling responsibility was that of deciding if and when to blow the vital bridges, leaving as many friends as foes on the far side. 3 RTR eventually arrived and occupied the high ground a few miles behind Dinant. When 23rd Hussars arrived at Givet they found there an American reinforcement camp which included some 101 Airborne troops. They had made no arrangements for defending the bridge, and no slit trenches or positions had been prepared. Few weapons were to be seen and queueing up for the cinema was their main preoccupation. The Hussars discovered: 'Mice had got at their abandoned Shermans. Some had no wireless sets, or sets that did not work, or the machine-guns were missing.' Some tanks broke down on the way to Givet via Charleroi, but they arrived – a good fighting unit – within thirty-six hours of their warning order in Ypres. On arrival every tank was whitewashed as snow-camouflage. Reliable information was sparse. German soldiers dressed in American uniforms had been 'seen'. A brigade of captured American Shermans were manned with German crews. Various minor bridges, road and rail between the three towns were reputedly unguarded. Refugees and American 'soft' traffic were streaming across the vital bridges. Carrier pigeons were taken on strength to pass back crucial messages. An American full Colonel from SHAEF visited Noel Bell: 'I want you to understand that you are Field-Marshal Montgomery's personal representative on the Dinant bridge.'

Jimmy Carson's CREME unit followed 29 Brigade, arrived at Givet, where he noted: 'the weather was so cold that a high rock on which the castle stands was covered in sheet ice down to the river'. But the need to process and check out the new Comets was paramount, so CREME returned to Ypres. The best way to counter the formidable Red Ball route with coloured American drivers belting their GMC 6x4 trucks, was to lead the CREME convoy with a Scammell 'Pioneer' tractor with counterbalance weights in front of the radiator.

On the 23rd Sergeant Baldwin, 8 RB, had blown to pieces an American jeep with a string of Hawkins mines. When challenged it had failed to stop. The three German occupants in American greatcoats carried detailed plans of the Dinant defences. On the following day Steel Brownlie was arrested as 'a spy' while working out defensive fields of fire in the Namur suburbs. By Christmas Eve the three armoured regiments had defensive screens put out on the far side of the river where excellent hull-down positions gave perfect fields of fire. It was good planning because a battle group from 2 Panzer Division attacked early in the morning at Foy-Notre-Dame, 5 miles east of Dinant, and received a bloody nose. At least three Panthers and a Mark IV were knocked out without loss. Moreover Browning fire accounted for many PZ in their half tracks. The machine-gun platoon of G Company 8 RB were, however, chased by a six-wheeled armoured car, found themselves cut off in the village of Boiselles and were saved in the nick of time by 3 RTR. By nightfall hardly a civilian was left in Dinant. Women and children, haggard and weary, stumbling along with their goods and chattels and bedding, were streaming over the bridge across the river – the way they had done in 1940.

Roland Jefferson's account was a little different: 'Most of the traffic across the bridge at Dinant was retreating Americans. In the darkness they were moving around with blazing headlights, and lighting fires as if there was no danger.'

Christmas Eve had been a great day for the allied airforces: for hour after hour the air was filled with the ceaseless roar of thousands of engines and with fuselages gleaming in the brilliant sunshine, planes of every size and description – hundreds of them – were seen flying east to spread havoc and chaos among the communication lines of von Runstedt's armies, hitherto spared by the weather alone, from the furious onslaughts of Allied airpower. The savage fighting around Bastogne was some 30 miles to the east.

Noel Bell wanted to send his carrier-pigeon squadron back to 21st Army Group at Brussels with suitable messages for Monty. Christmas Day was brilliantly fine and bitterly cold. Ted Harte and A squadron 23rd Hussars had moved east from Givet to Beauraing, then to Neuville, some 18 miles, where they took up 'marvellous defensive positions for possible targets'. The enemy never crossed the River Lesse so the Hussars had a peaceful four days. Christmas dinner consisted of iced bully beef and frozen cheese sandwiches. Improvised sledges provided some tobogganing. 8 RB at Dinant were greeted on Christmas morning by a salvo of shells which fell on widely scattered points in the town. 'Hardly a message of good will on this festival day,' recalled Noel Bell. That morning 3 RTR and 8 RB were ordered east to attack the villages of Sorinne and Boiseilles, to meet 2 US Armoured Division and keep on moving south-east. The British 53rd Division would then take over responsibility for Dinant. All went well and for several hours 3 RTR/8RB watched American Lightnings and a tank battalion fight a pitched battle in the village of Foy-Notre-Dame. Noel Bell was enthusiastic about the grandstand view: 'It really was a wonderful spectacle, and compensated for our Christmas lunch of bully sandwiches and a mug of tea. After the last wave of planes had disappeared from sight, from our left came a perfectly deployed formation of some fifty US Sherman tanks in drill movement with their machine guns blazing.'

That evening the 3RTR/8 RB group found Foy-Notre-Dame littered with German dead with several Panther tanks almost untouched and quite usable, the crews having hidden under them. Although the Americans had captured 200 Germans, 11 Platoon 8 RB searched the village thoroughly – barns, cellars, houses and church steeple, – and captured another forty-two prisoners. 'The mass of captured German equipment provided all with Christmas presents far better than we could have got in England.' The RB Colour-Sergeant arrived with a bumper Christmas mail, so morale was high. Boxing Day was spent patrolling from Sorinne, Foy-Notre-Dame and Boisseilles. The only two casualties were from American MG bullets. Many German vehicles were found intact, having run out of petrol. Despite the fury of the attack on Foy-Notre-Dame, its famous old church had miraculously escaped injury and the local priest was overwhelmed with gratitude. 3 RTR enjoyed themselves shooting up enemy half tracks. Steel Brownlie had a miserable Christmas guarding the crossroads at Lezfontaine, so cold he could not write letters home as his fingers were so stiff: 'no mail, and the cooks brought rations up – stone cold! Merry Christmas indeed!' But the news that the Americans were fighting back in Stavelot, St Vith, Malmedy, Vielsam and, of course, Bastogne, was the best boost to morale. Even Monty's ADCs visited to solicit information. In front of 29 Brigade were the tell-tale signs of defeat – abandoned equipment, deserted guns, burned-out tanks. 3 RTR and the American Shermans had captured, one way or another, over forty enemy tanks. RAF Typhoons caught a German column south of Celles, 8 miles south of Dinant, and destroyed it. Unusual 'friends' turned up – 61 Recce Regiment, 198 A/Tk Battery, the Herts Yeomanry 25-pounders, Belgian SAS, and for a week it looked as though the Black Bull's 'long stop' of the Ardennes battle was over, even though patrols found several villages, including Bure, still held by the enemy. Temporary masters changed every few days – from directly under 21 Army Group, to 30 Corps and then, rather surprisingly, to the newly arrived 6th Airborne Division.

Roland Jefferson spent New Year's Day, and his twentieth birthday, in a village called Heer, in freezing conditions. Digging in was impossible, vehicles engines needed to be started every half hour to keep them from freezing up, and greatcoats were worn all the time. Various practical jokes were played to celebrate Hogmanay and New Year's Eve. In Mesnil Eglise, G Company 8 RB's home for nine days, elaborately-dressed 'female' spies appeared, who answered '*Nein*' to all questions. Forfarshire troopers recited: 'Ma feet's cauld, Ma shin's thin, Gie's ma cakes, And let me rin,' dropping heavy hints about fags and treasured NAAFI bottles; and Trooper Grive's guitar playing was popular.

612 RE Field squadron was ordered to build a bridge at Chanley on the River Lesse, 15 miles east of Givet, with protection by 2nd Fife and Forfarshire, F Company 8 RB and some Belgian SAS. Brigade HQ was at Wellin and a near divisional attack was now planned with 7th and 13th Parachute battalions of 5 Para Brigade under command. The objectives were initially the villages of Bure and Wavreille and then eastwards to Grupont and Forrières. 3 RTR with 3 Parachute Brigade were left flanking to the north, the Fifes in the centre, and 23rd Hussars on the right to the south. On the morning of the 3rd the attack started across the Chanley bridge, advancing towards Bure, 6 miles to the east, which was dominated by the 2,000-foot high Chapel Hill. For the next three days there was a savage battle around Chapel Hill and Bure – the 6th Airborne troops fighting as infantry suffered 200 casualties, mainly from 13 Parachute Battalion. Steel Brownlie's squadron was in the thick of the fighting. AP shot from the Chapel, which was guarded on three sides by thick woods, hit several Fife and Forfarshire tanks. The unfortunate paras sat in the woods being heavily shelled. 'The battle in Bure raged furiously and the Airborne were in danger of being pushed back. Desmond still with them in his scoutcar reported a Tiger, unassailable at the far end of the village.' Corporal Dave Findlay knocked out a SP gun, but was in turn wounded: 'This High Noon encounter earned him the MM.' The Fifes repelled a German counter-attack, hitting SPs at a range of about 2 miles. Having taken Chapel Hill, Bure proved to be even more difficult, with Fife tanks knocked out by bazookas.

The night of the 3rd was very cold and rather dangerous. At dawn on the following day enemy medium guns stonked the Fife harbour area on Chapel Hill and in Bure a further three Fife tanks were brewed. There were times when C squadron seemed to be all out of action, the vehicles looked so shrapnel-scarred and mud-bespattered that they gave the appearance of being knocked-out. Jimmy Samson, 2nd Fife and Forfarshire 'seemed to have shrunk to half his normal size, face black and blue, encrusted with dirt, icicles and beard'. By nightfall the squadron was down to nine tanks out of a possible nineteen. C squadron was withdrawn to Tellin, where kindly nuns gave food and wine to the tired and shivering tank crews, until a direct hit on the convent put an end to the meal. The battle for Bure continued until the 5th with heavy fighting. The 23rd Hussars were now due to relieve the Fifes. Ted Harte's A squadron moved out from Beauraing, then to Wellin and Tellin. Their awkard top-heavy Shermans skated about on the icy roads like a stampede of drunken elephants. First Sergeant Huthwaite's tank went up on a mine; next Sergeant Roberts was bazookad and he was killed. When they reached Bure four more tank crews were killed. The Germans clung to the houses and ruins, hid in cellars and catacombs, fighting and sniping to the end:

There followed an afternoon of very bitter fighting in the village, which was in a hollow, and the main street [wrote Ted Harte] was littered with bodies both Airborne and Germans. Stanley Goss with his troop gave magnificent support, but both his own and his second tank were knocked out by a Tiger, one shot passing through the front of the tank and coming out of the rear engine doors.

The parallel attack through Tellin, north-east to Wavreille with 12 Para, was more successful. C squadron 23rd Hussars and F Company 8 RB occupied it but found minefields on the road to Ferrières and the River Homme. Having so painfully and brutally taken Bure, a planned withdrawal took place on the night of the 5th. Chapel Hill and Tellin were occupied. On the 8th and 9th minor support actions with 1 RUR and 12 Devons took place, and Grupont and Ferrières were taken.

The last few days in the Ardennes were rather more comfortable. There was rum and hot food, a piano in the Mess, hospitable Belgians, visits to the Grottos at Han-sur-Laize, and the Recce Troop of 23rd Hussars claimed to be expert wild boar hunters. Indeed Messrs Sudlow and Yetman of G Company 8 RB wounded an enormous beast with their pistols near Lavaux-St-Anne. The local hunter finally dispatched it and administered the *coup de grâce*. On the 13th the battered, grimy, camouflaged and still whitewashed Shermans of 29 Brigade struggled over the icy roads back and through Brussels to an enthusiastic civilian reception. The tanks were left for the second and final time at the reinforcement unit – and then back to Ypres!

All four regiments involved – 3 RTR, 23rd Hussars, 2nd Fife and Forfarshire and 8 RB – had acquitted themselves extremely well in daunting conditions against die-hard opposition. They had excellent unsung backup from 171 Company RASC, who supplied food, petrol, ammo and mail over the three-week period.

CHAPTER TWENTY-TWO

In the Bleak Midwinter:
January

In the first half of January, while the armour was performing nobly in arctic conditions along the Meuse in south-east Belgium, the rest of the division, with assorted 'friends', was performing by no means ignobly along the frozen reaches of the same river in Holland. On patrol with D company 4 KSLI on the river bank opposite Roermond, Signal-Corporal Ralph remembers:

> There had been a fall of about 4 inches of snow and I have never spent such a cold, miserable night standing in a trench about 3 feet deep, gazing out over the snow-covered fields. Small files of men could be seen moving about. Whether they were friend or foe I soon became too cold to care. On 8 January 4 KSLI were relieved and withdrawn to Weert in the midst of a snow-storm, there to become non-operational for nearly six weeks to rest, refit and re-train. With reinforcements they were again up to full strength and Colonel Max Robinson was back as CO.

Seventeen degrees of frost was recorded over the Christmas period. 44 RTR, briefly by our side on Hill 112 in Epsom, had temporarily replaced the Inns of Court, who went out of the line back to Helmond. Another temporary exchange on the 8th was 2 KSLI and 7 Seaforths for the 3rd Mons and 4 KSLI, who both badly needed several weeks to rest and train their reinforcements. The Mons spent six weeks at Baexam with replacements being trained and joint infantry/tank exercises with 4 Tank Brigade. Being out of the line meant leave to Brussels and locally to Weert, where there was a cinema and several canteens. In the evening Housey Housey, socials with the friendly Dutch families, and even dances. The Burgomeister was chairman of a vetting committee responsible for allowing girls of a good moral status to attend. Their mothers also attended as chaperones!

The Herefords left Baexem on the 21st, returning to the line in Heel sector where six hamlets had to be guarded – Pol, Heel, Beegden, Panheel, Wessem and Pennenhoi. There they stayed until 2 February when they handed over to 46 Marine Commando and withdrew to the relative comfort of Weert barracks.

During their rest at Weert, Reg Worton and his Hereford platoon were billeted with a Dutch family. He usually slept in two big green curtains which the hausfrau coveted. So he gave her one, she washed the other, and she gave him a pair of Dutch clogs, painted for the liberation.

Near Asten Peter Reeve, Inns of Court C squadron, relieved on a temporary basis a Commando unit who had been doing their best to stir up things in 'Spandau alley' with snipers, mortars and aggressive patrols. Fortunately the armoured car-less 'Devils Own' had a peaceful few days on the river banks, but the Commandos' provocation brought eventual retaliation. The infantry who relieved Peter Reeves' squadron lost three men killed and three prisoners to a German patrol.

Ayrshire Yeomanry spent a rare week out of the line at Deurne, where guns and vehicles were cleaned and painted and kit replaced. David Swiney, 75 A/Tk at Geystinger, near Bree/Haelen, enjoyed with twenty-four others a delicious roast pig lunch supplied and cooked by the friendly local farmers. In the next village four Germans were captured while visiting their girlfriends. Oh what a lovely war! 8 RB had expected to be sent back to Poperinghe, where they were sure of a warm welcome, but due to a shortage of infantry they were sent to Bree. Most units celebrated an 'ersatz' Christmas Day on 21 January. 8 RB celebrated in style with a huge dinner helped down by beer and Guinness, and in the evening held a dance in the largest café in Bree. The following day many men had hangovers as Monty presented medals at Bishops Castle, Weert. 'He was in great form and spoke with optimism and conviction about the future. He admitted that Runstedt's Ardennes offensive had set back our plans,' recounted Noel Bell. During their three weeks spent at Bree the Riflemen were also visited by General Dempsey and by General Roberts.

On the 16th Operation Blackcock started, with 12 Corps clearing the area between the rivers Roer and Maas. Buffaloes, tracked landing craft that could cross water hazards, were employed by 80th Assault Squadron RE plus No. 3 Commando under command of 'our' 4 Armoured Brigade. 13 RHA at Baexem and Ayrshire Yeomanry were in action continuously from 12 January. The smoke screens were fired in cold so bitter that the smoke froze into a dense and permanent fog. Targets were fired in support of 7th Armoured, 3 Parachute Brigade on Linne, Echt, St Joost and Montfort, often 100 rounds per gun per target. Propaganda shells were fired on the 22nd on Linne, Herton, Merum and Roermond. The large 'island' between the Maas and the Juliana Canal was duly taken. The Herefords occupied a small front around the small enemy pocket remaining south of Roermond and 2 KSLI and 7 Seaforths were returned to their respective owners. 15/19th Hussars operated gunnery and mines schools at Lommel, and wireless and D & M school took place in barns and sheds in the Kelpen area. Some exercises in infantry/tank co-operation took place around Weert, 15 miles west of Roermond. Leave to Brussels, Antwerp, Eindhoven, even back to the UK, was granted to many during January.

Trooper Broad of 15/19th KRH cooking a German pig in the tank harbour, Hellmannshof, March 1945

The three armoured regiments post-Ardennes were recovering happily around Ypres. The Fifes had their belated Christmas on the 20th and 21st.

Christmas Eve was a regimental holiday, so [Steel Brownlie] went to a dance at the Flamhuis. Next day it was visits from one Mess to another, then the officers and sergeants converged on the men's cookhouse to serve them their festival meal, a well-established Army tradition. We were surprised to be met by the whole regiment of other ranks armed with snowballs. There was quite a battle. I could write a slim volume about our spell in Ypres, the reputable and disreputable liaisons, the parties, the brief leave I enjoyed in Paris and other non-military matters. Better not.

Many old friends rejoined the armour after various spells in hospital due to wounds received in Normandy. The 23rd Hussars historian noted: 'Back in Ypres we were received with open arms and each man was quickly swallowed up by his old billet, the warmth of his welcome soon thawing the chill of the Ardennes winter from his bones.'

CHAPTER TWENTY-THREE

In the Bleak Midwinter: February

Initially the intense cold continued with inches of snow on the ground and all the canals frozen, but a rapid thaw with torrential rain fed the rising Maas. All roads became rivers of deep mud so that many units were cut off from supplies of food and ammunition. Indeed G Battery 13 RHA was destitute of shells and had to turn for a while to road repair to ensure continuity of supply. They also swapped their faithful Shermans for Cromwells. The Ayrshire Yeomanry supported the Commandos of 155 Brigade, who sent back a message: 'Thank you for your close and accurate support. We don't believe the island [between the Maas and Juliana canals] liked you.' FOOs from both regiments 'guarded' the Maas from a dozen OPs during the day. At night it was '*sauve qui peut*' with patrols active on both sides, with isolated farmhouses as sporting targets. The Inns of Court held a dozen farm hamlets, which were often comfortable but dangerous at night. It was a confusing time of order and counter-order (rarely disorder), plans and changes of plan.

8 RB moved from Bree on the 11th and moved to Helden, 3 miles from the Maas, as reserve to 5 Parachute Brigade (6 Airborne Division). 'We put in some practice at boating,' recalls Noel Bell. Shortly afterwards 8 RB moved via Eindhoven, Tilburg and Breda to Roosendaal, where the billets were very comfortable. Rifleman Kingsmill sold cakes of Blanco on the black market for 5 guilders each! A large number of flying bombs were seen and heard on their way to Antwerp, although the LAA shot a fair amount down. 13 RHA spent some time at Asten resting and refitting and Major R. Gaunt was awarded a DSO for his Le Bas Perrier actions. The Ayrshire Yeomanry harboured in a lunatic asylum near Wortel! 15/19th Hussars spent the third week of the month in a large monastery in Vught in the first warm spring weather.

Back in Belgium Comet training and testing went on. At the range at Gravelines Steel Brownlie fired the Comet 77-mm gun at a captured Panther's front plate. 'The shots did not penetrate so we knew that our new gun, however accurate, was still inferior to that of the opposition. A Brigadier Blagdon came to Ypres, invited criticisms of the Comet, got them and went back to UK!' The Fifes nevertheless enjoyed themselves. ENSA shows, entertainments, piano-playing in the mess. Eric Lamont later

Lieutenant Steel Brownlie with tank crew,
Bakel, September 1944

Brigadier Roscoe Harvey making an inspection of 23rd Hussars, Ypres, 1944. The Black Bull
emblem was blurred for security purposes

1 Battery 13 HRA officers, Asten, Holland, February 1945 (Author right front)

15/19th KRH officers relaxing near Bardowick, April 1945

married an ENSA girl and David Reid was engaged to Suzanne. Driver-mechanic Kenneth Kirkley, 15/19th Hussars, thought: 'the new Comets were the Bees Knees and the 77 mm was my passport home to Blighty, 11 inches of glossy plate! Sheer luxury.' The 23rd Hussars had the same reactions to the new tank: 'A vast improvement on the Shermans, possessing a higher speed, a lower silhouette, thicker armour and a very good gun, the 77 mm. We were amazed at its accuracy which compensated for its slightly lower penetrating power compared to a [Firefly] 17-pounder.' The Hussars had weekly dances and an occasional concert. Brigade church parades were held in the square and then a march to the Menin Gate. 'Now and then,' wrote the regiment's historian, 'we spared a thought for our comrades who were now fighting the bitter battle of the Reichwald Forest in which 4th Armoured Brigade took our brigade's place in the Division.'

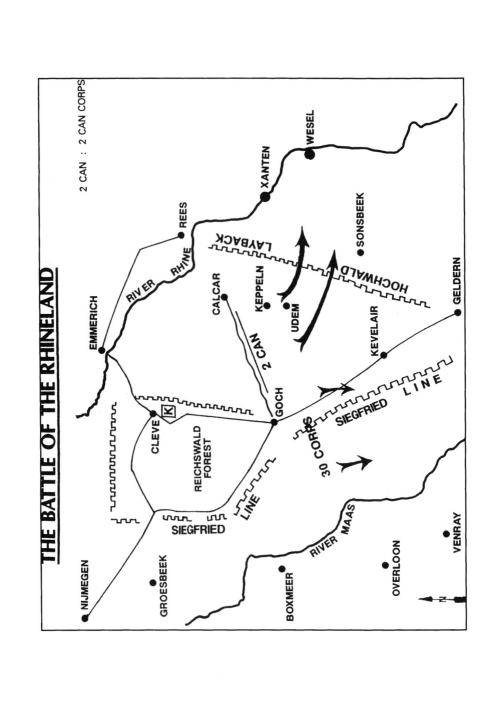

THE BATTLE OF THE RHINELAND

2 CAN : 2 CAN CORPS

NIJMEGEN

GROESBEEK

EMMERICH

RIVER RHINE

REES

SIEGFRIED

LINE

CLEVE

K

REICHSWALD
FOREST

CALCAR

KEPPELN

XANTEN

WESEL

LAYBACK

UDEM

HOCHWALD

SONSBEEK

2 CAN

GOCH

30 CORPS

SIEGFRIED LINE

KEVELAIR

GELDERN

BOXMEER

RIVER MAAS

OVERLOON

VENRAY

N

CHAPTER TWENTY-FOUR

Operation Blockbuster: the Hochwald Battle

General Horrocks's 30 Corps, including 11th Armoured Division, was lent to the 1st Canadian Army and the huge Operation 'Veritable' was designed to destroy all the German forces between the Rhine and the Maas. The German 1st Parachute Army had concentrated their battle groups to defend the Siegfried Line, with 1,000 guns and 700 mortars deployed. It was a last-ditch stand and they were to fight with a desperate fanaticism defending their Fatherland. In theory 30 Corps (51st Highland, 53rd Welsh, 15th Scottish, 2nd and 3rd Canadian, supported by 43rd Wessex and Guards Armoured) would sweep down south-east from the Cuyk/Nijmegen/Arnhem line to link up with General Simpson's 9th US Army moving northwards from the River Roer. The Germans had breached the banks of the Rhine and many areas were then flooded. For two weeks from 8 February the brutal battle continued to clear the Reichwald Forest and take the towns of Cleve (14 February) and Goch (21 February). On 23 February the 9th US Army crossed the swollen River Roer. 30 Corps had already suffered 15,634 casualties and 11th Armoured now came under command of 2nd Canadian Corps. 4th Armoured Brigade under Brigadier Mike Carver, was a welcome well-tried temporary addition to the Division. 159 Infantry Brigade concentrated south of Cleve while 4th Armoured Brigade, under command and 15/19th Hussars, remained at Nijmegen because of the congestion and lack of roads and tracks ahead. Operation Blockbuster was planned to make a breakout from the Reichwald Forest which ran in a semicircle from Cleve in the north to Goch in the south-west. The first objective was Udem, then the Hochwald Forest, Sonsbeck, and finally to the east, the town and vital bridge at Wesel. 13 RHA at Horst supported 115 Infantry Brigade, and Ayrshire Yeomanry were between Pfalzdorf and Keppeln. FOOs fired many substantial targets – even 'Uncle' and 'Victor', which needed approval of the CRA. A complex mix of twenty-five regiments of field, medium and heavy artillery was available to the Canadian and British forces. The 2nd Tactical Air Force was also on call. General Horrocks had a difficult choice when asked: 'Do you want the town of Cleve taken out?' – the lovely, historical Rhineland town which was home to Henry VIII's fifth wife. Squadrons of Lancasters flying low also flattened the well-defended Udem. It was the start of the demolition of western Germany.

The Hochwald defences and the Schlieffen Line were the western support lines to the famous Siegfried Line, which consisted of anti-tank ditches, minefields, concrete emplacements and barbed wire entanglements. General 'Pip' noted: 'We had a very narrow front and no outflanking moves would be possible so we must concentrate our resources and play some leapfrog, moving one armoured regiment and one infantry battalion in a series of successive phases, passing each group through its predecessor. The artillery would be concentrated to support each operation.' The brigades were grouped as follows: 4th Armoured Brigade; Scots Greys/4 KSLI and 44 RTR/2 KRRC, and 159 Brigade; 3/4 Country of London Yeomanry/3rd Mons, 15/19th Hussars/1st Herefords.

At 1800 hrs on the 26th the Greys and 4 KSLI crossed the start line and soon made their first objective. The support barrage, 'Caroline', was fired by Ayrshire Yeomanry and 13th RHA. Barely one hour of daylight now remained. 'This was the first time I had operated with artificial moonlight. The amount of light was roughly equivalent to dusk or to the best full moon. Individual people could be distinguished at up to 200 yards,' recalls Ned Thornburn. A few hours later a bit of shrapnel hit his knee 'and my fighting days were over'.

By 0500 hrs on the 27th the railway line south-west of Udem was reached despite increasing opposition, and 350 dazed prisoners, four SPs and two tanks were captured. So far so good. The infantry were the major factor as roads had crumbled, the fields were under water and the role of tanks was strictly limited. The battlefield appeared to be straight out of the First World War Battle of the Somme – a cratered landscape with almost total destruction of houses, trees and hedgerows. Anything that could shelter the enemy had been pulverized by artillery power. Finally it was to be a non-stop affair with searchlights turning night into day. All in all it was a nightmare of a landscape.

3rd/4th County of London Yeomanry tank brewed up south of Udem. Red Cross ambulances queue up in the background to collect casualties

Corporal H. Lucas, MM (second from left) with 15/19th KRH tank crew, Hellmannshof, March 1945

On the 27th behind fireplan 'Rebecca', the Herefords and 3/4 CLY passed Udem, now just a mass of rubble. It was ringed by an anti-tank ditch, the bridges were blown and odd pockets were defending Das Reich at the exits from the town. B Company rounded up twenty POWs and killed many more. By 1430 hrs the battlegroup was tackling the Gochfortzberg feature south of Udem. They reached the crest taking 120 POWs, but A Company had sustained casualties from shells, airburst, flying masonry and collapsing buildings. The company was composed of 50 per cent reinforcements in their first action and were in danger of 'going to ground'. But the CSM rallied his inexperienced men and encouraged, persuaded and forced them to go forward. The going was difficult for tanks and the enemy had ideal observation and brought down well co-ordinated heavy fire. A 20-foot wide stream had to be filled in with fascines before tanks could cross it!

By dawn of the 28th the Herefords had had an evening's hot meal and despite shelling and active enemy patrols, were still holding their objective. During the early evening 3rd Mons and 15/19th Hussars had passed through this so-called centre-line, and advanced a mile or so south-east to Amen Corner before being halted by A/Tk ditches and burning vehicles on the roads. The advance continued slowly and painfully for a few hundred yards under heavy shelling.

On the morning of the 28th, 44 RTR/2 KRRC battlegroup on the right, and Scots Greys/4 KSLI on the left, advanced slowly over waterlogged ground overlooked by the Hochwald and the high ground north of Sonsbeck. The left-hand group came to a halt, the KSLI in the face of intense MG fire from well-prepared defences, with the tanks completely bogged down. The right-hand group made slow but steady progress in spite

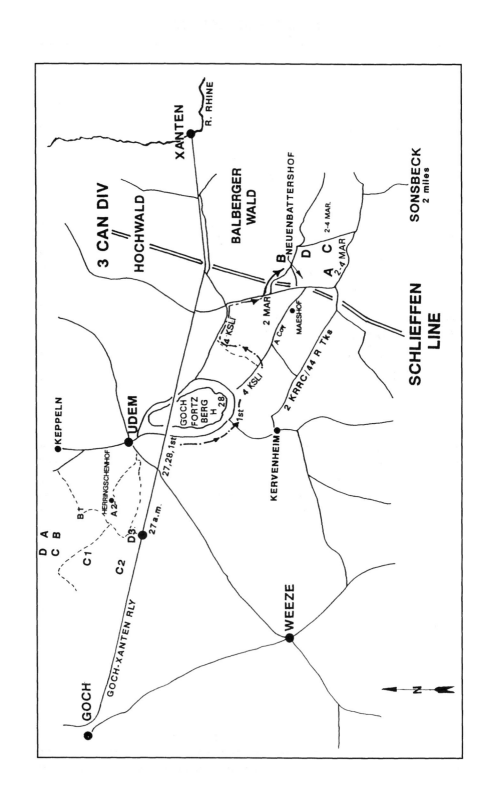

Lieutenant Ted Deeming 15/19th KRH with Challenger A 30 tank and crew, after breaching the Schlieffen Line, Hellmannshof, March 1945

of intense shell fire, SP anti-tank guns and pure bog. Further north the Scots Greys and C company of KSLI managed to find an unused road and the rest of their battlegroup painfully consolidated behind them. For two days, 1–2 March, 3rd Mons were static, under fire the whole time and unable to move forward. They had been badly mauled in bitter fighting. The 15/19th Hussars had two consecutive night actions under artificial and natural moonlight. Major Guy Courage, C squadron, said of the attack south of Udem: 'This was the beginning of the most unpleasant hour we ever spent – our tanks advancing at walking pace along the straight, flat, narrow track with bog on both sides with the AP shot cracking straight down the track just over our heads and all the time the knowledge that at all costs we must get on.' C squadron had three leading tanks knocked out, probably by A/Tk SPs using a new German infra-red nightsight.

On the second night attack with the Herefords on the 1st, B squadron were in open ground and took many casualties. RHQ and Herefords Battalion HQ were in the hamlet of Sandforth. By the end of the second night in action, C squadron had one fully operational tank after A/Tk damage and many 'boggings' in the thick mud. Ted Deeming wrote: 'tanks belly deep in mud in the German farmland south of Udem and crews crouched in wet slit trenches in our "pixie suits" trying to rest and being persistently shelled and mortared from the heights of the Hochwald – this was not the armoured warfare of the "*Schwerpunkt und Aufrollen und Blitzkrieg*" I had read about'. They had a long narrow bridgehead with scant and obvious cover, so they were relieved when the Scots Greys and 4 KSLI passed through them for an assault on the Hochwald. The Ayrshire Yeomanry, now south of Udem, supported them with a fireplan when the KSLI were counter-attacked. The main target was Sonsbeck which 159 Brigade were due to take from the south, but which was in the event taken by the Canadians from the north. Meanwhile 44th RTR/2 KRRC had closed right up to the Schlieffen Line, clearing woods into the dawn of 2 March. At 0300 hrs on that day the Scots Greys/4 KSLI attacked southwards between two lines of trenches on the edge of the forest. They crossed an anti-tank ditch by RE scissors bridge: 'With bated breath the COs of Scots Greys and Herefords watched as each successive tank negotiated the scissors. Two squadrons of Greys got across before the muddy approaches became impassable. It was enough to turn the scale', wrote Ned Thornburn afterwards. Then they captured the high ground on the edge of the forest overlooking the valley where the rest of the brigade was. They defeated a counter-attack but despite heavy shelling held their ground all day. 2 KRRC/44 RTR in the afternoon started to clear the southern end of the line in the face of bitter opposition which continued throughout the night into the morning of the 3rd. Then after the sappers built a bridge over a big anti-tank ditch the final push was made by 3rd Mons and 3/4 CLY, who linked up with the Canadians.

On the 5th D Company 3rd Mons with the Canadian Recce regiment, who took heavy armoured car losses in the process, finally entered Sonsbeck. To the east 43rd Division and 2 Canadian Division were investing Xanten, which, supported by the divisional artillery, they took on 8 March. On 10 March the small German bridgehead at Wesel was liquidated and the way to the Rhine was opened. All organized resistance west of the Rhine had ceased. In the Hochwald battle the infantry as usual suffered the heaviest casualties. In five days the Herefords had twenty-eight men killed and 124 wounded, the KSLI had twenty-five men killed and 108 wounded, 3rd Mons eleven killed, with the proportional casualties wounded. From 1 March A and C companies 3rd Mons worked as one company, and B company had also taken heavy casualties. Udem was certainly a battle honour richly deserved.

The Ayrshire Yeomanry did sterling work in this five-day battle. Captain 'Bubble' Spence was FOO with 15/19th Hussars, and not only brought down DF throughout the nights of 28 February and 1 March, but also searched for wounded men and carried one 800 yards back to the RAP. He noted: 'That night was utter chaos – mud, rain and brewed-up tanks. The rescue of wounded men, badly hurt in most cases, was an obvious thing to do.' 123 Battery was shelled at Keppeln and Captain Rolfe, Lieutenant Milne and others were killed by a large bomb which landed on their command post. Lieutenant Plummer, FOO with 3rd Mons, was wounded and evacuated.

Lieutenant Ted Deeming with Jagdpanzer Mark IV of 116 Panzer Division, knocked out by C Squadron, 15/19th KRH, March 1945

After the battle Ted Deeming wrote: 'The enemy paratroopers were tenacious fighters; there was a great number of Jagdpanthers in evidence and the largely increased volume of enemy shell fire was a feature of the Rhineland operations.' 15/19th Hussars had thirty-three casualties including nine killed, but they destroyed six tanks and hit another six.

At the end of 'Blockbuster', General 'Pip' wrote:

It was the most unpleasant battle I had anything to do with in the *whole war* – rain, wind, ruins and no possibility of manoeuvre! It was a slow, miserable and costly operation. We had been fighting our way through country where no armoured division could have been expected for one moment to fulfil a natural role. We had been confronted by impenetrable forests, impassable bogs, numerous craters, roadblocks, mines and every form of demolition.

CHAPTER TWENTY-FIVE

Another Interlude: March

After the Hochwald battle 4th Armoured Brigade left on 7 March for training in the Maastricht area. 159 Brigade moved back out of Germany into the rest area of Diest and Louvain, close to Brussels, 8 RB, who had been lent to 49 Division, had spent two weeks at Dreumel and Wamel watching the Waal. They had taken over from the Manitoba Dragoons and handed back to them on 12 March. Noel Bell's main problem was supervising two platoons of gun-happy Dutchmen. He nipped south to Poperinghe to stay with 3 RTR and check up that they knew how to use their new toys. The RB move back to rest in the divisional area proved to be complicated. Noel Bell called it 'Gulliver's Travels' – from Blauwberg to Hersselt to Ramsel and finally to Gelrode outside Aerschot. The riflemen called this interlude 'The last Frat' – before the fraternization ban in Germany took effect.

Wezemaal, north of Louvain, was home to 4 KSLI for two and a half weeks from 9 March. Private Joe Davey after being wounded at Asten returned to duty, and remembers the battalion being taken to Louvain to be 'shown over' the Division's new Comets, on which they were going to ride so many miles across Germany. Ned Thornburn wrote: 'The old Shermans were tall and difficult to climb on, the Comets were low-slung, child's play to mount and easy to sit on.'

The Herefords moved back to Haecht north of Brussels and licked their wounds from the Hochwald as reinforcements arrived to replace the 152 casualties. 3rd Mons were in Werchter and the 159 Infantry Brigade band from the three regiments beat the retreat each night in the village square. 15/19th Hussars were based on Liffeek, 30 miles north-east of Brussels, with good billets and in fine spring weather re-equipped with the new Comets. With sport, films, recreation and leave visits the Regiment's morale recovered from its pasting in the Hochwald. The Ayrshire Yeomanry were in three villages, Holsbeck, Gelrode and Rhode-St-Pierre. Their historian relates: 'Certain restrictions were imposed on the movements of 29 Armoured Brigade who had been savouring the fleshpots of Ypres for so long; it was feared that their personnel – especially the officers – might go soft, or softer!' Both artillery regiments exchanged Sherman OP tanks for Cromwells, better able to keep up with the new Comets.

Steel Brownlie commented how on 10 March Monty came to pin medals (a MC in his case) in the theatre in Peerbohmplatz in Ypres. Apparently he had six stock questions, of which he would ask each medal-recipient three:

15/19th KRH after Rhineland battle, en route to Belgium to re-equip with Comet tanks, March 1945

What were you in civvy street? (Music hall reply – 'Happy'); when did you come over? (D + 10, same as the King); what do you intend to do after the war? (No idea). Monty then told us 11th Armoured Division would be Army Reserve when we went into Germany, others would do the slogging at the Rhine, while we would burst out and belt for the Baltic. He was a great showman, a morale-booster and a great general as well.

The Fifes discovered that the new Comet was cramped compared to the Sherman. The sixty rounds of AP/HE per tank were increased to eighty-five and machine gun ammo by over 50 per cent. The Comet also bogged down more in soft ground than the Sherman. Perhaps as well they had not fought in the Hochwald; they might never have been seen again. The Fifes moved up from Ypres to Montaigne near Diest. 75 A/Tk regiment in Boschot/Shriek were briefed on their new infantry role since the main German armour had been so written down, and there was now an acute shortage of PBI. David Swiney wrote: 'The two SP batteries were to operate as two tank squadrons with a higher proportion of HE to AP and the two "towed" 17-pounder batteries became two lorry-borne infantry. The SP troop commanders were equipped with Locust light Airborne tanks, US made, small, fast armed with a 37-mm gun, and .30 machine guns. The force was named Todforce after our CO Lieutenant-Colonel Fred Tod.'

23rd Hussars moved north of Diest to the villages of Veerle, Vorst, Petit Vorst and Schoot, the cosy billets of Ypres being replaced by the floors of chilly schoolrooms.

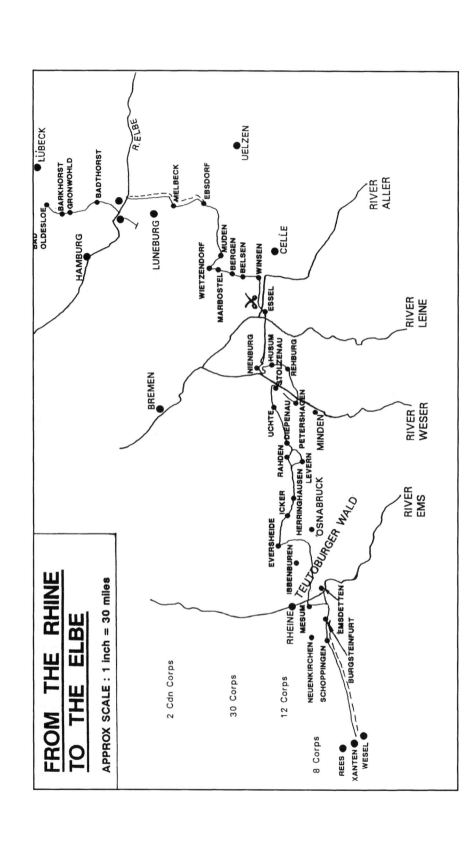

FROM THE RHINE
TO THE ELBE

APPROX SCALE : 1 inch = 30 miles

CHAPTER TWENTY-SIX

The Rhine Crossing and Advance

The General wrote that the Division was fortunate to get a rest of eighteen days after the brutal battle of the Hochwald. Certainly the infantry battalions needed rest and maintenance. On the night of 23 March, the first British troops, 1 Commando Brigade in 'buffaloes', crossed the Rhine at Wesel. Along a 25-mile front 3,300 guns fired an intense one-hour barrage. The divisional artillery were now to be in counter battery action more or less non-stop for five days. For instance Ayrshire Yeomanry fired 350 rounds per gun in a fire plan to support 51st Highland Division's attack and by the 26th had fired an average of 1,000 rounds per gun. 13 RHA had a ten-hour programme of non-stop firing and in just fifteen hours fired 16,800 rounds – 420,000 pounds of high explosive. Patrick Delaforce's I battery guns were 1,500 yards west of the Rhine and he recalled:

> The noise and pressure on the gun position was unbelievable. A normal regimental target might last twenty minutes, but from dawn to dusk non-stop was a really tough programme. The two gun position officers alternated one hour on, one off, as the need to sustain pinpoint accuracy of the creeping barrages and switched counter-battery targets needed acute concentration. One of our main targets was heavy A/A guns located by air photography. We supported 43 Division for 2½ days.

On the morning of the 24th, the main operation 'Varsity' started and the first Dakotas hummed low over the gun positions as the giant armada of the 6th British and 17th US Airborne Divisions launched their great airborne attack on the Germans waiting for them on the east bank of the Rhine. 6, 7, and 8 Parachute Division with 15 Panzer Grenadier and 116 Panzer Division were ready for the onslaught. 1,700 aircraft and 1,300 gliders were used to drop 14,000 troops across the river. An umbrella of 900 fighter planes shielded the vulnerable carrying planes plus 250 Liberators with immediate supply drops. The heavy anti-aircraft defences took their toll and fifty gliders and seventy aircraft were lost in the three-hour drop.

30 Corps under General Horrocks on the left, 12 Corps on the right were to lead the attack and head for Osnabruck, Celle and Velzen with 8 Corps in reserve. The Division was placed under command of 8 Corps along with 6

An American-built Bailey bridge over the River Rhine, March 1945

Airborne Division and 6 Guards Armoured Brigade under command of Lieutenant General 'Bubbles' Barker. From Wesel the first divisional targets were Holtwick and then north to Osnabruck on Operation 'Plunder'. 7th Armoured would be on the left under 30 Corps. Nobody knew it at the time, but it was to be a spectacular horse race up to the Elbe with the rank outsider nearly winning! Roland Jefferson noticed that the divisional post office address had moved from APO (Army Post Office) to BWEF in Normandy (British Western Expeditionary Force) to BLA (British Liberation Army) and was now BAOR (British Army of the Rhine).

The bridge at Wesel was 500 yards long and the pontoons in the four-knot river strained and creaked against the steel wire ropes. The three tank regiments had come up from Belgium on transporters. Steel Brownlie had made a recce via Beeringhen, Helchteren, Bree, Kinroy and Venlo to Issum. He passed hundreds of the 'strange stove-like contrivances that had produced the huge smoke-screen for the Rhine crossing'. Wesel after the bombardment was but a heap of rubble with paths still being cleared by sappers and pioneers. Brunen was the small village where the Fifes in their handsome new Comets were to harbour. Even there there were scattered gliders, bodies, weapons, equipment left over from the intense week's fighting. Noel Bell's 8 RB company headed for Brunen:

> The actual crossing of the Rhine was a great thrill, unending columns of every description were queuing up to take their turn on the pontoon bridges. In addition, overhead cover was provided by barrage balloons

15/19th KRH on the east bank of the River Rhine, March 1945

and by the vigilant patrol of RAF fighters. Numerous dead bodies, nearly all German, lay unburied alongside the roads and in the ditches. Congestion on the roads was very great. We were well and truly mixed up with 7th Armoured Division.

The RBs had covered 140 miles in the day and not one vehicle had broken down. By nightfall the whole of 11th Armoured Division was concentrated some 4 miles north-east of Wesel. It was clear very soon that the main problems were to be mud (twenty tanks were bogged down), the poor quality of the north/south roads and, above all, skilful defences by German bazooka teams.

On the first day of the advance in heavy rain 8 RB teamed up with 3 RTR and played follow-my-leader without opposition to the small town of Velen, where the local hotel served plates of bacon and eggs. 'There was no question of fraternizing on anyone's part and any friendly gestures by the German citizens were met by frigid British stares,' wrote Noel Bell. 13 RHA ended the day at Heiden after 20 miles of difficult going in this north-west corner of Westphalia. The Herefords advanced to Erle, joined the Fifes there and moved through Legden on to Osterwick. Steel Brownlie noted: 'The routes were signed by Military Police, then chaos. Our maps were reprints of German ones and inaccurate.' 3rd Mons moved through Raesfield and Heiden to Velen, passing scores of abandoned Airborne gliders. Trooper Ernie Hamilton, 15/19th Hussars, and his tank crew collected nylon ropes used by the glider troops, ideal for towing out tanks which got bogged down. For the first time 75 A/Tk regiment left their guns and quads with A Echelon and took over an infantry role.

6th Airborne gliders near Hamminkeln/River Issel, March 1945

Roland Jefferson remembers how in Heiden the RB turned out all the civilians from their houses 'while we occupied the comfort of their homes. If there were any creature comforts we simply helped ourselves to them!' The roads were so bad that 7th Armoured on the left made no advance at all over a two-day period. But on the right 6th Airborne, using anything on wheels (including a steam traction engine) made quite astonishing progress. The battle groups were 23rd Hussars/8 RB, 3 RTR/4KSLI and 2nd Fife and Forfarshire/Herefords, and 15/19th Hussars/3rd Mons. The Inns of Court were soon back ferreting out the roads ahead, on operation Steeplechase.

The second day's advance was similar – about 17 miles – and 3 RTR captured Holtwich and then Horstmar, while 2nd Fife and Forfarshire cleared Gescher and Legden. However, 13 RHA with their Sextons alongside 3 RTR/4 KSLI and 23rd Hussars/8 RB were in action several times on a 40-mile march through thickly wooded country to Emsdetten. Norman Young at Schoppingen had a private war engaging bazooka men, setting cottages on fire and chasing a small enemy convoy, of which he destroyed four vehicles and took twenty-five prisoners. In the village he blew up a lorryful of infantry and a half track, leaving fifteen men dead. The irony of this splendid action was that FOO's primary task is bringing down artillery fire from their batteries behind, leaving heroics to others! The Herefords/2nd Fife and Forfarshire group advanced to Erle, thence to Legden and on to Osterwick. But 23rd Hussars ran into a fairly large bazooka party on the outskirts of Holtwick. This cheap, portable, nasty little weapon, based on the 'hollow charge' principle, was fired from the hip.

Fortunately the Comet armour was far tougher than that of a Sherman. H Company 8 RB methodically winkled out the bazooka men who had damaged three tanks. A little later B squadron ran into a pitched battle. And the morning showed a dead Panther, four 88s, four half tracks and six lorries destroyed, but at a cost of five men killed, six wounded. In Geschen the Fifes had a small battle in the main square where two troops were surrounded by enemy infantry. Eric Lamont and Charlie Workman left their tanks and attacked with brens and grenades until reinforcements came up. Between villages the armour 'brassed' up every wood and bit of cover with BESA including tracer to scare off the ubiquitous bazooka men. A trail of burning woods and cottages marked the centre-line.

For the first time the Division encountered first hundreds, then thousands of displaced persons (DPs) and released POWs escaping from German captivity and plodding sadly southwards to relative safety, gratefully accepting cigarettes and biscuits on the way.

On the night of the 30th a well-balanced little operation took place. 3 RTR were held up by a stream near Burgsteinfurt. 4 KSLI, 8 RB and the Sappers combined to bridge over and keep up the advance momentum. On the last day of March the Division was directed north of Osnabruck, leaving that town to 6th Airborne and 6th Guards Armoured. And by 0730 hrs 3 RTR reached the River Ems at Emsdetten, but, the bridge being blown, they moved north to Mesum, where 4 KSLI crossed the river. Many prisoners were taken including a German colonel and several drunken Volkssturm, 'Dad's Army'. The Inns of Court accepted the surrender of Neuenkirchen, the first German town so to do on our front.

The 23rd Hussars and 15/19th Hussars had an unfortunate noisy fracas with the Inns of Court but then linked with the entire 8 RB and for the rest of the campaign this alliance continued. The 23rd Hussars followed through Horstmar and Emsdetten behind 3 RTR, and by midnight were across the River Ems, although the bridges over the Dortmund–Ems Canal were predictably blown. Noel Bell noticed: 'The civilians appeared glad to see us and relieved that the war had passed by them. Many of them waved and threw fruit to us but the non-frat orders were still deep set and no one wavered.' The RAF had difficulty in keeping tabs on the pace of the advance and yellow smoke had to be fired to keep enthusiastic Typhoons at bay. 23rd Hussars went east to Saebeck to look at the bridge over the Dortmund–Ems Canal and at Legden met a heavily defended Flak position. 13 RHA lost to a sniper 'Stonker Bill' Budgen, a brave determined FOO, a valiant friend to 23rd Hussars and 8 RB. So angry was this battlegroup that 'all rules were forgotten as the German position was savagely and bloodily overrun, and when resistance ceased, fifty Germans lay dead, 150 were POWs and eight 88s were in our hands', wrote the historian of the 23rd Hussars. Altogether 600 prisoners were taken on that day.

At Legden 3rd Mons had one of their patrols captured, but a follow-up quickly released them. A counter-attack by 15 Panzer Grenadiers moving south-east towards Münster was advised but failed to materialize. At the village of Wettringen A squadron 15/19th Hussars knocked out three 88-mm A/Tk guns and six smaller 'flak' pieces as well as taking prisoners.

On 1 April, Easter Sunday, the methodical British pushed their watches forward one hour to Double Summer Time, presumably to fit in with the host country requirements. The Inns of Court ranging far ahead reached Saerbeck and the outskirts of Rheine. The KSLI now crossed the canal against some opposition and the sappers built a bridge during the night. 3 RTR had found an abandoned ferry near the bridging site at Birgte and ferried A squadron across. 'Ironically with the Allies at last superior in armour,' noted Bill Close, 'it was the cheap, fire and throw away bazooka in the hands of Panzer Grenadiers which dominated tactical thinking. The best antidote was another infantryman but he was a rare commodity by then. The policy of protecting infantry with 2-, 6- and 17-pounders was abandoned.' Thus 'Todforce', the unhorsed 75 A/Tk, now did yeoman service with the Division. I Battery 13 RHA was in action 250 yards west of the canal. Suddenly from the north came a solitary FW 190 flying at about 500 feet. Patrick Delaforce in his half track fired a complete burst of .50 Browning in front of the plane, at the same time shouting to the BSM in another half track in the field. To his surprise – to everyone's surprise – the FW 190 rather pathetically crashed several hundred yards further south. 'My bird, Sergeant-Major', he boasted over the tannoy, but Regiment did not take the claim seriously. 58 LAA did bring down several other planes that day! Reg Worton, 1st Herefords, remembers being strafed by three Jerry Messerschmidts: 'We fired everything at them, three Tempests came over, downed two and the other went off smoking. Soon after a Jerry jet plane came over hedge height and put the shits up everybody.' And Horace Hughes, Herefords, recalls: 'There was a great big crater on the road leading to the canal bridge and a bulldozer tank put a chain round a house and pulled it down and filled the hole in.'

On standby to move, the Inns of Court were in a burning village west of the canal where Peter Reeve remembers: 'Every twenty minutes a move was delayed, so we settled into a café loaded with wine and schnapps. We passed the ensuing hours playing poker, calling SUNRAY for instructions and emptying a vast array of bottles.'

CHAPTER TWENTY-SEVEN

The Battle for Teutoburger Wald (Ibbenbüren Ridge)

Some 12 miles west of Osnabruck runs a long thin strip of dense woodland, some 30 miles in length and 2 or 3 miles in width. The three key villages are Ibbenbüren, Holthausen and Tecklenberg. This is the Teutoburger Wald, which runs roughly north-west/south-east a mile or so to the east of the Dortmund–Ems Canal. It was a magnificent natural defensive position, armour was useless on the tree-lined slopes and infantry was just sucked into its lethal maw.

No fewer than seven companies of young dedicated infantry cadets from a NCO training school in Hanover were dug in along the Ibbenbüren Ridge. Fire support for the attackers was limited as the shells burst in the upper branches of the tall trees, falsifying the range. Landmarks were few and it was only too easy to get lost in the woodland thickets.

The first attack at 1430 hrs on 31 March was across the 'new' bridge at Birgte, built by 612 Field Squadron RE. It was led by 2nd Fife and Forfarshire and 4 KSLI and was not successful against mortars and machine guns playing upon the exits of the bridgehead. Bob Bignell, KSLI, adds: 'It was quite a slog up the steep hill clearing the area . . . Lieutenant Cunningham became very annoyed because the Jerries kept firing till the last minute and then insolently put their hands up to surrender.' A company 4 KSLI had done a fine job. From their vantage point on the heights they now commanded the German forward positions and forced the enemy to fall back, thus leaving the new canal bridge less exposed. But the KSLI had five men killed expanding the bridgehead.

Ibbenbüren was technically within 7th Armoured's boundary. Since 11th Armoured had been 'poaching' ground recently by using roads and tracks belonging to 7th Armoured, it was felt that the north-west area of the ridge around Ibbenbüren should be cleared and handed over to them. It was not, however, to be. The two roads through the Teutoburger Wald are the Münster–Ibbenbüren highway and a secondary road which winds along the valley through Brochterback up the hill to Holthausen.

The battle that followed had two very different characteristics. 159 Brigade with 3rd Mons and 1st Hereford had the unenviable task of clearing the thick woods in the north-west area of the Ibbenbüren Ridge. Although 2nd Fife and Forfarshire blasted the outskirts of the woods with HE, and

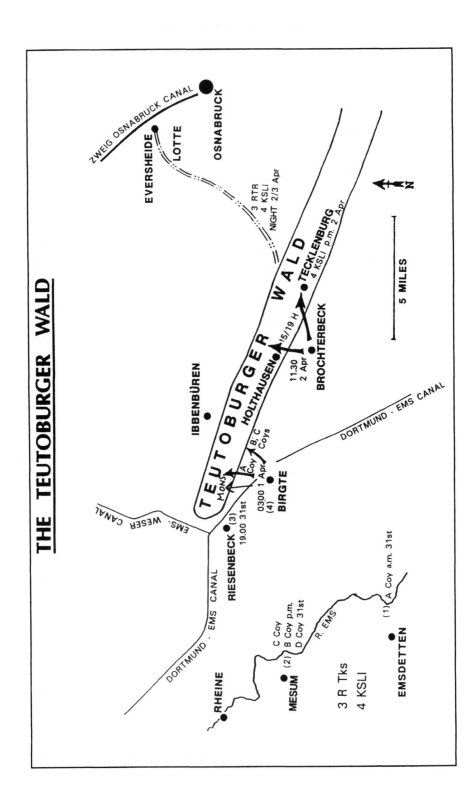

THE TEUTOBURGER WALD

Close support tanks of 15/19th KRH giving infantry support with their 95-mm howitzers, in the Teutoburgerwald battle, April 1945

divisional artillery rained down stonks on the Hanoverian cadets, it was to little avail. Major Mitchell and Captain Goer were the Ayrshire Yeomanry FOOs with 3rd Mons, the latter ending up fighting as an infantryman.

Two gallant attempts were made by the Mons to dislodge the enemy from the top of the crest. The thick undergrowth reduced visibility to a few feet and in the forest fighting C and D companies were pushed back 400 yards by a sudden counter-attack. Fighting became confused, the companies were disorganized and, with no information, sections lost touch in the dense woods. Many officers and key NCOs were killed or wounded and enemy sniping was constant. Major W.P. Taylor, Captain V. Mountford and Lieutenant S.M. Driver were killed in the woods. D Company was attacked in the rear by an enemy group shouting: 'Don't shoot, B Company'. Late in the afternoon of 3 April, Colonal Sweetman agreed a temporary truce to get wounded back to RAPs and stretcher parties were kept busy. There was torrential rain all night and at dawn a very strong enemy attack on Battalion HQ was only just beaten off by a troop of the Fifes. Corporal E.T. Chapman, a Bren-gunner from Rhymney valley, won the VC for conspicuous gallantry and then took the mortally wounded Captain Mountford back to the RAP. Private Roy Nash was with D Company at the time and wrote:

Our radios were useless so the signallers were laying lines for field telephones. The wounded should find the wires and follow them back to the RAP. As we moved forward I said to Corporal Chapman that the wood was full of Germans. I could see footprints in the molehills and on the soil outside rabbit warrens, and a lot of dew had been knocked off the bracken. I spotted three Germans walking over to the right. I fired my rifle as fast as I could. I shot one, wounded the second but the other got away. We moved forward again up a hill down into an old slate quarry. As we neared the top of the far side, we were cut down by murderous machine-gun fire. It was the worst I had experienced in ten months of action. Many were killed and wounded and the terrible screams of the wounded and dying haunt me. I kept firing until I ran out of ammo. I lay down behind the wall, picked up thirteen empty bullet cases and pushed them into the ground into the shape of a cross. The German fire was still devastatingly accurate and many more of our lads were killed and wounded. [Roy Nash was hit and the back of his right hand had been blown off.] Suddenly I felt pain, terrible pain, wicked pain and I cried, broken-hearted for my Mum. Corporal Chapman told me to lay down and that the stretcher-bearers were coming. He then picked up my Bren gun, put on a full magazine and said 'I'll kill the bloody lot of them, Waas' (that was my nickname). I could see him firing hosepipe fashion from the hip.

One company was cut off on the top of the hill and when the Dorsets of 131 Infantry Brigade came to their rescue they trapped two companies of the German NCOs and killed them all. The Mons eventually took 100 prisoners, but by the time they were relieved at 1100 hrs on 4 April, their casualties – forty-one killed, eighty wounded – were the heaviest in any action. That was the end of the magnificent Mons. Their casualties in the whole campaign were sixty-seven officers (twenty-five killed) and 1,089 ORs (242 killed). They had three commanding officers killed in action and C company had six consecutive COs killed. The battalion was taken out of

A Challenger, slave carrier and Cromwell of 15/19th KRH on the Teutoburgerwald, April 1945

B Squadron 15/19th KRH fitters at work on their Sherman ARV, Teutoburgerwald, April 1945

the line and was withdrawn to Wesel to join 115 Independent Infantry Brigade in guarding the Rhine bridges and assisting thousands of DPs in the area.

The General wrote: 'Unfortunately 3rd Monmouths had now fought their last battle with the division. They had received very heavy casualties during the campaign. We were very sorry to see them go.' A few days later their place was taken by the 1st Cheshire Regiment.

The Herefords had an equally difficult time between the bridgehead and wood clearing. During their attack on the wooded pass leading to Ibbenbüren they made little progress against the Hanover NCOs. Reg Worton wrote of his reactions: 'It was a training camp. We saw some stragglers, very young boys and if they did not put their hands up empty we shot them.'

At one stage A Company had reached the high ground in the woods but were counter-attacked three times and were finally surrounded. They fought their way back to the southern edge of the wood. It was a painful battle for the Herefords. Two officers, Lieutenant Spittal and Lieutenant Hopkinson, were killed and two more wounded; thirty-nine ORs were killed or wounded and thirteen taken prisoner. The battalion was glad to hand over to 7th Armoured Division on 3 April. It took a further three days for the infantry of 7th Armoured Division to make the final clearance of the north-west sector of the Teutoburger Wald.

Lieutenant Simon Fraser and crew, 1st TP, B Squadron, 15/19th KRH, Teutoburgerwald, April 1945

The 29th Armoured Brigade attack was altogether different. 15/19th Hussars, bit between their teeth, galloped their Comets due east from the bridgehead at Birgte on 2 April and took the village of Brochterback. One squadron stayed there and the other charged north up the road to Holthausen to assault the key pass. Despite many attacks by bazooka men no Comets were knocked out, and 'elan' carried them up the long winding hill.

Ted Deeming wrote later:

> The road or 'gorge' was a bazooka man's paradise and the only answer was to run the 1½ mile gauntlet at the Comet's top speeds. That all of C squadron's tanks reached the top, some 7–800 feet high, without being hit was incredible. Probably the bazooka men had not learnt the rules of 'aim-off'. They seemed to have an inexhaustible supply of panzerfausts – it was later calculated that one was fired at every other tank – but thank God they had no access to Teller mines or the support of anti-tank guns.

On the next advance 2 miles west, 15/19th Hussars enjoyed a good day's heavy shooting and killed or seriously wounded at least 150 Germans between 1130 and 1830 hrs. Near the top 23rd Hussars with 8 RB passed through 15/19th Hussars, wended their way through the undefended steep and narrow gorge, and entered the small town of Tecklenberg. It was quiet

Tank Gunner 'Tich' Croft of 15/19th KRH, Bardowick, April 1945

and no flags were flying, and battle soon raged. No quarter was given and the 'Volksturm' fought alongside the regular German troops. The tanks battled their way slowly down the narrow, twisty streets. Riflemen cleared houses and fought through trim cottage gardens. By nightfall the shattered town, in ruins and burning, was cleared. But following up behind were A1 Echelon, who were violently ambushed in the narrow gorge, and with assistance from 8 RB the Germans were beaten back into the woods. 23rd Hussars had three officer casualties that day.

Back at the bridgehead FW 190s, Stukas, Heinkels and ME 109s bombed and strafed the Herefords and the Fifes, but divisional AA plus every rifle and Bren belted up noisy deterrent barrages and four planes were shot down on 1–2 April. About a dozen bombs were aimed at the vital Birgte bridge, but fortunately none hit it. On the 3rd the enemy sent a platoon down to within 200 yards of the bridge but they were liquidated by the reserve squadron of the Fifes.

Meanwhile, from the shattered remains of Tecklenberg, 11th Armoured prepared for another 'cavalry' charge.

CHAPTER TWENTY-EIGHT

The River Weser Crossing

The General decided on another night march of 19 miles north-east to 'bounce' the bridge over the Osnabruck Canal at Eversheide, just north of Osnabruck. The clearing of that town was the task of 6th Airborne Division who had incredibly kept pace (well, almost) with 11th Armoured. Their supporting 6th Guards Tank Brigade had Churchills capable of 17 mph, far slower than Comets, yet day by day they kept up their strange but effective 'alliance'. At midnight on 2 April 3 RTR now led with 4 KSLI in drenching rain through close country intersected by bog and stream, without stopping for rest or sleep. Bill Close commanding B squadron recalls:

> My squadron was leading and the main bridge was literally blown up in my face just as I was about to follow Lieutenant Wadsworth, my leading troop commander, across. We moved down river to another bridge [at Eversheide over the Haase] which was also mined but Wadsworth got out of his tank, cut the wires of the explosives [for which he received the MC] and we then captured the bridge which was then used by 29th Armoured Brigade.

23rd Hussars were following 3 RTR and their historian noted:

> Tank commanders peered miserably by the light of waning torches, at rain-sodden and unreadable maps hoping, without much optimism that they were on the right road. A watery dawn [on 3 April] revealed morale at its lowest ebb and it needed a very strong brew of tea, with a dash of whisky, to improve the bedraggled condition of the crews. The downpour had more decisively defeated even the new tank-suit. Most tank commanders were soaked to the skin.

Out of the bridgehead formed by 3 RTR/4 KSLI, advanced 23rd Hussars and 8 RB. All afternoon they pushed north against infantry opposition and anti-tank guns. By dusk they reached the bridge at Herringhausen over the Ems–Weser some 8 miles north-east, but this time it was 23rd Hussars' turn. About 3 miles north of the Osnabruck suburbs three tanks were hit by AP and 13 RHA brought down a quick stonk. Three 88-mm A/Tk guns were left abandoned but by then it was 4 p.m. Two centre-lines were in use with C squadron and H Company 8 RB racing B squadron and F company

8 RB, leaving gaping German soldiers, dismayed and inactive in the ditches. Lieutenant Steinhart of C squadron won the race. Completely out of wireless touch he hurtled down the cobbled roads through the failing light towards the bridge, which he reached in time to prevent the startled Germans from demolishing it. Then B squadron arrived and in the twilight opened fire on the 'enemy' tank! The German POWs taken were very ancient and ineffective – some had been but four months in the Wehrmacht, a strange contrast to the demons of the Ibbenbüren Ridge who were still fighting on!

By 4 April the enemy had lost Osnabruck, the capital of Westphalia and three important canal lines. In the event they had decided to make a vigorous stand on the River Weser. Resistance was met in the villages of Levern and Rahden and 4 KSLI were involved until dark in tricky house-to-house fighting. The KSLI took forty prisoners in Rahden after 3 RTR had set the village on fire, and a Panther was found abandoned and an SP destroyed. But in Levern the defence was much tougher and the KSLI took twenty casualties including two company commanders. Of the garrison of 400, 150 were made prisoner and many of the others killed. Piles of manure in the fields ready for spreading gave cover to Private Davey's platoon when two MG 42s opened fire at 80 yards. Throwing phosphorous grenades A company worked their way forward. Bob Bignell recalls: 'The attack was short and sharp. I helped put down a smoke screen with the 2-inch mortar but Major Jackson was killed before the smoke had thickened up.' The Herefords now arrived via Lotte, Osterkappeln and Buttebohn. And Steel Brownlie with the Fifes in reserve recalls: 'We went through the narrow winding streets of Eversheide, then down the long hill beyond. There was an immense traffic jam said to be caused by a damaged bridge. Brigadier Churcher was going up and down the column bawling out any driver who got out of line. A rather nice "liberated" Mercedes was shoved in a ditch and left.' The divisional sappers were very busy with numerous damaged bridges over three canals that needed repairing, in heavy rain and none too warm.

Steel Brownlie described a typical farm he had selected for his squadron HQ: 'Huge hallway, raftered and cobbled stalls for horses and cattle, on two sides, family kitchen at the far end all scented by the hay in the loft. Warm, dry, comfortable.'

During the 4th 600 Germans were taken, including 100 collected during the night in the woods by Patrick Delaforce's I Battery 13 RHA. At Osterkappeln Roland Jefferson with 8 RB recounts: 'Here we relieved our first prisoner of war camp. They were mostly Russians and we could do no more than to let them loose into the German town, where they doubtless took their own retribution. There were hundreds and hundreds of them.'

The next day was reminiscent of a 'point to point'. On the 5th Brigadier Churcher had ordered his 159 Brigade on the right, led by the Fifes, to get to Stolzenau on the River Weser before 29th Armoured Brigade on the left, led by 23rd Hussars. A thrilling race ensued and B squadron of the Hussars starting from Esern, with F company 8 RB, reached the river five minutes ahead, in the early afternoon. Predictably the main bridge was blown. Steel Brownlie remembers:

A race to the Weser, 30 miles away. 23 H were on Chase Route, we were on Steeple Route a few miles to the south. Off, flat out at first light. This was more like it. Twiehausen, Espelkamp, Rahden, Linteln and seven more villages on the way to the Weser. At Glissen prisoners from 12 SS Panzer were taken, very young, blubbering and weeping as they ran back along the dusty road, urged by the boots of our infantry [Herefords]. Everybody shouting 'Schneller, Schneller'.

Lieutenant Frank Fuller's Comet was hit in the front in Glissen by a Panzerfaust and was halted in the midst of the 12 SS Panzer youths, who were in ditches on both sides of the road. Frank got out of the turret to climb down and get in on top of the driver, to try to drive out of danger. He was riddled by MG fire and blown off the tank by another Panzerfaust. His gunner lost his nerve, jumped out and was killed. Trooper Oxley, the radio operator, came on the air and said very quietly that the rest of the crew (Lance-Corporals Axtell, Grossmith and Marris) were dead, the enemy were all around and that he proposed to lie doggo till he could escape. He was told to do just that.

Divisional artillery fired quick stonks at 0950 hrs and 1030 hrs. G Battery 13 RHA put down DF fire and smoke screens to break up three attacks by the SS and 8 RB. Stolzenau was reached on the left and Schlusselburg on the right. The Herefords crossed the river at Musleringen with assault boats, rafts and ferry to form a bridgehead. 2 miles north at Stolzenau H and G companies 8 RB made a crossing by assault boats under 88-mm and 20-mm airbursts. Noel Bell described the Weser as 'wide and flowing fast – too fast to be pleasant'. Bridging began by the sappers at 1700 hrs, interrupted by a violent air raid. The Luftwaffe had the unusual assortment – outdated Stuka dive-bombers, FW 190s, JU 88s, Messerschmitts – anything that could fly. 58 LAA Bofors were in action and every form of small-arms fire was thrown up into the sky. Noel Bell recalls: 'Our own Brens and Brownings chattered constantly against the marauders but they were quite futile, the tracers visibly bouncing off the armoured bellies of the Boche planes as they swooped low over the rooftops.' C squadron, Inns of Court, were returning to harbour towards evening, 'as the lumbering Staghounds pulled into the road, two Heinkels flew low and parallel and wheeled to starboard turning to come down dead ahead on the column', reported Peter Reeve. His rear link car was gathering speed and its crew scrambled hastily inside leaving him sitting on the turret top. Having sworn rudely he grabbed the Bren and poured a stream of bullets into the nose and cockpit of the now diving Heinkel: 'I watched the tracer drift almost lazily into its centre front. The aircraft veered sharply to port, lost height, drifted over some trees and disappeared.' It was not until midday on the 6th that the RAF appeared and their Tempests patrolled the river length. In the interim 12 SS Panzer and 100 Pioneer Brigade put up determined resistance using the village of Leese as their base. During the night of the 5th the small RB bridgehead was continually under fire. Noel Bell's HQ in a farmhouse had the advantage of having vast quantities of preserves, bottled fruit and vegetables, plus bottles of Chianti and hams. But at 0900 hrs the following day 11 Platoon rang through to report infantry advancing in waves on to the companies' positions. 'Hundreds of 'em,' said Lieutenant Clark, 'hundreds of 'em.' Fortunately DF fire from 13 RHA and Ayrshire Yeo brought down 'an almighty stonk slap in the midst of the enemy. The attacking force was written off', noted Noel Bell. Kenneth Chabot, another RB officer, had been watching the DF fire come down from a top-storey window: 'He came down in great jubilation muttering "First class – that'll teach the bloody Boche."' By midday the Sappers were making good headway with the bridge despite constant shelling of 612 and 13 RE squadrons. Constant salvoes of 88 mm took their toll.

Dick Anderson explained that:

[the Weser was] a really big obstacle and required a floating bridge 346 feet long. The CRE took charge of the operation tasking 612 Field squadron with building the two ends (landing bays and end floating bays) and 13 Field squadron with the floating bays for the centre of the bridge. 224 Corps Troops Field company were under command of unloadings and to man assault boats for the infantry. But some six FW 190s swept in about 1600 hrs on 6 April, skip bombing from very low altitude with considerable courage in face of LAA fire. They destroyed 50 per cent of the bridge with direct hits on an end floating bay and both approaches. Much equipment was sunk and thirty to forty casualties incurred. On the 7th and 8th the site was again shelled and mortared and work rapidly became impossible.

Eighteen Sappers were killed – a real disaster.

Further bombing followed and destroyed the bridge, leaving just so much twisted metal. Now 8 Corps sent 1 Commando Brigade to help. 45 Royal Marine Commando arrived at 1000 hrs on the 6th. Captain Goer, Ayrshire Yeomanry, was their FOO and Captain Lucas the FOO with the Herefords 2,000 yards to the south. Both little bridgeheads were pinned down with fire and no tanks could get across to enlarge them. So now 15/19th Hussars and the newly-arrived 1st Cheshires moved 15 miles south-west to Petershagen, where the indomitable 6th Airborne had secured a bridge. Stolzenau with its grim memories was now abandoned. 8 RB withdrew across the river and the Sappers licked their wounds.

Combined Tank (15/19th KRH) and Infantry (1st Cheshires) advancing on the east bank of the River Weser beyond Heimsen, April 1945

The Rifle Brigade had never before fought alongside the Commandos, and Noel Bell reported:

We were amazed after daylight had broken on the 6th to see them walking about, seemingly quite oblivious of the enemy so close at hand, making no effort whatever to conceal their movements. In consequence, a considerable enemy artillery barrage came down on our positions, wounding many of them, some seriously. To us trained for years in fieldcraft and concealment of movement, their lack of same left us speechless.

The only good news was the discovery by F company 8 RB of an enormous wine dump in Stolzenau. For two days 23rd Hussars mounted guard on 'Hockpoint' as it was signed up. Brigadier Roscoe Harvey was one of the first to hear of this find and the General ordered Geoffrey Thwaites, the A/Q, to formalize the situation. All units got their share and a lorry load of hooch was sent to Corps HQ to keep them happy. Eventually the multitudes of DPs in the area were allowed supplies and the streets were filled with riotously happy 'United Nations' celebrating some kind of victory.

CHAPTER TWENTY-NINE

From the Weser to the Aller

The General had ordered 159 Brigade to drive north towards Leese, still strongly held by 12 SS Panzer, with the Cheshire/15/19th Hussars group on the left and Herefords/2nd Fife and Forfarshire on the right advancing towards Loccum.

At Harrienstedt, 3 miles west of the River Weser on 6 April, the 1st Cheshires, having left 115th Independent Brigade, joined 159 Brigade. Lieutenant-Colonel Kreyer was in command and for the next few, final weeks the Cheshires worked closely with 15/19th Hussars, with three companies up on the Comets and the fourth rifle company in reserve in its own TCVs. At 1000 hrs on the 7th the Cheshires were in action, having crossed at the Petershagen bridge, and soon captured the villages of Heimsden and Wasserstrasse on the way north to link up with 1 Commando Brigade bridgehead at Stolznau. By nightfall Leese had been reduced to rubble by RAF Typhoon rockets and divisional artillery fire programmes.

But the Herefords and Fifes, having pushed eastwards through Windheirm and Dohren, had a long sharp battle to take Loccum. The heaviest fighting was encountered by B company/C squadron who were engaged at close quarters for six hours with paratroopers and 88-mm guns. After Steel Brownlie had been photographed at Petershagen by the *Illustrated London News* in his fairly new Comet, and John Gilmour's tank was photographed for a 'Matchbox' kit, the Fifes found Loccum strangely quiet. A full-scale attack was planned but half the tanks were bogged: Steel Brownlie wrote:

> I reached the railway line with a platoon of Herefords and blazed away at likely targets in front. 400 yards to the left the line ran into a cutting and suddenly a stream of Germans came pouring down one side and up the other, obviously fleeing from C squadron's assault. I fired rapidly with HE and MG; they were soon in confusion and the Herefords went out to bring in the survivors. They were the crews and covering infantry of seven 88-mm guns which amazingly C squadron had overwhelmed without loss. Was it cruel to batter retreating troops? That night squadron HQ was in a café on the main crossroads. In the huge bar almost the whole squadron were crammed in, clouds of tobacco smoke and the aroma of suppers being cooked. The Herefords were dug in round the town and the Comets were parked outside. Half a dozen serving wenches

Lieutenant Ted Deeming, 15/19th KRH, with his tank loaded with a section of B Company, 1st Cheshires, moving north from Petershagen, April 1945

kept the steins of beer coming to all ranks. Within an hour we had drunk the place dry. I liberated the entire stock of cigarettes for distribution to POWs or DPs who might want them.

23rd Hussars having crossed at Petershagen on 8 April came under command of 1 Commando Brigade for the final attack on Leese. The Commandos had been finding life on the bridgehead opposite Stolznau rather tough, and 20-mm guns had caused many casualties. But they finally cleared Leese on the evening of the 7th and morning of the 8th with the help of a squadron of 23rd Hussars. At midday the KSLI/3 RTR group met obstinate opposition in Rehburg and it took five hours to clear the village. One platoon took heavy casualties, and Major Edwards killed two men with his rifle before that enemy position surrendered. But 7 miles north at Husum they met fanatical resistance from the Hitler Youth. Captain Hank Henry directed the fire of two Wasp flamethrowers to savage effect. Bazookas knocked out 3 RTR tanks and snipers killed ten KSLI in the village, seriously wounding Major George Edwards. Second Lieutenant Brecknell lasted less than a day, having joined the KSLI on 7 April. Private Dave Dalton, a Brengunner with 11 platoon, wrote: 'Those German snipers were deadly – their victims rarely got away with a bullet wound.' Altogether the battalion had thirteen killed and thirty wounded but in turn killed eighty Hitler Youth and captured another 120.

Peter Reeve's Inns of Court squadron was sent to Husum to support 4 KSLI:

> They were in the throes of a bloody battle with an SS unit who had looted the village and shot several KSLI prisoners in cold blood in the back of the head. We were met by a hail of fire from Schmeissers. An SS officer crouched with his machine gun cradled as we loosed off bursts from the Browning. He went on firing till he was cut almost in half. Late in the evening all opposition ceased – a grisly pile of burned bodies being the only memento.

A few Wasps, flamethrowers mounted on Bren gun carriers, were available to the Division and had been used in the Husum battle.

The 23rd Hussars found a large V Bomb factory at Landesbergen. It was a boiling hot day with a blue sky and they pushed easily through Loccum, Rehburg and east to the high ground at Schneeren, where they harboured the night.

After clearing Leese, the main objectives were the bridges some 20 miles east along the River Leine which linked with the River Aller near Hodemstorf. By 1500 hrs on the 8th the Cheshires had cleared eight villages and reached Eilvese, 3 miles west of the River Leine. In Eilvese strong opposition was met and bazookas claimed two tanks, but the Herefords and the Fifes took over and continued northwards through the villages of Hagen, Dudensen and Laderholz. Most of the villages were briefly defended and the woods near the centre-line roads harboured bazooka men.

Apart from the considerable number of displaced persons encountered, wandering back to safety along the centre-lines, the Division liberated the occasional POW camp and a great many ammunition dumps, explosive factories and V–2 sites between the rivers Weser and Leine. They were usually concealed in large woods, and had to be guarded, often by the invaluable Todforce/75 A/Tk Regiment.

Bill Close with 3 RTR wrote: 'No one wanted to take any risks any more. The men in lead tanks knew they would be the first to get it if we bumped into a last ditch battlegroup. It was necessary to ring the changes. People were reluctant to drive round corners. I gave orders that no chances were to be taken with bazooka merchants.' Cottages and houses were set on fire quite indiscriminately on the surmise that there just might be a bazooka group lurking within. Very few enemy tanks were now encountered. Very few minefields or nebelwerfers, but the ubiquitous 88-mm A/Tk guns turned up with discouraging frequency. The advance was now through rich Prussian cornland with large well-stocked farms, amply supplied with slave labour and Russian POWs. A peaceful and prosperous countryside completely untouched by war – until now. A captured U-Boat biscuit and chocolate dump showed that within this part of Germany food stocks were ample. It was difficult to predict which villages the Germans

A captured V-2 rocket site, Leese, April 1945

would defend whole-heartedly. At this stage there were two. Nienburg needed a combined attack by 3 RTR and 8 RB, plus SPs from 75 A/Tk, and was eventually cleared by 4 KSLI, with 13 RHA putting down supporting stonks. A Tempest pilot was shot down and he claimed furiously that David Swiney's SP troop (equipped with .5 Browning AA machine-guns) was responsible: 'I replied that we knew the difference between a Tempest and a FW 190.'

Another village that caused a great deal of trouble was Steimbke, half-way between Nienburg and the River Leine. It was defended by a company of the Hitler Youth, of 12 SS Training Battalion, who had killed several KSLI prisoners and a medical corporal near Schneeren. On the morning of the 9th, 23rd Hussars entered Steimbke, knocked out two towed 88-mm A/Tk guns and a 75-mm gun, but lost a Comet to a bazooka. Noel Bell with G company 8 RB recalls: 'Steimbke looked peaceful enough sheltering in a quiet valley under a warm sun in the morning sky. The small cottages with their thatched roofs, and a small pretty church presented a picture of complete tranquillity.' The first effort failed, so a set-piece attack took place and 13 RHA put a heavy regimental stonk into the village. A squadron of 23rd Hussars surrounded the village on three sides and fired HE non-stop. Two RB companies began to clear the village. 'The SS fought fanatically and every house had to be cleared individually. Our stretcher-bearers were fired on which spurred us on even more. No quarter was given or asked and very few SS prisoners lived to tell the tale,' according to Noel Bell. Lieutenant Eric Yetman was wounded and died. 'Here we practised house-to-house fighting as we had been taught in training,' remembered Roland Jefferson. 'We would throw a grenade into the house and as soon as it exploded, rush in after it and so on from room to room and house to house. Trouble was we used up our supplies of '36' grenades.' The 23rd Hussars historian wrote: 'From the village, sullen greasy-looking striplings with the SS flash came running, hands raised, their faces contorted with pain whenever the heavy boot of a rifleman was applied. Steimbke, smoking and wrecked, was clear after a model operation which cost the enemy 150 casualties.'

Seven miles further east a similar little battle was fought at Nord-Drebber, also by 23rd Hussars/8 RB. Here the defenders were Kriegmarine troops, many of whom were killed or captured, but the bridge at Bothmer was blown – as indeed were the bridges at Niederstocken reached by Herefords/Fifes, and Holstorf reached by Cheshires/15/19th Hussars. The situation was awkward for the Division. At the confluence of the Leine and Aller in thickly wooded country, with all bridges blown, it was a natural defensive position. On the northern, left flank, 7th Armoured Division had not yet drawn level and on the south, right flank, 15 Scottish had just replaced 6th Airborne. Nevertheless a 6th Airborne bridge at Bordenau was loaned to the Division and 15/19th Hussars/Cheshires crossed and swung north on the far bank to Helstorf, described as Norfolk-like country of heath and pine. Here 15/19th Hussars captured an airfield complete with twelve aircraft. The situation on the 10th was that the Herefords/Fifes had crossed by the Bordenau bridge and passed through the Cheshires/15/19th Hussars to capture Schwarmstedte. Steel Brownlie reported: 'It was strongly held, there was stiff fighting,' and the Herefords launched a two-company attack supported by the Fifes and a stonk from the Ayrshire Yeomanry 25-pounders. In the evening 1st Commando Brigade arrived to force a crossing of the River Aller at Essel some 2 miles to the north-east. During the night of the 10th they crossed by a railway bridge and established a small bridgehead, but in the early hours of the morning of the 11th the vital bridge at Essel was blown up, leaving a gap of 120 feet. That same morning 3 RTR at Schwarmstedte lost men and tanks to an 88 mm on the other side of the river.

Meanwhile the rest of the Division harboured in the triangle of rivers in readiness for the next breakout around Grindau, Esperke and Elze with 8 RB in Rodewald and 3 RTR at Wenden. The sappers had built a 170-foot Bailey bridge at Helstorf across the Seine, which Dick Anderson described

3 RTR Comet tank near the
River Rhine, March 1945

as the longest class 40 single-span Bailey built in north-west Europe. 612
and 13 Field Squadrons worked from 1600 hrs on 9 April to 0300 hrs on 11
April, then moved to Essel on the River Aller for rafting activities. The eyes
and ears of the Division, the Inns of Court, had been probing in front every
day and reporting back. A squadron lost Lieutenant Hills and Corporal
Trevett in a bazooka attack, Sergeant Cox was killed by an 88 mm near
Offen, Trooper Davies's scout car was hit by a bazooka near Romstedt and
he was killed – every regiment had its almost daily casualties at the sharp
end. During the night of the 11th 4 KSLI crossed the River Aller to widen
the Commando bridgehead and 1 Cheshire crossed at 1445 hrs, having
found a 4-foot wide foot-bridge south of Engenhausen. By 2100 hrs the
Cheshires, under cover of a stonk by 13 RHA, crossed and occupied
Engenhausen and took a few prisoners. Patrick Delaforce, FOO 13 RHA,
supporting KSLI, tells how:

> we crossed at dusk in black rubber boats with an 18 set. The KSLI
> occupied a crescent-shaped dense wood which was attacked throughout
> the night by young German marines. I kept up DF fire through much of
> the night but in the thick woods did little damage. In the morning [12
> April] my OP tank was ferried the 40 metres across with A Squadron of 3
> RTR on sapper-constructed rafts. Unusually the bridgehead was attacked
> by odd Tiger and Panther tanks which knocked out several KSLI A/Tk
> guns, although they were rather cautious in the dense pine trees. My
> stonks certainly deterred their protective infantry screen.

4 KSLI and 3 RTR then spent two days trying to break out from Hademstorf towards Ostenholz. Straight narrow roads through the immensely thick woods were easily defended by the German tanks and guns. The Cheshire bridgehead eventually was linked up with the Essel bridgehead. Another main bridge was blown at Winsen, but by the 13th the Sappers had built a new one at Essel and another new one at Winsen.

CHAPTER THIRTY

Towards the Elbe

The breakout from the bridgehead over the Aller took some time. David Swiney's 75 A/Tk SP troop supported 46 Royal Marine Commando in the woods in an attack on Hademstorf, which was eventually taken with sixty prisoners: 'The enemy were from a Marine Division and it was quite fortuitous that both British and German Marines should meet in battle so far from the sea. One of my guns hidden in a barn destroyed an 88 mm. The blast of the 17-pounder brought down half the roof which knocked out the gunner OP signaller upstairs. He was not amused.' The Cheshires soon met the exhilarated faces of several Allied POWs who, hearing gunfire approaching their prison camp at Fallingbostel, had escaped in the early evening of 11 April. Their excitement and relief at seeing the Cheshires was extreme. The infantry battalions moving through densely wooded country usually had two rifle companies leading clearing the woods on each side of the road. The third company followed up on the supporting squadron of tanks and the fourth was in reserve in its own TCVs. The companies were generally organized two platoons forward, one in reserve; platoons in turn were organized in a similar manner. The infantry moved in 'extended' order to clear as large an area of the wood as possible. If the woods were bounded by roads or tracks the carrier platoon moved along them keeping abreast of the rifle companies, rounding up enemy who attempted to escape from the woods.

During the 12th and 13th the Germans fought like devils to hold off the northerly thrust to Ostenholz, and 4 KSLI/3 RTR had a difficult time trying to clear thick woods, with each road and track defended by elusive Tigers, some heavy shelling and many MGs. In the two days the KSLI lost twelve killed, forty wounded, but a hundred enemy marines and panzer grenadiers were captured and about three hundred killed or wounded.

When on 12 April 3 RTR started meeting Tiger tanks on the way out of the KSLI bridgehead towards the little River Drebber, the textbook advance was little use. A Tiger suddenly appeared round a corner, knocked out one of John Langdon's Comets, a scout car and a half track: 'About 300 yards away I saw its 88-mm gun slowly traversing on us. We fired. Head-on as it was to us we could not hope to knock the tank out. We were out-gunned and if I wanted to save my tank and crew there was only one thing to be done.' The Comet was reversed into cover, knocking over 40-foot fir trees. Corporal Brindle's Comet was hit three times and knocked out. The

1st Cheshires and 15/19th KRH near Berkhof, April 1945

following day, the 13th, Sergeant Harding ambushed the Tiger at 100 yards broadside on, put two AP into its side and brewed it up. A second Tiger withdrew! But 3 RTR lost Sergeant Probert to a sniper, Lieutenant Michael Bullock and Trooper Bligh to an AP shot. They also had many tanks bogged down in the streams and marshes between the woods – sitting targets until ARVs recovered.

The 13th was Black Friday indeed. Three hundred Germans were dead around the enlarged bridgehead. 13 RHAs FOOs were all in trouble. Patrick Delaforce's OP had been shelled by a Tiger tank. Bill Smyth-Osborne's OP tank was hit five times at 200 yards range. Ernest Mather and Philip Kinnersley's OP tanks were also hit. The Cheshires pushed their way out of their bridgehead towards Winsen, with 15/19th Hussars taking ninety prisoners at Thoren Bannetze, having crossed the new bridge at Essel.

Unfortunately the 14th was another Black day. The Cheshires resumed their attack on Winsen, defended by the staff and students of a nearby Anti-Tank Officers Training Unit equipped with 88-mm, 75-mm SP guns and numerous panzerfausts. Nebelwerfers bombarded battalion HQ at 0530 hrs, firing at TCV loaded with petrol, which exploded causing many casualties including the 2 i/c and adjutant. All day long the slow, tedious and painful battle to clear the woods continued. Artillery stonks and rocket-firing Typhoons destroyed artillery pieces. By 6 p.m. the woods were cleared – at a cost. Three officers and eleven ORs killed, two officers and twenty-nine

Seventy captured Hungarians near Lübeck: Captain Chris Weatherby, second in command B Squadron 15/19th KRH, takes their surrender, May 1945

ORs wounded – the hardest day's fighting since landing in north-west Europe. The CO of the Cheshires, Lieutenant-Colonel R.G. Kreyer wrote: 'Some magnificent things were done by various individuals, notably Lance-Corporal R. Fields who was afterwards killed, Sergeant H. Birkby, Corporal G. Bagshaw. Lieutenant Wolpert, though badly wounded, refused to be evacuated.' In the evening the Herefords and Fifes made a dash along the final mile of the road to capture Winsen. All told about two hundred prisoners were taken and eleven A/Tk guns destroyed.

The Herefords took thirty prisoners of Battlegroup Totlech. The 15/19th Hussars were supporting the Cheshires in the bitter Winsen battle and Trooper Kenneth Kirkley was in the leading tank on the 14th:

We took a surprise 75-mm A/Tk hit as we exited from laager and started through the forest centre-line. Our commander was Sergeant John Finlayson who jumped out of the [disabled] tank and 'arrested' the German occupants of a trench. Afterwards Major Mark Pearson, our squadron leader, ordered me back into the turret to maintain possession of our tank. Afterwards I counted thirteen holes in the hull and turret. My birthday cake for the 18th was in the offside stowage bin. Later when we ate it, we picked out large pieces of shrapnel.

And Eric Hamilton remembers: 'the laager in a small green field, the only one in the very large forest; naturally the German Kriegmarines gunners had this earmarked as the only tank harbour so over came the airbursts'. 15/19th Hussars lost a dozen casualties around Winsen and Ted Deeming wrote: 'Here after the Volkssturm light resistance, we encountered troops from the German Marine Division and the bitterest fighting we had seen. It was the regiment's last real battle and it was the hardest.'

CHAPTER THIRTY-ONE

Belsen

A large German staff car with a white flag carrying Lieutenant-Colonel Schmidt and a major, both of the Medical Corps, arrived at the Cheshires' Battalion HQ early on 13 April. They stated that they had been sent by the camp commandant of Belsen concentration camp, 10 miles north-east of Engenhausen, to warn the Division not to approach within 3 miles of the camp as a serious typhus epidemic was killing many of its inhabitants. The camp, they said, housed '500,000 people, mostly Poles and Hungarians, of whom 5,000 were stricken with typhus. Dysentery was also rife.' Lieutenant-Colonel Kreyer, CO Cheshires, sent them back to Brigadier Churcher at Bucholz, and via Division to Corps HQ. The General wrote: 'It was arranged that the Germans would withdraw by 1000 hrs on the 14th and a corps medical team would follow our leading troops to investigate the camp. It all went according to plan and we went on with war.' In fact this terrifying place between Hermanaugberg, Bonstorf and Bergen and north of Winsen held 35,000 men and 25,000 women, mostly political prisoners, in two large camps.

Roland Jefferson with 8 RB had seen the staff car with its huge white flag and 'we thought, this is it – the war's over!' Not quite. Patrick Delaforce, FOO with 3 RTR, remembers the ignominious way white DDT anti-typhus powder was sprayed and sprinkled over every individual proceeding close to the camp, which Noel Bell describes:

> The yellow German road signs, edged in black announced 'Belsen'. It was just another name to us then. The sight of a concentration camp on our left as we drove through caused us no surprise. The whole place was surrounded by pretty young conifers and beyond them a barbed wire fence about 12 feet high. By the entrances there stood groups of Hungarian guards – we recognized them by the colour of their uniforms – and small knots of men, pyjama-clad. They were the inmates; those that could stand. We had been ordered not to fire at enemy personnel in the camps unless we were provoked. Unnecessary fighting would only spread the typhus disease.

Captain C.K.O. Spence with the Ayrshire Yeomany recalls his experience:

> It was a huge place covering several square miles lying in wooded country. The narrow roads leading to it were full of wrecked horse-drawn vehicles

filled with turnips and potatoes for the inmates. In the previous six weeks allied fighters had shot everything off the roads. At the gate was a small group of men and women – the 'civilian camp staff' including the infamous Kramer and his head woman assistant, Irma Grese. About one third of a mile separated the outer and inner wires. A few ragged figures, filthy and emaciated, had found their way to the space between. Seeing us they rushed to the outer wire and spontaneously some of our men pushed cigarettes and sweets through the wire or threw them over the top. The ragged band fell upon them with ferocious energy and when everything had been seized some were left dead or dying on the ground, torn to pieces by their comrades for the sake of chocolate or cigarettes. The stench is still in my nostrils.

There were 13,000 unburied corpses.

Trooper H.W. Drummond with 15/19th Hussars drove a scout car through the camp and noticed the guard houses, water tower, a new large red sign with white lettering, '*Achtung Typhus*', and the look of the inmates: 'As they watched us go by, we could have been from Mars. There were no emotions discernible.' Lieutenant-Colonel Bob Daniell, 13 RHA with 29 Armoured Brigade HQ, stopped outside the main gates, walked in, briefly walked around the camp and pistolled three aggressive Hungarian guards who tried to stop him. The historian of the 23rd Hussars commented: 'Lining the road were brown-uniformed swarthy little Hungarians with white armbands, quite unabashed and occasionally having the impudence to give the Fascist salute. On our side of the barbed wire barrier lay a Hungarian tensely gripping a machine gun on a tripod pointed unwaveringly at the mob of prisoners which clamoured at the gate.'

In 1944 Belsen had been designated a 'sick' camp by the German authorities. There were five categories: Extermination, Labour, Sick, Experimental and Training purposes. The 'sick' were internees whose death was not *immediately* required. The 'training' was for the SS in concentration camp techniques and 'extermination' was just that in the style of Auschwitz 1. Josef Kramer's staff of forty-four included Dr Klein who headed Admin., sixteen SS men, sixteen female members of the SS (Irma Grese was aged twenty when captured), plus twelve KAPOs including six Poles. Camp 1 was sited 2 km from Camp 2. Germans were the majority of the prisoners, then Russians, Poles and a great many Jews. Klein invented some of the tortures, one of which was injecting creosote and petrol into the prisoner's veins. When Major Charles Chapman, 58 LAA and his battery and then 63 A/Tk regiment took over responsibility for the camp, the German guards were forced to bring the dead bodies from all over the camp and bury them in huge bulldozed graves – 500 at a time:

One could only hope for a quick death for the majority [Chapman wrote]. The awful cloying stench of death was everywhere. There were piles of dead bodies, mere bags of bones from years of systematic starvation, but worst of all was the animal look and habits of so many of the prisoners still alive: all spark of human intellect seemed to have departed. The haunting memory of it will be with me till my dying day.

Alan Moorehead noticed 'the curious pearly colour about the piled up bodies, and they were small like the bodies of children'. He was told by the Pioneer captain in charge of burials: 'The doctors are doing a wonderful job. They are in the huts all day sorting out the living bodies from the dead and it's not easy sometimes to tell the difference. But they are saving a lot now with two meals a day at ten and six.' Kramer claimed that he was swamped with trainloads of new prisoners from all over Germany, that he did not have enough staff, nor enough food. The Allies bombed the electric water pump in the camp and disrupted cartloads of food for the camp. Patrick Delaforce looked carefully at the twenty guards lined up on the right as his Cromwell went through before spending twenty minutes in the camp. In late May he was diagnosed as having the Belsen bug, was put on a drip with a near lethal dose of penicillin, no food and 12 pints of water a day, and he recovered. Later he was junior member of several 'minor' war crimes trial tribunals, and on Friday 13 December 1945 was an official witness at Hameln when Pierrepoint hanged thirteen convicted Belsen staff – before lunch.

CHAPTER THIRTY-TWO

The Last Stretch

After the liberation of Belsen by 23rd Hussars and 8 RB on the 15th 3 RTR/4 KSLI pushed north from Bergen towards Wietzendorf. Patrick Delaforce, FOO with 3 RTR, remembers the shelling at dusk which delayed the advance: 'The airburst was unexpectedly heavy at a crossroads. It was so dark that a DF would have been pointless.' The Hereford/Fifes group moved due east to clear Walthausen, where Steel Brownlie reported:

> The Herefords dismounted to make an assault. I went round to the left to find a good fire position. I blazed away with HE and tracer to help the infantry forward and the attack went in past the wrecked road block and into the blazing streets. I followed through burning debris. The Herefords with our close support forced the defenders to retreat but a few snipers were left. They killed or wounded several of the infantry, but we tank commanders ducked up and down to present as small a target as possible while still seeing what was going on. House-to-house fighting like that in Walthausen was always exhilarating.

Colonel Alec's Comet was then blown up by a mine linked to an aerial bomb. He had been told the road was clear! The Fifes sped through the woods northwards through Sulze, Diesten and Huxahl, bypassing Hermannsburg towards Muden, brushing aside resistance and taking seventy-five Hungarian POWs. The Herefords had twelve separate actions that day and Ayrshire Yeomanry engaged targets at Sulze. 'Tam' Steven was the driver of Captain Lucas, Ayrshire Yeomanry FOO with the Fifes: 'A single squadron of tanks – B squadron under Major Voller – without infantry but with artillery support, relying solely on their speed and firepower might just pull it off before dusk.' The objective was the River Wiotze at Muden, ten miles away: 'This was to be a true cavalry advance. Eighteen Comets charging up the road in line ahead at about 35 mph, firing BESA into the woods by the roadside and farmhouses which conceal parties of bazooka-men, being the target for the 77-mm main armament.' Two troops of Fifes pitched up in the centre of Muden when the main bridge *behind* them was blown up. The Fifes then took to the high ground outside the town centre and, despite attacks during the night, held their ground. During the night of the 15th the Herefords forced a small bridgehead in Muden and the Sappers bridged the river so the seven surviving, battered

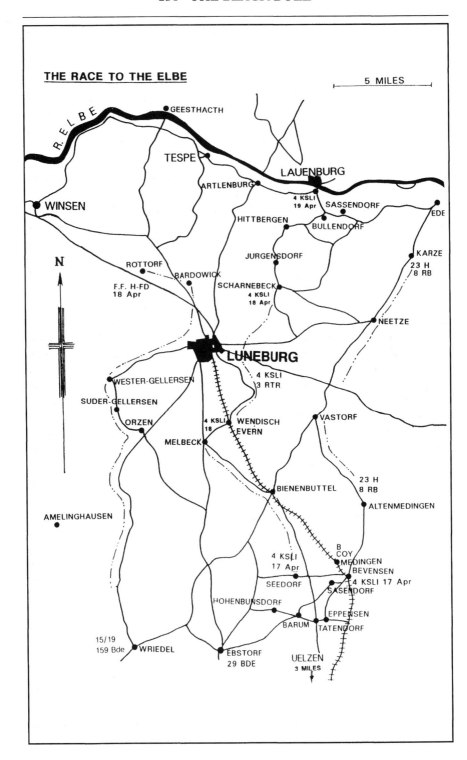

THE RACE TO THE ELBE

5 MILES

R. ELBE

GEESTHACTH

TESPE

LAUENBURG

ARTLENBURG

4 KSLI
19 Apr

SASSENDORF

WINSEN

EDE

HITTBERGEN

BULLENDORF

N

JURGENSDORF

KARZE
23 H
8 RB

ROTTORF

BARDOWICK

F.F. H-FD
18 Apr

SCHARNEBECK

4 KSLI
18 Apr

NEETZE

LUNEBURG

4 KSLI
3 RTR

WESTER-GELLERSEN

SUDER-GELLERSEN

ORZEN

4 KSLI
18

WENDISCH
EVERN

VASTORF

MELBECK

BIENENBUTTEL

23 H
8 RB

AMELINGHAUSEN

ALTENMEDINGEN

4 KSLI
17 Apr

B
COY
MEDINGEN

BEVENSEN

4 KSLI 17 Apr

SEEDORF

SASENDORF

HOHENBUNSDORF

EPPENSEN

BARUM

TATENDORF

15/19
159 Bde

WRIEDEL

EBSTORF
29 BDE

UELZEN

3 MILES

tanks drove back into Muden to greet the rest of 159 Brigade. Lieutenant-Colonel R.C. Fripp arrived to become CO of the Herefords.

Meanwhile 23rd Hussars/8 RB had occupied Bergen, north of Belsen. And at Hagen 4 KSLI liberated a large Allied prisoner-of-war camp and sixty German guards. Private Davey with A company 4 KSLI, wrote: 'At Hagen, our battalion was feted by crowds of liberated prisoners, mainly British and Dominion troops [including RAF]. They just blocked the road, making it impossible for the tanks to move, they were so happy, and we gave them what little food and cigarettes we had with us.'

The Hussars took another 100 captives at Bornstorf. Lieutenant Farquhar's Recce troop dashed across the river bridge and found itself in a hornet's nest of SS. Two 'Honeys' were knocked out but C squadron and 8 RB came to their rescue, set the village alight, killed seventy SS and captured even more. But from Bornstorf north to Reiningen all the remaining bridges over the Wiorze were blown.

The advance continued strongly on the 16th against sporadic but determined resistance by Hungarian SS with snipers, bazookas, spandau and many mines. Muden was on the edge of Lüneburg Heath, the German equivalent of Salisbury Plain. No wonder that once reaching the River Aller the quality of the opposition had unfortunately noticeably increased! Now 15/19th Hussars with the Cheshires pushed through Muden east and took Gerdehaus and Schmarbeck, where they encountered the defences of a large aerodrome. The SS held out for five hours but were smoked out, trench by trench, and 150 prisoners of war were taken. The Comet BESAs ignited the dry, dusty heath and heather and soon huge explosions of bomb dumps blowing up were seen and heard. At twilight the Hussars had advanced in broad naval formations across rolling heathland and occupied Wichtenbeck at nightfall – a day's advance of 30 miles. On the left flank 3 RTR/4 KSLI had made some progress. After the liberation of the POW camp at Hagen, 4 KSLI on the left route left a company to guard Bergen and moved north to try to reach Wietzendorf, 8 miles ahead. 3 RTR set the heathland on fire attracting two Messerschmitts which bombed the column, destroyed a truck and jeep and damaged a Comet, causing casualties. Nevertheless the advance of 25 miles had produced 300 prisoners and the battlegroup harboured amid a good deal of shelling and mortaring near Marbostel. In the early morning the poor quality of the roads and strong mortaring produced a change of plan.

Noel Bell's comment was: 'We had run into a certain amount of opposition [the bridges were blown and the tracks were of poor quality] so were switched from Bergen to Hermannsburg where a bridge had been taken intact. We followed 3 RTR and a short "swan" developed. By nightfall we reached Wriedel [overrunning a large poison gas dump in the Forst Lintzel].' 3 RTR actually reached Ebsdorf on a five-road junction in the midst of thick woods, which was swarming with Germans who showed no signs of surrendering.

The following day, the 17th, 7th Armoured on the left flank had reached the Hamburg autobahn, and on the right 15th Scottish (who had taken over from 6th Airborne at the Aller) were attacking Uelzen. 11th Armoured's task was to cut the roads north of Uelzen leading to Lüneburg. 6th Airborne, intrepid 'birdmen', still in the race to the Elbe, were to thrust round Uelzen from the east to trap the German defenders. 8 RB/23rd Hussars, starting from Wriedel, pushed on to Seedorf, where two 88-mm A/Tk guns destroyed two Hussar Comets. 13 RHA put down a heavy stonk and pink smoke targeted the area for a Typhoon strike. Noel Bell saw them:

> After circling the objective two or three times, down they came, diving to tree-top height and loosing their deadly rockets with incredible accuracy into the midst of the enemy position. Our grandstand, a few hundred yards away, was rocked by the explosions. Many dead Germans and several wrecked guns were the only testimony of what we had been up against and no live or even wounded German remained to tell the tale.

The Hussars now had a set-piece attack on Barun, 1½ miles south of Seedorf. It was a classic attack against bitter defence. Despite heavy RHA bombardment, it needed a Medium regiment's shells to reduce the village. The Hussars' tanks were belting in HE from all four sides and by nightfall H Company 8 RB finally cleared the totally stricken village. For the loss of four Comets, ten Hussar and four RB casualties, sixteen assorted 88s, 75s and 37-mm guns were destroyed, 150 prisoners taken and 60 Germans killed.

The Uelzen trap was closed. Meanwhile 3 RTR and 4 KSLI had captured Medingen and Bevenson a mile or so north-east and blocked the main railway line between Uelzen and Lüneburg. Altogether the nine key villages north of Uelzen were now captured. 15/19th Hussars made contact in the south with SAS troops and elements of 15th Scottish, who stormed Uelzen at dawn on the 18th. The Inns of Court now hurtled north for over 25 miles to the outskirts of Lüneburg and 15/19th Hussars liberated a large batch of Allied POWs at Kirk Gellersen, 5 miles west of Lüneburg. Although the Devils Own had put a patrol into the town, it was Major Courage and C squadron 15/19th who actually captured Lüneburg. Indeed for a day the Hussars acted as Town Major, Military Government, Conqueror, Advice Bureau and general factotum for the varied population of Germans, Russians, Poles, French, etc.

On the right flank 3 RTR/4 KSLI soon cleared Bienenbuttel and Melbeck, where 400 Allied POWs were freed, then moved east across the railway to Wendisch Evern. Then they cleared the western suburbs of Lüneburg and moved north-east to Scharnebeck. During the day 4 KSLI had advanced 28 miles, taken 250 enemy prisoners and freed hundreds of Allied POWs – one of their more satisfying days. The 23rd Hussars/8 RB group reached Barendorf and A squadron went into Neetze where they almost demolished and/or liberated Belli's Circus, where they found lions, bears, two elephants, many ponies, a monkey, several fat women and an overpowering smell. The Riflemen reported: 'A great reception was prepared for us. The fat lady, the lion tamer, the midgets and countless others turned out to greet us.' Unfortunately two lions had been killed by A squadron Comets, but two bears ambled off into the woods unscathed.

The Elbe now lay 10 miles north. The General wrote: 'The idea of capturing a bridge over the Elbe seemed an exciting objective. It was reported that the railway bridge over the river at Lauenberg was still intact.'

There was one final action on the morning of the 19th when 4 KSLI was ordered to clear the banks of the Elbe at Sassendorf on the south bank opposite Lauenburg and seize the railway bridge while 3 RTR backed up on the road from Hittbergen. Patrick Delaforce, FOO with 3 RTR, transferred to 4 KSLI and on foot with 18 set, sten and signaller took part in the fighting:

> It was a beautiful day, we had a mile and a half of lovely countryside with a dozen prosperous farms to clear. There was a maze of dykes and streams to cross with tanks and mortars barring the way to the railway embankment. Flak guns from the north side of the Elbe raked the approaches with fire. Unfortunately every farm was well defended and we had to winkle out the SS from deep well-stocked cellars where it was easy for the few survivors to hide, reappear and try to shoot us in the back. So we had to turn around, several times, to retake the farms. Curiously enough we failed to take any prisoners. During this time German artillery on the north bank of the Elbe was shelling us. Eventually by mid-afternoon the south bank was cleared and from a farmhouse on the river embankment I started 13 RHA firing some brisk targets. There was certainly plenty of activity from troops, vehicles and guns. Suddenly a grenade or small mortar bomb came through the window of the OP where we had a KSLI O group, and wounded everyone. That night Dr Cree, 13 RHA MO, took out four shrapnel fragments, left two in and said to me: 'You look rather pale, you need a good iron tonic.'

For the KSLI it was one of the bitterest battles of the whole campaign. Joe Davey wrote:

> Although between the Rhine and the Elbe we advanced about 20 miles per day and took casualties on most days, the majority of our actions consisted of nasty little skirmishes lasting just an hour or so. Up to the Rhine our casualties had been 80 per cent from shrapnel, in the last phase of the war it was 75 per cent from bullets. Most actions were Company attacks, almost always with help from the tanks. Our two main actions in Germany, at the Dortmund–Ems Canal and at the River Aller against nasty and fanatical troops, did not compare with those in Normandy or the Rhineland.

When, by 1730 hrs, 3 RTR got within 200 yards of the railway bridge it was blown. But 11th Armoured were the first British troops to reach the Elbe and 4 KSLI was the unit concerned.

The Division now took up positions south of the river at Wittorf, Westergellersen, Winsen and Bardowick and spent a peaceful ten days while bridges were being built at Artlenburg on the left and Lavenburg on the right.

This was the end of Operation Plunder, a magnificent advance of 300 miles over twenty-one days, involving the crossing of three major rivers; the Ems, the Weser and the Aller. The German army had been destroyed as a fighting force. All that remained now was the final round-up.

CHAPTER THIRTY-THREE

Round-Up

While the Division occupied the banks of the River Elbe between Winsen and Tespe – some 15 miles – rumours were current that the Americans had linked up with the Russians and also that there was Werewolf activity in the forests behind. Although for over a week the Division sunned itself, maintained and cleaned vehicles and played football, the RASC were bringing up huge loads of bridging equipment and ammunition from as far back as Goch. David Swiney with 'Todforce' was directed to take Munster Lager, a large enemy training area south-west of Lüneberg: 'There we found a large Army hospital full of amputees, a sizeable gas dump and a vast ammo dump. 'Todforce' stayed in Munster for a week guarding the spoils, taking hundreds of prisoners and keeping Russians, Poles et al from looting German stores.' A battery of 58 LAA garrisoned Belsen and the Inns of Court kept up contact with 7th Armoured to the west. Peter Reeve recalls: 'The 11th Hussars leading 7th Armoured had dropped well behind and we were compelled to sit and wait protecting our left flank. There was relish and delight for us, as a junior outfit, to greet the Cherry Pickers with a glance at our watches and a casual "Where have you been, Charles? – we've been here for *hours*."' The Cheshires patrolled vigorously from Bardowick, killing or capturing an enemy patrol, while the A/Tk Platoon had some 'opportunity' shoots on enemy boats in the river. The Herefords too moved up from Winsen to Hoopte on the river and repelled enemy raids. The Fifes cleared the villages between Winsen and Niedermarschact. The divisional artillery fired at fleeting targets on the north side of the Elbe while the 23rd Hussars, 8 RB and other regiments relaxed at Westergellesen and Bardowick. There were no signs of surrender from the German army pinned north of the river.

The General wrote:

Eisenhower ordered Montgomery NOT to go to Berlin, but this instruction was given *after* bridges had been built over the River Elbe at Lauenberg and Artlenberg by 29 April. If we had crossed the Lauenberg railway bridge on 19 April I feel sure that we could have had our leading troops 25 miles EAST within twenty-four hours before Eisenhower was aware of the fact. Could he, or would he, have kept the British out of Berlin? And had we, and by 'we' I mean 21st Army Group, got to Berlin, what a much more suitable 'West' Germany could have developed after the war.

The River Elbe crossing at Artlenberg pontoon bridge, May 1945

However, it was not to be Berlin but Lübeck and the Baltic as divisional objectives. 15th Scottish with 1 Commando Brigade had made a bridgehead by the morning of 29 April. 13 RHA and Ayrshire Yeomanry fired 200 rounds per gun at 0200 on the 29th to soften up the opposition. 11th Armoured and newly-arrived 5 Division were to move through on the 30th and resume the advance. The battle-groups were to be 3 RTR/Herefords, 15/19th Hussars/4 KSLI, 23rd Hussars/8 RB, 2nd Fife and Forfarshire/Cheshires. The main difficulty initially was not shelling or bombing of the bridgehead at Artlenburg but a monumental traffic jam! 23rd Hussars led the breakout from Schwarzenbeck at 2200 hrs under a protective screen of RAF fighters. All through the pitch dark night of the 30th the Comets pushed on as far as the village of Sahms. Here an SP knocked out two tanks, causing six casualties. Fallen trees, blown bridges, shelling and minefields held up the advance both at Sahms, where 100 prisoners were taken, and at Kankelau. Noel Bell wrote after the battle for Sahms: 'The situation was very strange as during the shelling by the battery of 88-mm guns we lay alongside our prisoners, all flat on our faces on the bed of the stream and all as frightened as each other. The day so far had been unpleasant – one of the most unpleasant since crossing the Rhine.'

The Fifes and Cheshires on the left, despite encountering A/Tk guns and a mined road between Niendorf and Breitenfelde, reached Wentorf by nightfall on the 1st – an advance of 20 miles.

On the far left 3 RTR/Herefords had a fight on their hands at Trittau, after taking Haverost and Mohnsen. Ayrshire Yeomanry fired stonks to cover 3 RTR/Herefords into Trittau at 1715 hrs on 1 May – their last target of the war!

The General wrote: 'by the evening of 1 May we had Sandesneben on the right and Gronwohld on the left'. 2 May was a very satisfying day for the Division. Despite bazooka teams, 15/19th Hussars and Herefords on the left flank pushed through Eichede, Barkhorst and knocked out a 'flak' train on the outskirts of Bad Oldesloe, having cut the vital Hamburg–Lübeck autobahn. By mid-afternoon they had taken Bad Oldesloe and Reinfeld without opposition. 3 RTR and Herefords took the village of Rethwischdorf nearby, capturing twenty guns and 500 prisoners. The Ayrshire Yeomanry FOOs detailed the abandoned enemy equipment and the many Luftwaffe girls who were surrendering. Trooper Ernie Hamilton with 15/19th Hussars liberated a large swastika flag flying over Bad Oldesloe post office: 'We found a beautiful Mercedes-Benz saloon car in a garage, poured in two jerry cans of 100 octane fuel and handed it to four RAF officers who had spent some years in POW camps. They were delighted and I hope they managed to motor all the way to England in luxury'. The Fifes/Cheshires had liberated at Westerau a prison camp with 1,600 RAF officers. 23rd Hussars, despite having most of their Comets 'absolutely sunk and stuck' in bogland near Talkau, hauled themselves out and tried to overtake the Fifes as they hurtled down the autobahn into Lübeck itself. The historian of the Cheshire Regiment describes this charge:

In a heavy rainstorm the Cheshire/Fifes column crossed the autobahn at 1445 hrs, having met no opposition, turned north-west towards Lübeck. Then followed an amazing race against time. With only forty-five minutes left before the main bridges were due to be taken and with some 25 miles still to cover, they accelerated along the smooth spacious autobahn until the average speed of each vehicle had reached 55 mph. A fantastic sight with 200 vehicles, tanks, carriers or half tracks – all speeding for Lübeck. [The Germans had now given up.] The column still moving at about 50 mph reached the outskirts at 1520 hrs ignoring the laden trams, buses and civilian cars which blocked the route.

The German policemen were bewildered. The German population was bewildered. The streets were soon lined with thousands of prisoners. High ranking Staff officers mingled with the troops as they were herded into a POW camp south-west of the town. By the evening 20,000 prisoners had been taken. A private soldier often found himself in charge of 500 prisoners. Bedridden limbless patients from the hospitals donned their clothes and crutches and joined the queue. 159 Brigade had captured Himmler's private train. Geoffrey Downam, 171 Company RASC, thought that the DPs were more trouble than the Germans. On the way to Lübeck his unit was provided with tea by a Salvation Army van!

On the outskirts of Lübeck the 23rd Hussars encountered, according to the Hussars historian:

a wild delirious crowd of Allied POW who surged forward, many of them British. They swarmed round the tanks, white, emaciated, hungry, footsore but riotously happy. Down the road came crowds, more German soldiers, a hopeless, defeated mob, caring nothing but that they should be able to surrender, lie down and sleep and not worry about fighting any more. They came in large cars, small cars, dusty yellow lorries, in carts, bicycles and on their weary legs. They came in hordes – Marines, Panzers, Gunners, even the once redoubtable SS.

Generals arrived in twos and threes, politely or arrogantly, but all to surrender. Simon Frazer, 15/19th Hussars, reported that every visible roof in Lübeck was painted with huge red crosses, or white crosses on red roofs:

There they were, literally hundreds of them, tired, cold and wet and hungry German soldiers. They had been lying down so thick on the ground that little grass was visible. They were dragging themselves to their feet. We were literally surrounded by thousands of exhausted men. They posed absolutely no threat. They had not eaten for three days, many were ill or wounded. There was no room for them in Lübeck, which had been converted into a vast hospital.

Corporal Alastair Tait, RASC/3rd Mons, was given the task of getting the many abandoned trams off the Lübeck streets. 'We could only make them go in the direction they had been travelling. So clang, clang, and off we would go. Don't say we didn't have fun!'

23rd Hussars/8 RB pressed on towards Travemunde and Neustadt, north of Lübeck on the Baltic coast. The great bay was full of shipping and the following morning ships and U-Boats were attacked by RAF Typhoons and the Comets of 23rd Hussars. The Fifes also sank a ship in Lübeck harbour. The U-Boats had AA guns but the Typhoons destroyed two large ships which blazed from end to end and capsized. Unfortunately the SS had imprisoned their own political prisoners on board one of them. The majority had had no food for eight days. On the appearance of the RAF the SS guards had opened fire, run up the Nazi flag and made off, leaving the exhausted prisoners to burn alive. The Inns of Court, ever in the lead, had assembled a great many prisoners in front of the Hussars, and they were passed back down the line. Watches, cameras, useless marks, and trinkets of all kinds were acquired by 'searchers'. Everyone waited for orders to head for Copenhagen, perhaps to meet up with the Russian armies – rumours spread. David Swiney with 'Todforce', who had appeared after the Kankelau battle and arrived at Niendorf, wrote: 'We looked after some of the 20,000 prisoners at Lübeck and prepared for the assault on Kiel. Enemy aircraft, including MG 262 jet fighters, flew around looking for somewhere to land, even using the autobahn.' The situation in Lübeck was chaotic, particularly after a vodka depot had been discovered. Early on the 3rd the Royal Scots Fusiliers from 5 Division appeared as the new garrison of Lübeck.

Altogether the Division took 70,000 prisoners in the period 2–4 May, including twenty-five generals and admirals. But a strong force of SS in the Forest Segeberg had not got the message and the captured 8th Parachute Division was ordered to operate against them. This they did and in due course the SS yielded! 3 RTR/Herefords then accepted the surrender of Bad Segeberg.

David Swiney's 'Todforce' troop occupied a camp at Elkenforde: 'My troop escorted several U-Boat crews to Kiel. They were arrogant, defiant and sang most of the way, including the song [translated] "We're marching against England."'

The last few hours of 4 May will remain clear in our memories for ever [wrote Noel Bell]. We were sitting in our headquarters [in Strukdorf], with the wireless booming out dance music. Suddenly a little before nine o'clock the music stopped and all was quite. Then the voice of the announcer rang out – you could have heard a pin drop in the room. 'The German armies facing the 21st Army Group have surrendered to Field Marshal Montgomery.' Everyone went crazy with joy. Very lights and tracer bullets were soon making a crazy pattern in the sky and people were madly rushing about shaking hands with each other and slapping each other on the back. Fantastic rejoicing went on till the early hours and every drop of liquor accumulated during the past months was soon exhausted.

Suffering from a colossal 'victory' hangover, Bill Close's squadron of 3 RTR was sent to Forst Segeberg on 6 May:

A unit of SS had refused to surrender in the middle of the forest. We, the squadron commanders, tossed up for the privilege of going to fetch them out. I chose the short straw! The anti-tank unit recently returned from Russia was drawn up in full review order. I had the pleasure of making the CO and Adjutant of the SS unit ride on the front of my tank back to Segeberg followed by his unit.

The rejoicing on 8 May – the official Victory in Europe day – was another day of celebration. By now strange mildly drunken meetings had taken place with the Russian troops on the new 'frontier' and the newly arrived Military Government officials came to restore order, slowly, in the unmitigated chaos. There were sweeps for war criminals and the tattoo-marked SS, which were carried out with enthusiasm. The feeding and medical care of

B Squadron 23rd Hussars celebrating Victory in Europe, 8 May 1945

the thousands of DPs was a priority. Vast quantities of drink bricked up in a burgomaster's cellar was equally distributed throughout the Division. The Division was to occupy the province of Schleswig up to the Danish frontier at Flensburg, as pleasant an area in Germany as one could wish for.

But there was one final military manoeuvre required of the Division. SHAEF controlled the newly-formed 'puppet' German government under Grand Admiral Doenitz, the new Führer. By 19 May the British High Command had become greatly disturbed by the manner in which the Doenitz Government was working. It was thought that a number of high-ranking Nazi officers and Reich ministers who were listed as war criminals were serving with the 'puppet' masters. The buildings they occupied contained vital documents relevant to future war crime trials. So 'Operation Blackout' took place on 23 May. At 1000 hrs the Cheshires and the Herefords with 15/19th Hussars in support swooped on the government buildings in Flensburg. A naval patrol of two destroyers cruised along Flensburg Fiord to ensure no escape by sea. A very detailed and well-planned 'attack' on the massive Schloss Glucksburg took place although no shots were fired and by 1130 hrs 5,000 prisoners were taken including Admiral Doenitz, Admiral Von Friedeburg, General Jodl, Generals Reinbecke, Dethleffssen and Reich Minister Speer. The VIPs were escorted to 159 Brigade HQ, thence to Flensburg aerodrome and flown back to England for interrogation. Apart from one suicide the final tally of 6,000 prisoners was dispatched to their various prison camps. The day ended with a thundering drive of the Hussar Comets through the narrow cobbled

13 RHA: Kiel victory parade, May 1945 (Author in centre)

streets of Flensburg – a demonstration of the Division's panache. Roland Jefferson recalled:

> The whole battalion [8 RB] paraded in a field two weeks after VE day and we held an open-air thanksgiving service. We sang the hymns listed in a booklet which we had been issued with and when the Padre spoke there were many wet eyes as we remembered the 209 members of the Battalion who had paid the full price and were lying in graves scattered all over the Continent. When we started out the Battalion was at full strength of a little over 800. Over 200 were dead and more than twice that number had received wounds. We were the lucky ones, and we remembered the many friends we would never see again.

Every regiment now took part in Operation Eclipse – the practical business of Occupation. The enforcement of Allied authority was paramount, disarmament of all three services and de-nazification. For instance 23rd Hussars 'Kreis' was centred on Husum and their CO became the 'Führer' with almost total responsibility for a large territory, using the new docile German military and civilian police to carry out appropriate orders.

In January 1946 the Division was disbanded. General 'Pip' Roberts led many of his young no longer virgin soldiers into our old rivals and comrades-in-arms the 7th Armoured – the Desert Rats of yore. Sadly all the formations were merged or disbanded, with the exception of 3 RTR.

Major General 'Pip' Roberts DSO, MC, at 11th Armoured Division memorial, Flers, Normandy

And Noel Bell wrote: 'And so eleven months packed with thrills and boredom, interest and fears, had come to a close. None of us would like to live through them again, and yet on the other hand, I don't think there are many of us, who on looking back would have missed it for the world.'

Contributors to
The Black Bull

8th Rifle Brigade has two literary heroes. Major Noel Bell MC has allowed me to use extracts from his *From the Beaches to the Baltic*, and Trooper Roland Jefferson BEM has done the same for his journal *Soldiering at the Sharp End*. Their many anecdotes enliven this book. Trooper Norman Habertin also provided both tales and photos.

The most exciting tank man's journal I have ever read is that by Lieutenant-Colonel W. Steel Brownlie MC, TD, MA, then a Troop Leader with the 2nd Fife & Forfarshire Yeomanry. I am also grateful to him for allowing me to quote extracts from his book *The Proud Servant* – a history of the Ayrshire Yeomanry (in this case the 151st Regt RA). Trooper John Thorpe's letters and articles of his time with the Fifes have been included. Moreover he gave me the great benefit of his knowledge of the Division's Old Comrades Associations.

From the 23rd Hussars came (from Trooper 'Bob' Walmsley) the loan of the superbly written regimental history and some photos. Trooper Tony Matza recounted a funny story and Major Ted Harte sent me an account of the Ardennes battle, plus the loan of the privately printed diary of the late Lieutenant Geoffrey Bishop MC.

3 RTR were the most battle-hardened unit serving with the Black Bull, and Major 'Bill' Close MC was rudely unhorsed on seven occasions. He has sent me useful letters, advice and notes. Major John Langdon MC and Jim Caswell have also sent me accounts of some of their skirmishes.

The 2nd Northants Yeomanry had a particularly tough time in Normandy, and Trooper Corporal Reg Spittles and Major 'Sandy' Saunders have sent me some of their recollections.

The glamorous 15/19th Kings Royal Hussars joined the Division in time for Bluecoat. 'Ted' Deeming has been a tower of strength with the loan of the War Diary, some stories and an excellent quiverful of photos. Simon Frazer, Trooper Ernie Hamilton, Sergeant Ernie Nicholls and Trooper H.W. Drummond have also helped me.

Sergeant Hedley Bunce supplied me with a network of old comrades of the 3rd Mons which helped me to chart the many fine, but bloody, affairs in which they were involved; in particular Major L. Moody MC TD, Captain Arthur Cadell, Privates Roy Nash and Joe Logan. Unfortunately Major Joe How MC died some time ago – a very brave Company Commander indeed.

The best infantry history that I have ever read is a trilogy by Major 'Ned' Thornburn, a Company Commander of 4 KSLI. It is interlaced with scores of individual contributors from *inter alia* Major Tim Ellis, CQMS Rowley Tipton, Lieutenant 'Jenny' Wren, Lieutenant Mike Sayer and Major Jack Clayton. I am doubly grateful to Ned for permission to include extracts from his fine trilogy, but also for the use of his maps as well.

Last but not least of the infantry of 159 Brigade was the 1st Herefords. Major Ken Crockford has provided advice, Sergeant Frank Moppett and RQMS Reg Horton have sent me stories to ensure that the HEREFS got a good showing in this book.

John Collinge for the Inns of Court provided advice and a network of 'Devils Own', which included a number of stories from Captain Peter Reeve and Signalman Roy Gillespie.

David Swiney (now Lieutenant-Colonel but then a Troop Commander) sent me half a dozen vignettes about 75th A/Tank Reg RA, plus some excellent action photos.

For the Sappers Colonel Dick Anderson OBE MC and Captain Jack Lockyer provided helpful information about their vital bridge-building operations which were needed to bridge every river and canal in front of the Division's advance.

Although I was possibly the main spokesman for 13 (HAC)RHA, it was a nostalgic pleasure to record some of the adventures of my Troop Commander Norman Young MC, 'Stonker' Bill Budgen and BSM Pedro Powdrill MC and others.

Helpful contributions came also from Major Jimmy Carson 2 i/c CREME, from Christopher Mackonochie RAChD and Sergeant John Hooper's 'Seven Christmasses' with 171 Coy, RASC, plus Sergeant O.R. Wilson with the Corps of Military Police who marked our centre-lines, kept an eye on POWS and kept law and order when needed.